Talking Trash

The Cultural
Politics of Daytime
TV Talk Shows

TALKING
TRASH

Julie Engel Manga

New York University Press • New York and London

NEW YORK UNIVERSITY PRESS
New York and London

Library of Congress Cataloging-in-Publication Data
Manga, Julie Engel, 1953–
Talking trash : the cultural politics of
daytime TV talk shows / Julie Engel Manga.
p. cm.
Includes bibliographical references and index.
ISBN 0-8147-5683-2 (cloth : alk. paper) —
ISBN 0-8147-5684-0 (pbk. : alk. paper)
1. Talk shows—United States. I. Title.
PN1992.8.T3 M36 2002
791.45'6—dc21   2002010094

New York University Press books are printed on acid-free paper,
and their binding materials are chosen for strength and durability.

Manufactured in the United States of America
10 9 8 7 6 5 4 3 2 1

For Manuel and Gabi—
My partners in curiosity and wonder

CONTENTS

Acknowledgments

This book marks the completion of a transition that began in the summer of 1987. That summer, while I was an organization development consultant, I took my first sociology course, "Introduction to Sociology," at Northeastern University summer school. I remember driving back from my family's vacation on Cape Cod with my stepson Pablo in order to take the final exam. Pablo quizzed me in preparation. Given that I had not attended college for many years, and that, even at that, I had attended art school as an undergraduate, this was new for me. This start, followed by a five-year hiatus as I focused on work and parenting and finally a full-time reentry into graduate study has culminated in the work of this book, which began as my doctoral dissertation.

Without the support of my husband, Manuel, this process would not have been possible. His support has taken many forms. Most concretely, his willingness to be the main source of income for our family facilitated my being able to move through my graduate study smoothly and relatively quickly. In addition, while I still accuse him (too often without enough compassion) of being a "recovering sexist," he has made great strides in assuming equal responsibility for parenting our son, Gabi. For example, he has become an official "hockey dad," brining Gabi to the cold, cold hockey rink for practice and games each week of the (long) hockey season so that I could finish up my work on this project. No small accomplishment for a cold-averse person from the Caribbean! This material support was supplemented by his unending moral, emotional, and intellectual support during my career transition more generally. The heart of our relationship is our shared passion for learning, something which imbues us both with curiosity, a sustained sense of wonder, and a willingness to challenge taken-for-granted commonsense both intellectually and in everyday life.

My now thirteen-year-old son Gabi has become the youngest social theorist I know. Being his mother keeps me grounded in the grittiness and immediacy of the everyday. Having conversations with Gabi about what I was studying and writing made me think about explaining my work in a nontechnical, understandable way. It has been satisfying to see his own curiosity, wonder, and critical sensibilities emerge over the several years I have been working on this project. One of my greatest pleasures has been to sit in my office with Gabi playing outside in the parking lot behind our apartment, rollerblading, shooting on his hockey net, or riding his bike. Sometimes he would call up to me with a question, asking for something to drink, or wanting me to see a new trick or skill he was working on. I'd open the window, stick my head out, and we'd talk. I characterize my work as embodying the transition Dorothy Smith speaks of between the local, immediate, and particular and the abstract and conceptual. While it's often frustrating to move between these modes of thinking and understanding, I think that having to transition has kept me grounded in the "real world" as a sociologist. It has also facilitated a critical reflexivity about the most mundane routines of everyday life. Doing chapter revisions in the warming hut next to the hockey rink as Gabi's team practice kept this all alive and well.

My cadre of fellow graduate students in the Department of Sociology at Boston College, where this project began as my dissertation, provided crucial moral and intellectual encouragement and support. Ongoing phone conversations and e-mail correspondence with Karen McCormack were instrumental in my moving through the early stages of proposal writing, interviewing, and analysis. My many conversations with Steve Farough, Heidi Bachman, Julie Boettcher, and Danielle Egan have empowered me to trust myself as a researcher and writer.

As this study took form, David Karp consistently provided me with encouragement. His feedback helped me work harder at trying to effectively explain complex ideas in a relatively straightforward manner, though I fear I am not always successful. His respect for my work, even those parts of it that are not "his thing," has been much appreciated. I am also intellectually indebted to Stephen Pfohl. Through my numerous conversations with him, I have tapped into most of the theoretical orientations informing this work. I have learned from him the importance of having a healthy disrespect for orthodox disciplinary boundaries, including the view that social science and art are not necessarily so far apart. Furthermore, he has always made it clear to me that this is *my* work.

Thanks to Sadie Fischesser for preparing my bibliography, a task that allowed me to stay focused on the substantive work of the project.

Finally, I thank the women who participated in this study as interview subjects. Their openness and willingness to give their time to a stranger never ceased to amaze me. This study would not have been possible without the generous sharing of these women.

1. TALK SHOWS, PUBLIC DISCOURSE, AND CULTURAL POLITICS

Television Talk Shows as Contentious Culture

> The objects of our criticism are not close calls. They are shows that typically cross way over the line. We have described their contents as cultural rot. How else could one describe shows whose typical subjects include a 17-year-old girl boasting of having slept with more than 100 men, a 13- year-old girl talking about sexual experiences that began when she was 10, or "Women Who Marry Their Rapists"? (Bennett 1996: B9)

> The talk show can be seen as a terrain of struggle of discursive practice . . . because of the nature of the format . . . What is conceived as confrontational devices become an opening for the empowerment of an alternative discursive practice. These discourses do not have to conform to the dictates of civility or the general interest. They can be expressed for what they are: particular, regional, one-sided, and for that reason politically alive. Few other shows on television today can make that claim.
> (Carpignano et al. 1993: 116)

"Alternative discursive practice," "cultural rot," something else entirely, or many things at once? Why is it that certain television talk shows are so controversial? Why do those who criticize these shows consistently seem to have such strongly felt, often morally tinged opinions about them? Why, on the other hand, do millions of people watch these shows daily?[1] And, who, if anyone, takes these shows seriously? This genre has become so pervasive that the Bush campaign lobbied for a talk show format for one of the three debates sponsored by the U.S. Presidential Debate Commission during the 2000 presidential elections. In the previous election, Elizabeth Dole used a talk show format in introducing her husband, Bob Dole, as a Republican presidential candidate at the Republican National Convention. Microphone in hand, she moved around the audience, soliciting testimonials of personal experiences with Bob (all attesting to his exemplary character) from selected individuals in the audience. Furthermore, as various congressional representatives confessed to their own past infidelities during the unfolding of the Clinton/Lewinsky affair leading to President Clinton's impeachment in December 1998, a *Boston Globe* article cited a University of Virginia political scientist as commenting, "I'm worried that we're going to have an interminable national *Jerry Springer Show*" (Fick 1998: A21). On his late-night show *Vibe*, Sinbad did a talk show spoof of the Clinton/Lewinsky affair, featuring actors playing Bill and Hillary Clinton and Monica Lewinsky as guests. These examples provide evidence that the talk show form has entered mainstream cultural sensibility as a paradigm for making sense of things: the privileging of the personal experience or testimonial of ordinary people over professional expertise as a way of framing issues. At its extreme, this sensibility emphasizes the outrageous, bizarre, unbelievable, and sensational: sex, sordid relationships, adultery, and other assorted betrayals. Like other popular cultural forms such as soap operas, for example, talk shows are trivialized and devalued and, in some cases, considered damaging.

The shows I examine in this study are those commonly referred to as "trash talk" in popular and television industry discourse. This category includes the shows *Jerry Springer, Ricki Lake, Jenny Jones, Maury Povich, Montel Williams,* and *Sally Jessy Raphael,* all of which share the distinction of being on various lists of "the worst" talk shows. This type of talk show is distinct from other television genres in that while all television genres feature talk, the talk is generally scripted dialogue among actors (e.g., sitcoms, soap operas) or dialogue, monologue, interviews, or commentary by experts or celebrities (e.g., newscasts, public affairs shows, sportscasts, late-night shows, morning "magazine" format shows). In contrast, the talk shows that are the focus of this study are live (taped for broadcast), at least seemingly unscripted interactions among guests, host, and studio audience members. These shows generally feature guests who are apparently "ordinary" people, albeit often with issues or problems that would be considered extraordinary by most. In addition, all feature studio audiences whose members have the opportunity to interact with the guests. Not only do they feature a mostly female viewership, but some of the shows have a viewership that is skewed toward black, Latino, working-class, or lower-income viewers.[2]

I study talk shows as a matter of culture. Any attempt to sort out what talk shows "are" entails an examination of the competing explanations through which individuals make sense of them, an issue of cultural intelligibility. However, these varying explanations do not necessarily peacefully coexist in society. Rather, it is generally the case (as it is for talk shows) that competing explanations vie for acceptance as mainstream common sense. This becomes, then, not just an issue of cultural intelligibility, but of cultural politics. As particular explanations categorize cultural forms along a hierarchy of more or less value, those using these explanations attempt to determine the extent to which a form is regarded as "legitimate." Making determinations of value and legitimacy is an implicitly, if not often explicitly, political process. That is to say, some groups' understanding of what is more or less valued or "legitimate" prevails over others'. This compels one to ask whose terms for legitimacy prevail in a particular social context or setting.

Herman Gray suggests that "media and popular culture are the cultural and social sites where theoretical abstraction and cultural representations come down to earth, percolating through the imagination of America" (Gray 1995: 35). While Gray makes this statement in the context of his discussion of the new right and African Americans' claims on representations of race and "the sign of blackness," I suggest that his insight is more broadly applicable. Popular culture and mass media forms can be studied as key "expressive sites and vehicles" (Gray 1995: 35) through which a range of issues facing society are expressed and engaged, and through which claims to legitimacy are contested and sorted out.

Before I introduce the substantive and theoretical issues central to this study, let me recount how I came to study talk shows, since this is directly connected to the issues of cultural intelligibility and legitimacy that I raise. I didn't start out with the intention to study talk shows. I began with an interest in the intersections of public discourse, public life, and culture. Reading Habermas (1991), Fraser (1994), Young (1990), Ryan (1992), Sennett (1992), Dewey (1991), Putnam (1995), and others who are concerned with the historical and contemporary construction of the public sphere and public life, more generally, I wanted to study how people located themselves in relation to public life and public discourse and how or if they participated therein. This interest took an unexpected turn one night as I was working out on my NordicTrack in the living room of my home. While I worked out, I usually liked to watch what I call "mindless TV." That night, as I flipped through the channels with the remote, I happened upon the *Ricki Lake Show*. I had heard about this type of talk show, but had previously only glanced at several.[3] My initial reaction "I can't believe this is on TV!" gave way to fascination as I found myself compelled to keep watching. At some point (I think during a commercial break), noticing that I continued to give the show my rapt attention, I became privately embarrassed that I could get so hooked by it. I found this rather multilayered reaction of disgust/fascination/embarrassment intriguing. Having discovered these shows for myself, I began informally asking other people I knew what they thought of them. The responses I got were consistently similar to my own initial reaction: "I can't believe they show that on TV!" or "What trash!"

Spurred on by my own complicated response and the consistency of the responses among most people with whom I spoke who were much like me (mostly white, middle to upper middle class and well educated), I became interested in finding out a bit more about this popular and contentious cultural form. My research found that the most popular of these shows (at the time *Ricki Lake* and *Jerry Springer*) were each watched by approximately four to 5 million viewers every Monday through Friday (Nielsen Media Research 1996). Furthermore, approximately 80 percent of the viewing audience were female, skewed toward women between the ages of 18 to 35 with low income and lower levels of education. In addition, while in raw numbers the audience was predominantly white women, black women watched at three times the rate of white women (Nielsen Media Research 1996).

While talk shows are a contemporary televisual form, my familiarity with popular-culture analyses led me to suspect that the kind of controversy that surrounds these shows was not historically unique. Supportive professors and fellow graduate students guided me to several works of social and cultural history. Key among these were Stallybrass and White's *The Politics and Poetics of Transgression* (1986, a study tracking the "carnivalesque" across a range of European literary and social contexts), Allen's *Horrible Prettiness* (1991, a study of "intelligibility" of burlesque in the United States), Levine's *Highbrow/Lowbrow* (1988, a study of the emergence of high culture from popular culture forms in the United States during the nineteenth and early twentieth centuries), Rosenzweig's *Eight Hours for What We Will* (1983, a study of working-class leisure practices in a New England city in the late nineteenth century), Ventura's "Hear That Long Snake Moan" (an essay on rock-and-roll in the United States), and Kathy Peiss's *Cheap Amusements* (1986, a study of the leisure practices of young working women in the early twentieth century). All confirmed my hunch that while the form of talk shows is unique, the social phenomenon it embodies is not. This allowed me to situate talk shows historically as a cultural form.

I was struck by three factors that seemed to be consistent both in the talk shows and in these earlier popular-culture forms. In each case, the form was associated with the lower classes, women, or other marginalized groups in society. In addition, the various forms and practices all embodied similar characteristics. They were rowdy, boisterous, and otherwise hyperexpressive and collective, often involving the body, sex, or sexuality. Third, in each case, the dominant (bourgeois) class of the time responded to the form or practice with repugnance, disgust, or moral outrage, devaluing it, often regarding it as "dangerous," and making efforts to either contain or eliminate it from the mainstream of society. This was the case, for example, with European fairs and carnivals (Stallybrass and White 1986) and with saloons (Rosenzweig 1983), burlesque (Allen 1991), popular theater and opera (Levine 1988), as well as with voodoo spiritual practices of slaves in the American South involving music and dance (Ventura 1985). The rhetoric of critics of these earlier forms and of contemporary talk shows was strikingly similar. At this point, I was convinced that I was onto something that was both intellectually interesting and potentially useful in terms of understanding the workings of culture and cultural classifications as they relate to what gets construed as "legitimate" and appropriately "public" in a society.

I study talk shows, then, as a site of "contentious culture," more specifically as an explicitly *discursive* contentious cultural form. It is this second aspect that most attracted me to study the shows. I argue that talk shows can be considered, if not a site of "public discourse" in the orthodox sense, at least a site for very (if not radically) public talk.[4] In fact, while the overarching question guiding my inquiry was, "How do people who watch talk shows make sense of them?," my initial question was, "Who, if anyone, engages with these shows as legitimate public discourse?"

Other Studies of Television Talk Shows

While there has been scholarly study and popular commentary about television talk shows, to date, people who actually watch the shows are interviewed in only three studies. A number of studies focus on the development of talk shows or their content, making claims about what the shows "are" or the possibilities they represent, taking a range of positions. Munson (1993) provides an account of the history of the development of the contemporary talk show, showing how it emerged as a form of radio and television programming. He suggests that talk shows are both a "utopian fusion of the human, the social, and the technological in a rhetorical mastery—and a democratic scaling down—of technology that puts even political 'outsiders' in," as well as "a dystopian place where problems come to light and one can hear America snarling," "a new public sphere," "one of the new cyberspatial neighborhoods we now live in" (Munson 1993: 155).

Abt and Mustazza (1997) and Abt and Seesholtz (1994) examine the institutional practices within which talk shows are produced and distributed. Writing firmly and unreflexively from a mainstream position, they condemn the shows as "toxic talk" (Abt and Mustazza 1997: 6). Heaton and Wilson, both of whom are mental health professionals, contend that "in their current form, talk shows contribute to, and even create more problems than they solve" and provide viewers with suggestions for being more reflexive about their talk show viewing (Heaton and Wilson 1995:

4). Masciarotte (1991) analyzes *Oprah Winfrey* and the now de-funct *Donahue*. Characterizing *Donahue* as privileging a male dis-course of rationality and reason, always working to achieve closure or provide solutions, she positions the *Oprah Winfrey* show, as it ex-isted in the early 1990s, as an oppositional discursive form. Mas-ciarotte argues that Winfrey and her show's mode of discourse emphasize the rich display of narrative in its entire nuance and difference, with less commitment to arriving at consensus and so-lutions.[5] Carpignano et al. (1993) suggest that the talk show is a form that privileges neither rational-critical debate nor experts. Rather, in featuring "ordinary" people and privileging their ex-perience and particularistic talk, they suggest that the shows con-stitute the potential for an "alternative discursive" practice.

Priest (1995) conducted a study in which she interviewed peo-ple who appeared as guests on the shows. Among those who in-terviewed talk show viewers, Livingstone and Lunt (1994) spoke with sixteen viewers as part of their British study, which examined what in the United States would be categorized "public affairs" programming, focusing on the possibility that these shows serve as a "public sphere" of debate. Shattuc (1997) argues that talk shows have their origins in the identity politics of the 1960s. Her analysis focuses on pre-1994 shows, the generation of talk shows just prior to those that are the focus of this study. While she pri-marily conducts historical and content analysis, she did interview four viewers, most of whom did not represent the "target" demo-graphics of the shows on which I focus, thereby rendering this as-pect of her study inconclusive. Gamson (1998) conducted focus groups of viewers as part of his study of talk shows. He focused on the relationship of the shows to sex and gender nonconformity. In particular, he emphasized the way in which the shows rou-tinely make sex and gender nonconformity public and visible, serving to exploit marginalized groups, but also serving to nor-malize them in some ways.

The Focus of the Study:
How Viewers Make Sense of the Shows

The focus of my study is squarely on how viewers make sense of the shows. I did not begin with the intent to either condemn or valorize the shows. Being interested in understanding how culture operates, I am as suspicious of simplistic, morally tinged condemnation as I am of quick valorization of "the popular" or "the marginalized." It is because the shows' are so fundamentally constituted by talk among at least purportedly "ordinary" people rather than experts or celebrities that I was attracted to them (as opposed to an equally outrageous form like World Wrestling Federation, for example).

Because so much thorough work has already been done by others in analyzing the content and form of the shows from a number of perspectives, I focus on how viewers make sense of these shows. I do this primarily through interviews with thirty women who watch talk shows on a regular basis.[6] Following Brunsdon, who, in the face of scholarly emphasis on audience reception in the past decade or so, argues for the importance of retaining the notion of text as a meaningful analytic category (Brunsdon 1989: 120), I take seriously the fact that the shows are produced according to particular industry conventions whose objective it is to make them intelligible in particular ways to the viewers. Recognizing this, my focus on how women make sense of the shows does not simply dissolve the "text" (the program, in this case) into the viewers' readings of it. This is apparent, for example, when I discuss "the lure" of talk shows for millions of viewers in chapter 5.

I analyze how the women make sense of talk shows by paying close attention to how the women talk about them. I pay attention not only to the substance of what the women say, but also to the systems of meaning and classificatory systems through which they make sense of the shows. For example, what are the terms through which they encounter a particular show as "legitimate," as "meaningful" or not?

Given my initial interest in how individuals situate themselves in public life generally, and in respect to public discourse more specifically, I also approach what these women share with the question, "What kind of subject would make sense of the show this way?" In paying attention to the terms of the women's discourse, I seek to understand how each woman situates herself, how she positions herself relative to talk shows. Taking poststructuralist insights seriously,[7] I recognize a relationship between language and the construction of subjectivity.

While the heart of my study focuses on how women who watch talk shows make sense of them, my analysis would be incomplete without recognizing that this sense-making occurs as part of a wider social field. Poststructuralist insights are instructive in illuminating the relationships between what are distinguished as "macro" and "micro" levels of analysis in traditional social science analysis. The macro and micro levels of analysis are generally distinguished by examination of institutional structures and practices and individual or interpersonal or group structures and practices, respectively. Taking these insights seriously, I examine the institutional structures and practices of the television industry, since these are the basis for the existence of talk shows and thereby make it possible for them to become interwoven into the everyday routines of those who watch them. "Experience" is socially constructed not just discursively, but through material relations with institutions we encounter in everyday life.

Furthermore, talk shows emerge and exist by virtue of the television industry that produces and distributes them in a network of relations upon whom the industry relies for its own existence. I summarize the development of the talk show from the industry's perspective, using television and marketing industry journals as my primary source of data. This also provides a means for comparing and contrasting industry discourse with that of the women who watch talk shows. I examine how producers, network and local station management, sponsors, media buyers, and media commentators speak about and represent talk shows.

Fundamentally this is a study of intelligibility, subjectivity, and culture. Within a particular context, at a particular historical moment, how is it that individuals encounter a particular form of talk the way they do and subjectively situate themselves in relation to it? What, if any, are the implications of this for how these individuals situate themselves in society more generally? I consider all this against the recognition of how these shows are constructed in mainstream discourse. Intelligibility, or how we make sense of phenomena we encounter in the course of everyday life, is for the most part unreflective, appearing as "natural," taken-for-granted common sense. Following Garfinkel, Foucault, Bourdieu, Butler, and a host of others, I argue that intelligibility is socially, historically, discursively and, in some ways, even psychically constituted.

Theoretical Framings

I approach theory pragmatically. Therefore, I am not bound to some theoretical approach as "right," but rather I use theory in two ways. I use it to help me frame initial sensitizing questions as I move into my research and analysis. It allows me to orient myself as I step into my research, but it does not bind me to a particular perspective or understanding. Then, as I try to make sense of my reams of documentary and interview data, theory helps me make sense of it. Given my task of trying to understand how women who watch talk shows make sense of them, I have reached for a range of theoretical/conceptual tools. This is important because each theoretical perspective and its concepts emphasizes certain aspects of a phenomenon and minimizes or even ignores others.

Foucault's Poststructuralism

Michel Foucault's poststructuralism is primary to orienting most of my analysis, in particular Foucault's central concern with the operation of language. Language is understood as being structured as varying *discourses*, or systems of meaning through which individuals organize and make sense of what they come to call their "experience," through which they come to be constituted as particular types of "subjects," and through which social practices emerge and institutions are organized. Foucault challenges the taken-for-granted common sense of these systems of meaning and the associated practices through which they are continuously reproduced in both the organization and conduct of everyday life. Through his detailed historical studies, he shows how these discourses and practices are socially constructed in particular times and places. These discourses have bearing on the material, social, economic, political, and cultural. For Foucault, language is not "just words," it has tangible consequences for "real life"—for individuals, institutions, and societies.

Foucault's influence will be seen in my interest in the discursive categories through which women make sense of the shows they watch, the categories or classificatory systems they seem to have available to make their experience intelligible. I pay close attention to what the women I interviewed say, the way they say it and the underlying categories and systems of meaning through which what is said is constituted. (As we will see in chapter 5, what is not, and perhaps, cannot, be said is also a function of these systems of meanings.) Foucault suggests that such issues are central in that "each discursive practice [the "fixing" of norms for the elaboration of concepts and theories] implies a play of prescriptions that designate its exclusions and choices" (Foucault 1977: 199). This is evident, for example, in our society's ubiquitous practice of identifying the color blue with baby boys and pink with baby girls, or in the attribution of certain qualities or behaviors as characteristically (and usually unambiguously) male or female. In Foucault's terms, these are discursive practices that emerge as part of a particular discourse of gender, one that has actual (material) effects on members of society.[8]

By his own account, the key objective of Foucault's work is to "create a history of the different modes by which, in our culture, human beings are made subjects" (Foucault 1983: 208). This commitment figures centrally in my own analysis, as I find that each woman's understanding of herself as a certain kind of subject is inextricably interwoven with how she makes sense of the shows. This is a dimension connected to, but at the same time distinct from how each woman is positioned in society in terms of socioeconomic status, race, and gender. Taking Foucault's suggestion, I pay close attention to who is speaking, the position from which they speak (in terms of status and social structure), and the authority they are afforded, both by themselves and others in their particular context (Foucault 1977: 222).

Audience Research

I did not set out to do an "audience reception" study. However, it became apparent to me, whatever my initial motivations, that the kind of study I was doing would generally be identified as such by other scholars. Initially, I resisted this framing, since I was not entering into the study with an interest in individuals as members of an "audience" per se, nor was I primarily interested in or focused on television as a specific media form. I was interested in talk shows as a forum of public discourse and, more specifically, in the extent to which individuals who watched these shows on a regular basis engaged with the shows as such. This form just happened to be on television. Nonetheless, I found that the kinds of questions I was most interested in asking were consistent with those doing work on "media reception." These questions focused on issues of intelligibility ("How do individuals make sense of the media form with which they engage?"), subjectivity ("How are individuals' senses of themselves influenced by their engagement with a particular media form?" and "How do individuals' senses of themselves influence the way they make sense of a particular media form with which they engage?"), and the operation of power. (The Foucauldian- influenced questions are: "How do individuals come to experience a particular media form the way they do?" "What discursive practices or modes of categorization are operating?" "With what effects?") This substantial body of literature provided me with a rich array of substantive, theoretical, and methodological resources.

Orientations toward understanding the encounter between audience members and that which they view, read, or listen to can be understood as falling along a spectrum. One end of this spectrum grants a highly deterministic role to the text of media message. (In its most simplistic form, this is apparent in the idea that watching portrayals of violence *causes* violent behavior in viewers of these portrayals.) On the other end of this theoretical spectrum is an understanding of "the text" as being created in the moment of the encounter between the audience member and the textual form. In this view, the "text" is not some static assemblage of messages and images that acts on the individual. Rather, the "text" is the interpretation the individual makes (Fiske 1987). There is much theorizing between these two poles that presents more complex and nuanced analysis, taking into account the context in which the individual encounters a media form, including his or her familiarity with other media forms.

The tradition of "media effects" represents the more deterministic end of the spectrum. Morley characterizes this perspective as a "hypodermic model of media influence," in which the media are seen as having the power to "inject" their audiences with particular messages that will cause them to behave in particular ways (Morley 1989: 16). Paradoxically, this behavior can be catatonic due to the addictive and anesthetizing effects of television, or dangerously active (as in compelling an individual to carry out violent acts). Here, the audience is generally viewed as an undifferentiated mass. This perspective is embodied, for example, in critical theorists' Horkheimer and Adorno's work on the "culture industry" (Horkheimer and Adorno 1987).

Psychoanalytic theory, while more sophisticated in some ways, also grants a high level of determinacy to the media text. Developed in film theory, this perspective focuses not so much on behavior effects, but on the dynamic psychic process through which the viewer comes to have a particular interpretation that is understood as "coded" into the media text. The media text (film in most of these writings) is understood as being structured to "offer" the viewer specific particular positions they may take up or "assume" in engaging the text. Rather than seeing the text as producing certain types of "effects," the text is understood as "producing" a certain kind of subject since it triggers the audience members into particular psychic processes. From their position as a certain kind of subject, they can have only certain types of interpretations of the text. Imagery is considered central to how the media engages the audience member in these psychic processes.

Morley notes that, as with the hypodermic model, this view implies that certain psychic processes are universal, producing uniform experiences in audience members. In addition, most work from this perspective is based on the authors' analysis of a particular film, not by interviewing actual audience members. Moreover, a number of television researchers (e.g., Seiter et al. 1989; Modleski 1983), show that television viewing is generally a very different process than watching film, considerably less focused and more fragmented (Morley 1986).

Hall's (1981) encoding/decoding model of the 1970s began to theorize the media text in a more nuanced way, incorporating a less deterministic model of the individual. Hall's model presents mass communications as structured by institutions that have the power to establish agendas, define issues, and offer "preferred readings" of particular media texts. (For example, the producers of Fox News would like us to interpret their stories in a certain way.) However, Hall also incorporates the model of a more active viewer, but one whose interpretations of media are mediated by socially and culturally structured patterns for "decoding" meaning. Evidencing a materialist analysis, Hall recognizes individuals as being situated within a set of actual specific circumstances in society, a particular positioning from which they encounter mass media texts (e.g., a woman or man, age, socioeconomic status, ethnicity, race, etc.). Drawing on Parkin's (1971) earlier model, Hall theorizes that individuals "decode" mass media texts in one of three modes: the *preferred* reading, the *negotiated* reading, and the *oppositional* reading, depending on whether the individual shares, partly shares, or does not share the code or ideas embedded in the text (Morley 1989: 18). These varied readings were based mostly on the audience members' class position in society. Recognizing this as incomplete, other scholars (e.g., Hobson 1982; McRobbie 1978) extended the focus of socioeconomic class as a differentiator to include gender as a fundamental dimension of analysis.

Hall's work and that of others at the Birmingham Center for Cultural Studies opened theoretical space for more complex considerations of the audience member/text relation. Through Hall's synthesis of the work of Althusser, Gramsci, and poststructuralism, he developed his theory of *articulation*.

"Articulation," in Hall's usage, refers to the process through which certain meanings or practices "take," that is, how certain understandings or practices come to be accepted by particular individuals or groups at particular moments in particular social, political, cultural, and economic contexts. Integrating poststructuralist insights regarding language and discourse, Hall theorizes the idea of *historical conjunctures*, or specific convergences of social and discursive forces. While some poststructuralists (e.g., Laclau) maintain that there is "no necessary correspondence" in terms of what articulates for whom, Hall suggests that some elements in a social formation operate from more privileged and powerful positions than others, and thus have more influence. For example, the institutions of the media (e.g., newspapers, television networks and stations, radio) work from a position of power that is clearly greater than that of the individual audience member. Hall suggests that researchers must examine the way in which various societal forces

> at a certain moment yield intelligible meanings, enter the circuits of culture—the field of cultural practices—that shape the understanding and conceptions of the world of men and women in their ordinary everyday social calculations, construct them as potential social subjects and have the effect of organizing the way in which they come to or form consciousness of the world. (Hall cited in Slack 1996: 124)

Work in the field continues to extend Hall's formulation, considering the convergences of the broad historical moment in which media representations are constructed and distributed as well as the more particularistic biographical moment in which these representations are encountered and made sense of by individuals. Two key concepts figure explicitly and implicitly in this body of literature: concern for the *context of viewing* and *intertextuality*.

Further specifying the concept of articulation, Silverstone (1994) and Morley (1981) suggest that watching television be understood as a *situated practice*. Morley (1981) and Silverstone (1994) emphasize *context of viewing*, that is, that such everyday practices occur within specific material contexts, which, while biographically particularistic, are also occurring in their relation to macrostructural forces. The everyday, therefore, is a point of convergence for the discursive and the material, the biographical microstructural, and the more institutionally based macrostructural. Macrostructural factors include institutional structures, practices, and discourses (e.g., those of the media industry, as well as those of the economic and political domains) within which an audience member is situated and which shape the broad contours of everyday life. For example, Gray (1995) examines the representations and readings of African Americans in his study of how "blackness" has been portrayed since the Reagan era and with the advent of the "narrowcasting" practiced by networks since the 1980s. Browne (1984) emphasizes the structure of network programming practices as they emerged in relation to the post–World War II structure of work and everyday life. Spigel (1992) examines how television was incorporated into the home and family life during post–World War II suburbanization in the United States, focusing on its gendered aspects. Understanding the watching of television as an everyday, mundane practice locates processes of interpretation (and the related process of subject formation) within this practice, rather than as an autonomous process. In this approach, to be *situated* means to emphasize the reciprocal connections between macro and microstructural factors, and further specifies the method of studying *historical convergences*.

Intertextuality refers to the notion that as individuals encounter media texts, they do not make sense of them in isolation but in relation to other texts and cultural knowledge more generally. This concept gives rise to debate about what exactly constitutes "the text" as an object of study. While "the text" can be considered any configuration of literary, spoken, visual, or musical representation, what the text *means* is a function of intertextuality. In this study, for example, the women I interviewed do not encounter or make sense of talk shows in isolation, but rather through a process in which a range of cultural knowledge is brought to bear on their viewing and making sense of the shows. Fiske notes that intertextuality, in its narrowest sense, can be based on genre and character (Fiske 1987: 109). Genres, or types of shows (such as soap operas, sitcoms, game shows, newsmagazines, and talk shows) are characterized by certain conventions by which they are structured. This applies not simply to narrative conventions, but to the conventional ways in which imagery is used in each. (Production conventions such as types of camera shots used are also included, since these conventions influence the type of imagery distributed to the audience.)

Fiske points to a more complex intertextual relation between a television text and what he refers to as "secondary texts." Secondary texts explicitly refer to a particular primary text. They include, for example, publicity, criticism, or other forms such as *Soap Opera Digest, Hollywood Access,* and *Talk Soup,* all of which "work to promote the circulation of selected meanings of the primary text" (Fiske 1987: 117).

A third level of intertextuality involves talk among audience members about a media form. Most scholarship on this has been focused on television (Fiske 1987; Liebes and Katz 1990; Brown 1994; Hobson 1982). This may take the form of informal conversation among friends or coworkers and interaction on Webpage chat rooms afforded by some shows, as well as any other form of audience response circulated publicly. Publication of ratings, which may be used to affirm or negate the meaning a show holds for a viewer, is included here (Fiske 1987).

Intertextuality can be viewed even more broadly, however. Barthes, for example, argues that "intertextual relations are so pervasive that our culture consists of a complex web of intertextuality in which all texts refer finally to each other and not to reality" (in Fiske 1987: 115). This echoes Baudrillard's (1993) even more radical view that "signs" no longer have "meaning" per se but reference only other signs in our media-saturated society. The current pop music practice of "sampling" in which a song is composed of pieces of others' songs is a good example of this level of intertextuality.

A Map of the Chapters

While each chapter of this study constitutes a distinct dimension of my analysis, each is "nested" within the others. In chapter 2, I examine the matrix of institutional structures and practices within which television talk shows are produced, distributed, and watched. As discussed above, apparently "individual" routine practices exist in relation to institutional structures and practices. This includes, perhaps most importantly, that it is by virtue of the television industry management's prerogative, and on their terms, that talk shows emerged as a genre and continue to exist at all. Flowing out of this discussion of daytime programming practices in general, and in the context of the changing situation of the television industry, I follow the development of the talk show as a popular daytime programming form, relating it, for the most part, from the television industry's perspective.

In chapter 3, before exploring how women who watch talk shows make sense of them substantively, I focus on the women's watching the shows as a mundane, everyday, routine *practice*. This analysis takes into account when the women watch, where they watch, how they watch, how their viewing practice fits into their larger scheme of daily routine practices, and how they make sense of their viewing practices, including what significance their practice of watching talk shows holds for them.

Chapter 4 addresses my initial research question, "Who, if anyone, engages with talk shows as 'legitimate public discourse'?" My research finds that, indeed, some of the women do engage with certain shows this way. I explore the character of the classificatory system the women seem to use in discerning the extent to which particular shows are intelligible as legitimate discourse. I find that the criteria the women use in making such discernments is strikingly consistent across most of the interviews, yet these criteria are used quite differently by different women. I account for both the consistency of the criteria the women use and the variation with which these criteria are deployed by them, identifying several distinctive cultural discourses that I find pervade the women's accounts of talk shows.

Recognizing that all viewers do not encounter talk shows as "legitimate public discourse," I shift the terms of my analysis in chapter 5. Here, I examine the women's experience of watching talk shows as entertainment. First, I situate trash as a form of *symbolic inversion* and then argue that trash talk shows embody characteristics of a particular kind of symbolic inversion, the *carnivalesque.* I demonstrate how this contemporary form is both consistent with historically earlier carnivalesque forms, as well as distinct from them, given the modes by which the shows are produced, distributed, and consumed. Second, I focus on a distinctive feature of the women's accounts—the way they consistently spoke of how the shows "grab" or "get" their attention, "lure" them, "fascinate" them—in general, using language indicating that something is *pulling* them to watch the shows or keeps them watching once they start. Counter to much commentary about trash talk shows, I suggest that the simultaneous attraction to and repulsion from trash talk shows evidenced by many of the women can be understood symptomatically as something more profound than cheap entertainment or guilty pleasure.

Finally, in chapter 6, I address several issues raised by my analysis: the implications of women's engaging certain talk shows as legitimate, the implications of contemporary society's lack of non-commodified collective rituals of symbolic inversion, and the impulse toward ecstatic experience understood in its sociological rather than psychological sense.

My methodology is discussed in appendix A. In addition, a summary in which I provide a brief description of each of the women who participated in the study can be found in Appendix B.

2. THE BUSINESS OF TALK

From a TV executive's perspective, programming is the sideshow that lures advertisers to the tent.

(Dominick, Sherman, and Copeland 1996: 173)

While the heart of my study focuses on how viewers make sense of talk shows, I recognize that how one "makes sense"— that is, how the world is encountered or made intelligible—always occurs within a particular social, political, and economic context, a context that is dynamic. A key dimension of the context in which the women of this study make sense of talk shows is the institutional structure and associated practices of the television industry. These are structures and practices with which the women participate by virtue of watching talk shows.

Whatever personal meaning the women derive from the shows they watch, the fact remains that talk shows exist at the prerogative of television industry management, for whom talk shows are first and foremost a business. Understanding the business of talk shows provides some background necessary to understand how the phenomenon emerged at the time that it did and, subsequently, has become a part of the daily life of many individuals such as the women with whom I spoke.

Talk shows have emerged as a viable, low-cost programming option for daytime television in a volatile media business climate, generating an increase in advertising revenues from $76.1 million in 1987–88 to $274.7 million by 1992–93 (Advertiser Syndicated Television Association 1993: 80). Over the past decade, networks have experienced radical declines in audience share due to new competitor networks and cable and satellite television. As a result, the networks have relinquished their hold on the daytime programming schedule of their local affiliate stations, allowing affiliates to shop around for their own programming. In many cases, affiliates are attracted to shows produced by syndicators, including talk shows.

The Unplanned Beginnings of Audience-Participation Talk Shows as We Know Them

While all but one of the talk shows that are the focus of this study are part of a flurry of newer shows that debuted starting in 1991,[1] the talk show as a distinctive television genre originated with *The Phil Donahue Show* in 1967, a show produced by a local station in Dayton, Ohio, owned by the Avco Broadcasting Group. The show did not move into national syndication until 1977. Talk/variety shows have been a popular daytime programming form since the early days of television. Among the most popular during the 1960s were *The Mike Douglas Show, The Merv Griffin Show,* and *The Dinah Shore Show.* All had a standard format featuring a celebrity host, various entertainment acts, and celebrity interviews. In addition, early public affairs programming like *Meet the Press* and *Face the Nation* also constituted a form of talk show, with their own traditions that continue to the present.

The contemporary talk show initiated by Phil Donahue (who had previously worked as a the host of a popular local radio show, *Conversation Piece*) was, like the variety/talk shows, produced under the category of "entertainment television." *The Phil Donahue Show,* though, from its beginning, was not entertainment in the strict sense of featuring entertainment acts (e.g., music and comedy routines). On the other hand, while not produced as public affairs programming, the show initially blended discussion of social issues with lighter topics and was, from the start, oriented toward women. For example, during its November 1967 debut week, the show featured atheist Madalyn Murray O'Hair, who had worked to eliminate prayer in public schools; men who discussed what they like about women; a gynecologist; an undertaker; and a discussion of an anatomically correct doll (Haley 1992b:S8).

The Phil Donahue Show was touted as "an overnight hit" (Haley 1992b: S10) and dominated its time slot in its local Dayton, Ohio, market. Ironically, the live studio audience component of Donahue's show was not part of the show's original plan. Rather, it was included in order to accommodate women who had made up the studio audience for the talk/variety show Donahue was replacing, *The Johnny Gilbert Show*. While studio audience members were relatively passive at first, merely watching the discussion, during breaks they fed Donahue questions to ask guests, which Donahue acknowledged as "great, some of them much better than anything we'd thought of" (Haley 1992b: S10). The shift to more active audience participation occurred spontaneously and unintentionally, according to a twenty-fifth anniversary advertising supplement in *Broadcasting*. Gunilla Knudsen, a Swedish model best known for her Noxema Shaving Cream commercial in which she seductively beckoned men to "Take it off . . . Take it all off," was the featured guest on Donahue's show. The anniversary supplement tells the following story:

> During a commercial break, a woman from the audience asked Knudsen why she never appeared with her long blonde hair in braids. The model replied that she'd never learned to braid her hair and accepted the woman's offer to show her how. Donahue decided to go along with the rapport developing between Knudsen and the audience. As the show went live again,

the woman from the audience came up to the set and began braiding Knudsen's hair. There was a new electricity in the room, when that woman began participating in the show," Mincer [the show's original producer/director] says. "Phil and I talked about it later in the day and decided to make the audience a part of the process every day." (Haley 1992b: S10)

About his viewing audience more generally, Donahue commented:

Back then [in the late 1960s], I had people come up to me all the time and say, "Where did you get those bright women in the audience?" As though women weren't supposed to be bright. It's important to remember how sexist we were, back there in the *Father Knows Best* days. Housewives were condescended to, patronized. Most certainly by the white male figures that were in the power management places of broadcasting. Women care about soap operas, covered dishes and fashion. And what we discovered early on, almost by accident, was that women were reading more parts of the newspaper than men. Women were more likely to ask a question and then listen to the answer. Less likely to give you a long oration about absolute truth. . . . Now I think we're past that terrible condescension. And men who have daughters realize, as I did, that it was really a waste for a culture to encourage women to aspire to nursing and men to aspire to doctoring. Not to say that there's something wrong with nursing. But who's going to deny that we really did try to put women on a certain track, and we had a place for them? That's no longer the case. Today, the audience, I think, is more diverse. We have more males watching us today, perhaps for bad reasons. Maybe it has to do with unemployment. I am very pleased to be recognized by cops, cab drivers, males who don't work nine to five.

And increasing numbers of them don't. (Haley 1992c: S16–18)

By the end of 1969 *The Phil Donahue Show* was being broadcast successfully across Ohio. By the fall of 1971, forty-one stations carried it regionally (Haley 1992b: S10). In April 1974 the show was moved to WGN-TV in Chicago as part of a strategy by Avco to expand the show's audience. Its base in Dayton, Ohio, had hindered the show's potential since, despite high ratings, producers found it difficult to attract big-name guests and to continue to energize audiences, since many women in surrounding communities had been to the shows several times since its 1967 debut (Haley 1992b: S12). Not yet popular in the Chicago market because it had earlier been broadcast there in a middle-of-the-night time slot, the show had to get its studio audience by bussing women in from Wisconsin, where the show had been airing during a popular time slot.

Avco sold the show to Multimedia, which was able to provide new resources and pursue syndication opportunities more aggressively. In 1977 *Donahue* acquired a clearance in New York through WNBC-TV. The show was a success in that market, and by 1978 it had a national audience of about 8 million viewers each day; it was syndicated in forty-nine of the nation's top fifty markets (a total of 135 stations) and was ranked number one in its time slot in 68 percent of them (Shah and Maier 1978: 85). By 1979 the show was carried by more than two hundred stations, which made it the most popular syndicated television show in the country (Haley 1992b). Still, the show was considered controversial for its day; in the words of a *Chicago Tribune* television critic, it "reduced the Mervs and Mikes and Dinahs to the level of Tupperware parties" (Shah and Maier 1978: 85). With one guest or couple and one topic per show, *Donahue* featured, for example, an episode on artificial insemination, with a couple whose friend carried their unborn child (well before the public controversy about surrogate mothering); another episode on homosexuality and impotence; and one on a home childbirth. (Donahue's Chicago station censored the latter episode before his move to New York.) While the issues *Donahue* examined would likely be considered "mild" by today's standards, in the 1970s they set the standard for controversy.

Oprah Winfrey: Conquering Phil's Home Turf and More

In September 1984, using a Donahue-inspired format, Oprah Winfrey became a ratings success with the Chicago-based show *AM Chicago*. Winfrey had hosted a morning show in Baltimore for seven years before moving to Chicago. She had once been the youngest woman (at nineteen) and the first black to serve as a news anchor in Nashville, Tennessee (Noglows 1994: 52). A December 1984 *Newsweek* article commented on Winfrey's rising popularity in Chicago:

> Talk about disparate styles of talk-showmanship, and going mouth to mouth at that. Every morning in Chicago, there's Phil Donahue, a silver-thatched, Notre Dame Irish, national-television icon and prototypical New Man, while . . . *clickety, click* . . . over there is Oprah Winfrey, nearly 200 pounds of Mississippi-bred black womanhood, brassy, earthy, street smart and soulful—and possessed of the merest shadow of Donahue's fame. Obviously, this looks like a hopeless Nielsen mismatch, at least until one looks at the bottom line. Since winning the hostess job on WLS-TV's "AM Chicago" last January [1984], the 30-year-old Winfrey not only has been outrating

the rival "Donahue" show, but has conquered Phil's home turf so completely that his recent shift of base to New York could almost be viewed as a discreet retreat. . . . Oprah carries unpredictability to its outer limits—try to imagine Whoopi Goldberg imitating Mae West. (Waters and King 1984: 51)

Maury Povich, who began hosting his own talk show in 1991, characterized Winfrey's success:

Nobody was talking about their own problems like Oprah. . . . The closest thing Phil Donahue ever talked about was the fact that he was a wayward Catholic. Other than that, talk-show hosts didn't talk about themselves. Oprah opened up a lot of new windows for viewers because they could empathize with her. (Cited in Noglows 1994: 52)

It took less than a year for the half-hour *AM Chicago* hosted by Winfrey to become the leader in its time slot. The show was expanded to a full hour and its name was changed to *The Oprah Winfrey Show* (Noglows 1994: 52). Due to its success in the Chicago market, syndicator King World Productions launched the show in national syndication in 1986, selling the show to 136 television stations that covered 90 percent of the United States. *Oprah Winfrey* emerged as the highest-rated show in twenty-two of thirty-two markets ranked by the industry in 1986 (Schleier 1987: S30). By 1991 the show was the highest-rated talk show in television history. By 1994 the show reached sixty-five countries and had approximately 15 million viewers daily; it grossed $180 million a year, of which Harpo Productions (the production company owned by Winfrey) received approximately 57 percent. In 1994 the show drew 55 percent more viewers than *Donahue*, its closest competitor at the time (Noglows 1994: 52). King World continued as the show's syndicator, but Winfrey owned her show as well as her own production company, which includes a 100,000- square-foot television and movie studio where the Winfrey show is taped. In 1991 she had projected revenues of approximately $39 million from her television projects (Goodman 1991: 52).

Sally Jessy Raphael: Ordinary People with Stories to Tell

Like Phil Donahue, Sally Jessy Raphael started her career as a talk-radio host. As a promotion for her NBC late-night advice radio show, she appeared as a guest on a daily television talk show, *Braun and Company*, based in Cincinnati and syndicated in the Midwest (Haley 1993: D7). When her appearance was announced, viewers called the show to confirm the day, causing Burt Dubrow, the executive producer of the show (and later, of *Sally Jessy Raphael*), to take notice. Given her popularity with the show's viewers, Raphael was invited back for a second guest appearance during "sweeps" period. Dubrow asked her to guest host a week of shows while the regular host, Braun, was on vacation. Dubrow reports that at this point he knew he wanted to sign Raphael for her own talk show (Haley 1993: D7–8). Raphael's show, produced and syndicated by Multimedia (which also syndicated *Donahue*), debuted as *In Touch with Sally Jessy Raphael* on October 17, 1983, on WSDK, a St. Louis station owned by Multimedia (Haley 1993: D8). The show followed *Donahue* in the morning line-up. Ratings exceeded those of the show it replaced, and they continued to climb. In the fall of 1984, Multimedia syndicated the show to other stations, and in the spring of 1985 it introduced it at the annual NATPE (National Association of Television Programming Executives) program conference, a major industry conference of programming executives (Haley 1993: D9–10). By May 1985 Raphael's show, now called *The Sally Jessy Raphael Show,* was syndicated in fifty-seven markets, including Atlanta, Boston, Miami, Seattle, Washington, D.C., and New York (although it aired at 2 A.M. in New York). During this time, Raphael continued her NBC radio talk show (Haley 1993: D10).

While *The Sally Jessy Raphael Show* had featured controversial issues and celebrities, and only occasionally had ordinary people as guests, in 1985 it shifted its focus to storytelling by ordinary people. A woman who had been a rape victim had called into Raphael's radio show and several months later offered to tell her story on the television show. Dubrow commented in an interview, "It was as if the audience took a deep breath at the beginning of that show and held their breath for the next half hour." Dubrow characterized the show as simply "someone telling her story to Sally" (Haley 1993: D10). The show's focus was shifted to feature "ordinary people with stories to tell, and in particular, stories that would illuminate an issue if told on the air" (Haley 1993: D10). The show moved to New Haven in 1987 and expanded to a one-hour format as ratings climbed. By 1989 *Sally Jessy Raphael* was carried by 131 stations. In 1992 Raphael's show was the highest-rated syndicated morning talk show. In 1993 it was rated among the top three syndicated talk shows.

Geraldo Rivera: Trying to Cut through the Bull of It

In September 1987 Geraldo Rivera's talk show debuted on over ninety stations (most of them network affiliates) covering 80 percent of the United States (Jones 1987: sec. 2, 21). Trained as a lawyer, Rivera was "discovered" by WABC in New York in 1970 when he acted as the spokesperson for the Young Lords, a Puerto Rican activist group. He worked as an investigative journalist for

ABC News's *20/20* news magazine show and developed a reputation for being theatrical.[2] A *Los Angeles Times* article written on the day of the show's premier notes that Rivera characterized his style as "more . . . newsman Ted Koppel's on *Nightline* than the cozy studio approach of Winfrey or Phil Donahue. Using news footage and occasional on-location shooting, Rivera wants things hot, controversial, visual" (Haithman 1987: 1). Rivera commented,

> The only thing that counts is the accuracy of the facts and the fairness of the broadcast—all the rest is packaging. . . . You can choose to package it the way Peter Jennings does, with a handkerchief in the pocket of his tailored English suit, or you can package it the way I do. I'm trying to cut through the bull of it. If I wear my emotions or my biases on my sleeve, I think that is more honest than say, Vietnam coverage with an eyebrow being raised or a sarcastic tone of voice that doesn't show up in the transcripts. To me, that's hypocritical; it's commentary disguised as something grand called objectivity. (Haithman 1987: 1)

The first week of Rivera's show included

> the handicapped and their families; Marla Hanson, the New York model whose face was slashed with a razor; high-tech dating; the medical procedure of using fetal material to treat Parkinson's disease and its implications for the abortion issue, and "AIDS Assassin," about carriers of the HIV virus who do not inform their sex partners. (Haithman 1987: 1)

Like Oprah Winfrey, Geraldo Rivera distinguished himself by asserting the validity of emotion as a key part of the program. While the show's co-producer and syndicator, Tribune Entertainment, marketed the show to women between ages 25 and 54,

Rivera commented, "I don't just want white women, the tribe, there. . . . I want men, women, younger, older, darker, lighter" (Jones 1987: sec. 2, 21).

According to the industry journal *Electronic Media*, in 1989 Rivera found himself faced with advertisers who pulled their time, and he had difficulties negotiating renewals with local stations for the fall 1990 season because of advertiser and local station management concern over "sensational" topics. The advertisers included, among others, General Foods, Procter & Gamble, McDonald's, BurgerKing and Kellogg—for the most part national rather than local spot advertisers. Rivera himself noted that the objectionable topics (e.g., battered lesbians and topless doughnut shop operators) were aired during the November sweeps, as a reaction to the producers' insecurity about the show airing opposite *The Oprah Winfrey Show* in one hundred markets. Rivera (who co-produced his show) promised to change the style and admitted to "pandering" to audiences in an effort to rate well in a highly competitive time slot.

Of the shows emulating *Donahue's* format that debuted in the 1980s, only *Oprah* successfully overtook *Donahue* in several large markets (Haley 1992b: S14).

A Flurry of New Shows in the Early Nineties

When *The Oprah Winfrey Show* went into syndication in 1986, it was one of only a few nationally syndicated talk shows. By the 1989–90 season, fifteen talk shows were in syndication, and by the 1996–97 season there were 19, according to Nielsen Media Research (Heath 1998: 48–53). By the early 1990s, the talk show was recognized within the broadcasting industry as an important genre: starting in December 1992 (commenting on the fall 1991 season), *Broadcasting and Cable*, a major television industry journal, has been devoting a section of its December issue to an analysis of the talk show market.

The predominant demographic groups to whom talk shows are targeted are females aged 12–34, 18–34, 18–49, and 25–54. However, the president of programming and development for the CBS (affiliate) station group commented at the time that "the key is to find fresh blood and new faces to lure in the younger demographics, the core 18–34 demos that drive the ratings for any talk show" (Freeman 1992b: 26).

In fall 1991 four talk shows using a Donahue-like format premiered and, in some cases, were given a slow, staggered rollout, as this method had proven successful for both *Donahue* and *Oprah Winfrey*. *Montel Williams* was tested in eighteen markets and expected to go national in January 1992. *Jenny Jones* and *Maury Povich* also premiered (Freeman 1992a: 35–36). In the flurry of new shows, *The Oprah Winfrey Show* continued as the ratings went far ahead of *Donahue*, which placed second, and *Sally Jessy Raphael*, which placed third.[3]

By December 1992, sixteen talk shows were broadcast, with a dozen predicted for the fall 1993 season (McClellan 1992: 22, 24). Already in 1992, there was industry concern about oversaturation of the genre, but producers and distributors nonetheless regarded the shows as a potential for huge revenues, having relatively low production costs at around $150,000 to $200,000 per week (Williams 1993: S6). For example, in its first six seasons, *The Oprah Winfrey Show* grossed $705 million, with estimated annual profits of close to $100 million. *Donahue* was estimated to have annual revenues of at least $700 million as of 1992, *Sally Jessy Raphael* approximately $40 million, and *Geraldo* an estimated $10 million, taking into account advertising revenues and licensing fees paid by network affiliates and independent stations (McClellan 1992: 24). Network affiliate stations were using talk shows for daytime and news lead-in programming, although in

1992 independent stations were beginning to include the shows in their line-ups as well (McClellan 1992: 24).

In late 1993, well after the start of the fall 1993 season, the lead article in the second annual talk show section of *Broadcasting and Cable*'s December issue stated, "The daytime talk genre finally has hit the wall—there are now more syndicated shows than stations have room for, and the anticipated shakeout has begun" (McClellan and Freeman 1993: 54). The article cites an industry programming executive as commenting, "I think the audience is saying 'enough is enough with the Oprah wannabes'" (McClellan and Freeman 1993: 54). Two of the season's most anticipated and hyped offerings, *Oprah* syndicator King World's *Les Brown* and Twentieth Television's *Bertice Berry*, were cited as "on the cancellation watch list" (McClellan and Freeman 1993: 54). There was still uncertainty about their fate, however, since industry executives acknowledged that "we all know these shows take time to build," given the fact that *Donahue* was broadcast for ten years before making it into national syndication (McClellan and Freeman 1993: 54). The late-blooming and revamped *Jenny Jones* and the slow start of *Montel Williams* served as examples of this development (McClellan and Freeman 1993: 54, 60). A show's rise in the ratings may result in upgrades, moving it into more desirable and competitive time periods at many stations. This, in turn, leads to the possibility of even greater ratings growth.

Ricki Lake and the "New Generation of Talk Shows"[4]

According to several industry journals, the fall 1993 season's surprise success was *Ricki Lake*. By December (after a September premier) the show was receiving important time period upgrades to 4 and 5 P.M., serving as a lead-in to local news programs

(McClellan and Freeman 1993: 60). The show was aired in both early fringe (4–6 P.M.) and daytime time periods and showed improvements in audience share over the programs it replaced in the two time slots in which it aired (McClellan 1993a: 12). The Nielsen Syndication Service Ranking Report for August 30 through November 14, 1993, once again rated *Oprah* the number one talk show, with almost double the rating (10.1) of second-place *Sally Jessy* (5.1), with *Donahue* a close third (4.9) (McClellan and Freeman 1993: 54). *Montel Williams, Jenny Jones,* and *Jerry Springer* continued to show substantial ratings gains, though they were only in the 2.8 to 2.0 range, far below the leaders.

Even with a disappointing season of new shows, a January 1994 *Broadcasting and Cable* survey of station executives showed that 23 percent of respondents indicated that talk shows were their top programming need (*Broadcasting and Cable* 1994a: 66). Industry executives anticipated yet more talk show offerings for the fall 1994 season. Among those cited and much anticipated in the annual December talk show section of *Broadcasting and Cable* in 1993 were shows featuring Gordon Elliot, Rolonda Watts, Suzanne Somers, and Susan Powter, of which some lasted just one season, others several, but none were on the air in 1998.

Results of the May 1994 sweeps indicated that syndicated talk shows that targeted women ages 18–34, including *Ricki Lake, Jenny Jones,* and *Montel Williams,* were reaching this audience demographic in "unprecedented numbers" (McClellan 1994: 18). A *Broadcasting and Cable* article entitled "Young-Targeted Talkers Take Off" specified some key results:

> *Ricki Lake* nearly quadrupled its time period rating and tripled its share among women 18–34 in daytime, where it was top ranked. *Jenny Jones* doubled its rating and was up 7 share points and ranked second in the demo in daytime. *Sally Jessy Raphael* was third but down 2 share points and almost half a rating

point. *Montel* also posted strong gains in the demo, placing fourth. (McClellan 1994: 18)

Donahue continued to show a drop in women's demographics. While *Oprah* continued its dominance as ratings leader, in early fringe hours (4–6 P.M.) *Ricki Lake* was number one among women ages 18–34 and 25–54 (McClellan 1994: 18). Debuting in fall 1993, the show was initially sold as an 18–49 show, with a focus on the "twenty- and thirty-something" demographics as part of a strategy by Columbia Pictures Television Distribution, the show's syndicator, to sell the show as a "transitional lead-in to local news" (Freeman 1992b: 26).

Ricki Lake was distinguished in the industry press as drawing a "new young audience to daytime," with ratings growing 104 percent in its first year (from a 2.6 national Nielsen rating to 5.4) and having broadcasts in 99 percent of the U.S. market. This surge made the show the fastest-growing talk show in television history (Tobenkin 1994: 47; *Broadcasting and Cable* 1994b: 56). While the *Oprah Winfrey Show*, with a 9.7 November rating, captured twice the number of viewing households, *Ricki Lake* was the first show to exceed *Oprah* in the female 18–34 demographic since *Oprah's* debut in 1984.

In an interview in *Broadcasting and Cable*, Ricki Lake responded to a question about why she appears to have connected so well with young viewers. She responded:

> They [the producers] wanted a young woman in her 20s and that's exactly what they got–who struggled through a weight problem, who had financial problems, who had been through a lot for my 24 years when they found me. The viewers can see through someone who pretends to be someone they're not. . . . I'm not this glamour girl who had everything sort of magically happen for her. For some reason they

related to me and feel I'm one of them. (*Broadcasting and Cable* 1994b: 56)

Responding to the accusation critics make of her show as being "trash TV," Lake commented:

I don't think talk shows are for everyone, but luckily they're for most people. Sure, a lot of the stuff we discuss is really tasteless. Some guy's infidelities can be hard to watch, embarrassing and even considered trashy. But I don't think we're trashy to the level a lot of other talk shows are. We won't put someone on a stage to laugh at them, belittle them, make fun of them and basically destroy their life. (*Broadcasting and Cable* 1994b: 57)

While *Ricki Lake* was experiencing success, seven of the nine talk shows premiering in fall 1994 were characterized as "on the ropes," with one already canceled (Tobenkin 1995b: 48, 56). The low performance of the new shows was attributed to "a tidal shift in talk that has seen the rise of faster-paced, audience participation-intensive, younger-skewing shows like . . . *Ricki Lake*" (Tobenkin 1995a: 60).

By December 1994, *Broadcasting and Cable* was crowing that a "[b]umper crop of talk shows hopes to tap Ricki's success"; "A new constellation of stars is rising on the talk show horizon, with *Ricki Lake, Jenny Jones* and *The Montel Williams Show* surpassing more established shows—and even denting the ratings of talk queen Oprah Winfrey" (Tobenkin 1994: 47).

In light of *Ricki Lake's* success, thirteen new talk shows were cited as in development for national syndication in the fall 1995 season, even as some in the industry expressed concern over the intensification of competition with "so many of the new shows . . . attempting to skew to the same youth-targeted, fast-paced format mined so successfully by *Ricki Lake*" (Tobenkin 1995b: 48). Emulating *Ricki Lake*, the new shows scheduled for 1995 for the most part featured young hosts, including Carnie Wilson (of the singing group Wilson Phillips), Tempest Bledsoe (formerly of the *Cosby Show*), Stephanie Miller (a late-night talk show host in Los Angeles), Mark Wahlberg (an ESPN host), Gabrielle Carteris (of Beverly Hills 90210), Charles Perez (a former talk show producer himself), and Danny Bonaduce (a child-star of the *Partridge Family* and Chicago radio host). Each show attempted to distinguish itself by virtue of its host's personality and qualifications and program content, but all vied for the same 18–34 female demographic (Tobenkin 1995b: 48, 56; Tobenkin 1995c: 26). By December 1995, these shows had already gained clearances (commitments for broadcast) in 50–70 percent of the country (Tobenkin 1994: 47). In line with the attempt to capitalize on *Ricki Lake's* success, *Jenny Jones, Montel Williams*, and *Jerry Springer* were described as "already hav[ing] increased their pace and audience participation levels and successfully hav[ing] captured large portions of the younger audience" (Tobenkin 1995b: 48). By February 1995, for example, the *Springer* show was cited as having "engineered a dramatic increase in ratings rise during the past year precisely by remaking itself to appeal to audience member's young enough to be Springer's children." It showed a February 1994 to February 1995 ratings increase of 53 percent, to 4.6, which placed it ahead of *Ricki Lake, Jenny Jones*, and *Donahue* in the young (and most hotly contested) demographic (Tobenkin 1995d: 22).

What the industry press referred to as a "glut" of talk shows created a more competitive environment affecting both new and old shows, including the "traditional leaders" (Tobenkin 1994: 48). Longer-standing shows like *Donahue, Oprah, Sally*, and *Geraldo* all experienced a drop in ratings, although *Oprah* continued to have double the audience of any other talk show. An industry executive noted: "What's happening here is that because of the competitive nature of the business, we have a natural leveling situation. . . . You are going to see 4s and 5s [in terms of ratings] now, not 6s and 7s" (Tobenkin 1994: 48). In addition, while shows like *Ricki, Jenny, Jerry,* and *Montel* had the benefit of a "three year growth curve . . . to remain in syndication," given the competitive environment in 1995, an industry programming executive suggested that new shows would not have that much time to prove themselves (Freeman 1995b: 16).

"Trash," "Cultural Rot," and Other "Prurient Tones": Renewed Concerns over Talk Show Content

On the March 6, 1995, taping of a *Jenny Jones* show using a "surprise" format popular among some of the talk shows, a male guest, Jonathan Schmitz, was brought on to meet someone claiming to have a secret crush on him. Unbeknownst to Mr. Schmitz, the secret admirer was another male, Scott Amedure. Embarrassed (and apparently enraged), Schmitz murdered Amedure soon after the episode was taped. The show was never broadcast, but industry press reports that *Jenny Jones*'s ratings "soared to a 5 [Nielsen] rating" after "averaging about a 4.5 rating, up from a 3.5 last season, largely on its move to increasingly salacious topics" (Mandese 1995: 34). A *Mediaweek* article maintained that the "*Jenny*-related shooting" caused advertisers to be more hesitant about the "surprise-guest gimmicks" used by many syndicated talk shows. While these made for the high level of emotion and conflict that viewers seem to enjoy, as indicated by higher ratings, and while local stations enjoyed the resulting higher ad rates, media buyers were reportedly concerned for their clients (Freeman 1995a: 9). The "disturbing, prurient tone" of syndicated daytime talk shows was attributed to the crowded, competitive market of the genre, in which shows attempted to emulate *Ricki*

Lake's success in encroaching on *Oprah Winfrey's* audience and brining in younger viewers (Freeman 1995a: 9).

Although most syndicators and local station management, as represented in the industry press, considered the *Jenny Jones* incident a "freak occurrence that does not reflect on either *Jones* or the genre," they also contend that the adult viewers who comprise the shows' primary audience want these "edgy" shows (Tobenkin 1995d: 23).

While some advertisers indicated that they would not continue to buy time on talk shows like *Ricki Lake* or *Jenny Jones, Mediaweek* noted that

> so far, *Jenny Jones* seems to have weathered the story. Procter and Gamble, the nation's largest player in daytime, recently bought time in the show. . . . A representative for Warner Bros. [the shows distributor] said no advertisers have asked to be taken out of the show. (Freeman 1995a: 9)

While on the one hand media buyers indicated that some of their clients were concerned about the content of talk shows, even advertisers characterized as "hypersensitive," such as Kraft Foods and Procter and Gamble, were cited as routinely buying time on the shows in question, although they reportedly review each episode (Mandese 1995: 34). The *Jenny Jones* producer, Warner Bros., is reported to have devised a "brilliant marketing strategy to get the best of both worlds: titillating topics that goose its ratings and safe havens for sensitive ad budgets" (Mandese 1995: 34). Each week, Warner Bros. produced two "advertiser-friendly" shows and three "advertiser-unfriendly" shows, thus allowing the show to elicit revenues from "sensitive" advertisers while also being able to feature the kinds of topics that keep their ratings average high. Ironically, the secret- admirer episode that preceded the murder of one guest by another was considered one of the "advertiser-friendly" shows (Mandese 1995: 34). While there appeared to be no immediate negative repercussions resulting from the *Jenny Jones* incident, the concern it elicited presaged more sustained concerns that would emerge in fall 1995.

Fall 1995 saw the initiation of a campaign spearheaded by former education secretary William Bennett and Senator Joe Lieberman (D-Connecticut) aimed at "cleaning up" daytime TV talk shows. This same partnership had previously been concerned about gangsta rap music. At a press conference announcing their campaign, Bennett asserted, "What is happening today is a pollution of the human environment" (Halonen 1995: 1).[5] Senator Lieberman concurred: "It is clear that talk is indeed cheap, and too often demeaning, exploitative, perverted, divisive or at best amoral" (Halonen 1995: 1). Bennett and Lieberman also clarified that they were not seeking to regulate talk show content, but rather appealed to producers as good citizens, looking for them to voluntarily "clean up" their shows. Lieberman noted, "We're looking for better citizenship, not more censorship" (Halonen 1995: 1).

Responses to the Lieberman-Bennett campaign varied from enthusiastic support to concern about infringement on First Amendment free speech rights. A spokeswoman for the National Association of Broadcasting affirmed the pair's right to make their views heard, "as long as they're not advocating government intervention" (Halonen 1995: 1). The executive director for a media watchdog group was supportive of the project to curb talk show content but noted, "This is why they [talk show producers] need rules. When it comes to programming decisions, the bottom line always wins"; it is not clear, however, whether he advocated a voluntary, industry-generated set of guidelines or legislative action (Halonen 1995: 1). In the television industry, some executives took a predictably pragmatic view. The president of a large firm that produces talk shows (including some of those cited by Lieberman and Bennett as chief offenders) commented, "I'm not sure this is as much a matter of morality as taste, and I think our audience may not be as culturally advantaged as some of your critics." He, as did others in the television industry, predictably tended to frame the issue in terms of the audience's right to choose their entertainment.

October 1995 Nielsen ratings showed a "near-total disaster" for talk shows. Of twenty-three talk shows being broadcast, twenty-two showed no growth or "modest-to-significant losses" compared to their time periods a year earlier. (The only show posting ratings gains was "advertiser-friendly" *Live with Regis and Kathie Lee*; Freeman 1995c: 13). While it was tempting to attribute the poor ratings to audience disapproval of talk show content, industry members tended to attribute the ratings to the "glut" of talk shows being broadcast, which sustained their assessment of the situation in a business rather than a moral discourse (Freeman 1995c: 13).

Advertiser responses were hard to read. For example, Proctor and Gamble, one of the biggest advertisers on daytime television, reduced its spending, with a spokeswoman for the company asserting,

> During the past twelve months, we made some decisions to stop advertising on some shows and reduce spending in others. We can't name names, but it is over content. Content fell outside our guidelines, and if shows fall outside our guidelines, we stop advertising. (DeCoursey 1995: 79)

Yet, while the company did reduce overall spending on talk shows from approximately $28.3 million to $18.5 million between July 1994 and January 1995, it actually increased its spending substantially on some of the shows considered among the "worst offenders" by the Lieberman-Bennett campaign.

(Increases amounted to 314.1 percent on *Ricki Lake*, 210.9 percent on *Jenny Jones*, and 92.8 percent on *Montel Williams*; De-Coursey 1995: 79).

By November, the Bennett-Lieberman campaign had begun to move its attention to sponsors of the talk shows regarded as objectionable. Bennett promised that his advocacy organization, Empower America, would set up a multimillion-person mailing list in an attempt to mobilize viewers to call sponsors of the offending shows. In addition, he claimed to be "enlisting supporters on boards of major corporations who sponsor shows and on the boards of TV and cable networks" (Mundy 1995: 20). An executive vice-president of a major producer-syndicator tempered Bennett's claims of progress. He faults Bennett for his lack of understanding of the talk show business. For example, while Bennett pointed to *Live with Regis and Kathie Lee* as an exemplar of what talk shows ought to be, the executive pointed out that *Regis and Kathie Lee* is not a talk show, but a variety show. Moreover, the show is geared toward an audience of viewers who are fifty years old and older, a much older demographic than targeted by shows like *Ricki Lake, Jenny Jones*, and *Montel Williams*, for example. In addition, he noted that "[t]hese shows are entertainment. The audience knows they are a hoot and we're all having fun" (Mundy 1995: 20).

With respect to Bennett's success with advertisers, the same executive noted that Procter and Gamble had had a practice of monitoring shows well prior to Bennett's current campaign. He noted that

> P&G has monitored their shows for years, looking for titles, not even content. They don't just avoid sex; they avoid anything controversial. . . . We have put on shows about women who are abused by their husbands, and P&G won't do it. Even if it were

the most responsible format, they won't touch it anyway. They won't do a show on AIDS. I don't think they will sponsor a show about public awareness of domestic violence. (Mundy 1995: 21)

Procter and Gamble also issued a statement charging that Bennett's accusations were based on outdated information and did not reflect Procter and Gamble's spring 1995 efforts to encourage talk show producers to "raise their standards and improve content," which had resulted in Procter and Gamble's pulling advertising from five shows in October 1995 (Reuters, Limited 1995). After a December 7, 1995, news conference in which Bennett, Lieberman, and Senator Sam Nunn (D-Georgia) launched a television campaign pressing advertisers to "refuse to sponsor this cultural rot," Kraft Foods (a division of Philip Morris), another big daytime advertiser, issued a statement asserting that, for more than the past twenty years, Kraft had "followed a policy of not advertising in programs that make gratuitous use of sex or violence, or that demean human dignity, a policy the company spends two million dollars a year enforcing." The company noted that it had already stopped advertising in seven high-rated talk shows while continuing to advertise on shows that met company guidelines, including, for example, *Oprah Winfrey* (Reuters, Limited 1995; Mifflin 1995: A22).

Some syndicators were reported to fear that "some stations [would] find a way to turn the content controversy into a legal means of yanking low-rated shows off the air before the contracts expire," thus capitalizing on the publicized controversy (Littleton 1995b: 64). This conflating of morality and business is evident, for example, in the decision of a Palm Springs, California, ABC affiliate to drop *Sally Jessy Raphael, Ricki Lake,* and *Donahue.* While on the one hand the station manager positioned the station as "getting out of the trashy talk business, he admits this decision had as much to do with ratings as with standards" (Littleton 1995a: 12).

Because of the controversy, most talk shows being developed for fall 1996 were being promoted as "advertiser-friendly" (Littleton 1995b: 64). In addition, a December 1995 *Mediaweek* article noted that "[w]ord in the advertising and TV communities is that the campaign, which began in October, is setting off a migration of ad dollars from syndicated talkers to alternative media, such as the broadcast and cable networks, print and direct mail." Media executives confirmed that advertisers were responding to pressure from Empower America and requesting that their agencies negotiate out of daytime talk shows (Freeman and Dupree 1995: 5). One major syndicator noted concern that "CPMs [cost per thousand viewers] are going to go lower as a result from their moves to cable and other media. . . . It could destroy some of these talk shows, and it will certainly spot dollars away from stations. Things will certainly get worse before they get better" (Freeman and Dupree 1995: 5).

One response to the concern about "trash talk" was the collaboration of Television Production Partners (TPP), a consortium of ten national advertisers (including Sears, Reebok, Procter and Gamble, General Motors, Campbell Soup, Coors, AT&T, Coca-Cola, MasterCard and Clorox), with Norman Lear's production company, ACT III Productions, on a new talk show hosted by Maya Angelou. One media expert positioned Lear as "reinventing the talk show genre" (Friedman 1995: 5).[6] While this arrangement was cited as appealing to controversy-shy advertisers, it was represented as an arrangement in which advertisers would provide overall direction in terms of the type of program, but would not be close enough to production to be perceived to be in a censorship role (Friedman 1995: 5).

The Healthiest Business in Daytime

By year's end, *Broadcasting and Cable's* annual talk show section declared that "this year's youth movement among new syndicated show hosts isn't paying off in the ratings" and noted that "the old guard of daytime has successfully, almost effortlessly, beaten back the onslaught of youth sparked by *Ricki Lake's* meteoric rise last year" (Littleton 1995c: 50). Another, more downplayed reason cited was that the fall premieres coincided with the climax of the O. J. Simpson murder trial. Even so, most industry press cited the "cannibalization" resulting from the intense competition between "all but the highest rated of the twenty-three talk show strips airing in syndication this season" (Littleton 1995c: 50). Again, as earlier in the year, the trend of talk show topics becoming "more sensational and bizarre" was attributed to the intense competition for shows to distinguish themselves (Littleton 1995c: 50).

In December 1995 *Oprah Winfrey* continued to be "firmly entrenched" while *Jenny Jones* and *Ricki Lake* tied for second place for most of the fall 1995 season (Littleton 1995c: 51). Again, *Jerry Springer* was noted as posting the best result, returning for its fourth season. The show's ratings increased 21 percent overall, 29 percent among women aged 18–34 and 40 percent among women 18–49 (Littleton 1995c: 51).

Donahue was cited as dropping 65 percent over its prior year's time period for women aged 18–34 and 50 percent for women 25–54 (Littleton 1996b: 66). Based on their ratings increases, *Ricki Lake* and *Jenny Jones* had received numerous upgrades from daytime to early fringe markets. Both shows experienced drops in household ratings attributable to this change but continued to have strong young-adult demographics (McClellan 1996a: 26). Industry leaders noted that the season's failures should not be interpreted as a sign that viewers are "tired of talk." Rather, a production/syndication executive noted that "[t]alk as a genre has never been more popular. . . . The gross ratings points generated by talk shows have grown over the past five years. Whenever you have a phenomenon like that, there are always some growth adjustments that need to be made. . . . It's just the normal sign of a maturing marketplace" (Littleton 1996b: 66).

In *Broadcasting and Cable's* annual January 1996 NATPE survey of 101 television station general managers, 41 percent of managers indicated that daytime constituted their most important programming need, with 25 percent responding that early fringe was most pressing. Eighty-three percent agreed with a statement criticizing talk shows for "sleazy, tasteless subject matter, with little, if any, redeeming value," with 63 percent agreeing that they should be changed or taken off the air, listing *Jenny Jones* (31 percent), *Ricki Lake* (28 percent), and *Jerry Springer* (20%) as the chief offenders (McClellan 1996b: 34). However, when asked, "Have you ever considered canceling a talk show based solely or primarily on content?," 37 percent responded yes and 57 percent responded no (6 percent responded "not applicable"). Forty-three percent responded that it was more difficult to sell talk shows to advertisers because of content, and 49 percent responded that it was not more difficult (McClellan 1996b: 34).

Even with the disappointing ratings of new shows, at least twelve new talk shows were cited as being in development for launch in 1996 (Littleton 1995d: 56). *Broadcasting and Cable's* January 1996 issue declared, "Talk toughs it out: through preemptions, low ratings and content bashing, genre proves resilient." Veteran observers are cited as commenting that "the future still looks bright for the genre" (Littleton 1996b: 59).

Given the poor performance of 1995's mostly younger-skewed offerings, the prediction for fall 1996 shows in development was that "[p]erversion, dysfunction and scandal are out as talk fodder; wholesome, wacky and topical are in" (Littleton 1996c: 46).

While not all talk shows featured the kinds of topics attacked by Bennett and other critics in fall 1995, industry press reflected a concern that Bennett's campaign had influenced program buyers to think that the entire talk genre is "trash" (Littleton 1996c: 48). In addition, market research by programming production companies was cited as indicating that "for the first time in five years, our research shows that people are looking for alternatives to talk. . . . They're saying there's too much of the same thing out there" (Littleton 1996c: 48).

Rather than trying to imitate the success of *Ricki Lake* (which no one else seemed to be able to duplicate), program development centered on a strategy of competing through differentiation. In this context, *The Rosie O'Donnell Show*, scheduled to debut in 1996, was positioned as a return to the Mike Douglas talk/variety format. Game shows and reality shows were also cited as efforts to counterprogram talk shows in many markets (Littleton 1996d: 34). However, in the opinion of industry veterans, talk shows were considered "likely to remain the dominant force in daytime and early fringe for many years to come," with some predicting that "the new push to counterprogram talk will only benefit the genre in the long run" (Littleton 1996d: 35).

One of the "advertiser-friendly" talk shows in development for fall 1996, *J&I*, a talk show co-hosted by a mother-daughter team, was noted as being produced with a new model, an alliance of syndicator, advertiser, and station, in this case CBS's new syndication unit CBS/Group W/Maxam and the parent company of Foot, Cone and Belding Advertising. The advertising firm was given an equity stake in exchange for "upfront commitments" from agency clients (Littleton and Coe 1996: 21).

With changes in FCC syndication and finance rules effective in late 1995, allowing networks to own and distribute programming on a much farther-reaching scale, as well as the growth of the Fox, WB, and UPN networks, "distribution is where the battleground is," according to the executive director of the Advertiser Syndicated Television Association. As a result, the industry press noted that syndicators were reportedly looking for "long-term deals" with sizable station groups" (Littleton and Coe 1996: 22).

By December 1996, *Broadcasting and Cable's* annual talk show section announced that "talk remains the healthiest business in daytime television, although it is not immune to the boom-and-bust cycle" (Littleton 1996g: 26). While almost two dozen talk shows failed within a three-year period, industry forecasters predicted that "the talk marketplace is headed for a recovery next year as the gap between supply and demand narrows" (Littleton 1996g: 26). The success of *The Rosie O'Donnell Show* was cited as a "boon to the daytime landscape," although, given the number of shows that failed in trying to imitate *Ricki Lake*, distributors were characterized as being more cautious in attempts to imitate *O'Donnell*. *Rosie O'Donnell* was referred to as "appointment television for four million to five million people a day [with an average Nielsen household rating of 4.5 for early December]. The overnight success of the show . . . has made most talk show producers wonder why the Dinah Shore/Merv Griffin talk/variety format ever disappeared from daytime" (Littleton 1997a: 40). While weekly production costs were estimated to be between $400,000 to $500,000 (in addition to $2–$3 million for marketing and advertising), the show was expected to earn more than $100 million during the next two years for Warner Bros., the show's producer (Littleton 1997a: 40). *Rosie O'Donnell's* success and *Oprah Winfrey's* dominance were noted as quieting controversy over "trash talk" (Littleton 1996g: 26–27).

While *Ricki Lake's* household ratings were down for 1995–96, the show continued to dominate the young-adult audience in major markets including New York, Los Angeles and Chicago (Littleton 1996g: 27). *Sally Jessy Raphael* was reported as "holding steady," and *Montel Williams*, who won the 1996 Emmy for best talk show host, as having ratings "inching up at a time when some veterans are slipping" (Littleton 1996g: 27). Shows characterized as "mid- range performers" (*The Geraldo Rivera Show, Rolonda, Jerry Springer,* and *Gordon Elliott*) were reported as down for the year. In December 1996 MCA bought Multimedia Entertainment, distributor of *Sally Jessy Raphael* and *Jerry Springer,* from Gannett Co. for a reported $40–$45 million (Littleton 1996f: 12). While *Sally Jessy Raphael* was indicated as being at the heart of the deal, an MCA executive noted that "*Springer* is 'a very profitable little show,'" thus recognizing that while the new owners expected to "tweak the content," they did not expect the show to be more than a "tad more advertiser-friendly" (McClellan 1996d: 39, 42).

"Feel-Good, Celebrity-Friendly Gossip is 'In'" . . . But *Springer* Is on the Rise

The forecast for 1997 was that fewer shows would be offered for syndication and that the "shows with the best buzz" would be those meant to counterprogram to talk shows (Littleton 1997a: 44). The increasing costs and lower returns were noted as prompting some program suppliers to cut back on their development and examine the possibilities of cable, with lack of good time period availability as a central concern cited by one programming and development executive. However, as in the prior year, "despite all the negative flap about talk shows in the past two years, the genre remains the most in-demand form with potential buyers on the eve of the annual National Association of Television Program Executive convention," with 21 percent of general managers interviewed for *Broadcasting and Cable's* annual survey indicating that talk shows were their greatest programming need (McClellan 1997: 24). Fifty-six percent of those surveyed responded that they thought talk show content had improved; 52 percent indicated that it was no easier or difficult to sell advertising on the shows, 28 percent thought it was more difficult, and 11 percent reported that it was actually easier. It was noted that "[d]ysfunctional families and mothers-who-dress-like-tramps haven't disappeared from the daytime scene, but they no longer rule. The feel-good, friendly celebrity gossip of *Rosie O'Donnell* is in" (Littleton 1997a: 40). In addition, *Martha Stewart,* a new half-hour show, was being positioned in daytime as appealing to a different demographic than *Ricki Lake.* An executive of the show's producer/distributor noted:

> We're simply going for the pot of gold: the American housewife . . . Over the last twenty-five years, daytime television has become a lot more fragmented and basically, syndicators have forgotten how to program to American housewives. Today, there are fewer housewives because of the movement of working women, but housewives in the twenty-five to fifty-four demographic group are by far the dominant viewers of morning television. (Freeman 1997a: 27)

The February 1997 sweeps period proved that talk shows were still willing to air the type of content condemned by critics. Station representatives reported that there was little negative reaction on the part of advertisers. In particular, Jerry Springer, who achieved above-average ratings during the sweeps, was noted as "pledg[ing] that he will not bow to activist groups' or legislators' efforts to tone down his show, as two of his February episodes were given a TV-M rating [equivalent to an NC-17 movie rating] by the show's own producers" (Freeman 1997b: 13).

By November 1997, the media press announced that "[o]nce-maligned chat shows are up in ratings and ad dollars." Both *Jerry Springer* and *Jenny Jones* were cited as posting "significant gains" in

October ratings. Springer was up 56 percent to a 4.1 rating in the women aged 18–49 demographic in the early fringe time period, higher than *Rosie O'Donnell* (3.1) in the same demographic and time period, although this was a 33 percent increase for *Rosie*. *Jenny Jones* was up 47 percent in daytime (Freeman 1997c: 9). *Oprah Winfrey* was down (to a 5.1) in this demographic, as were Montel Williams (2.0) and Geraldo Rivera (1.1). *Jerry Springer* was noted as the "biggest surprise in talkers' resurgence" (Freeman 1997c: 9). In the afternoon he placed second overall behind *Oprah Winfrey* and placed ahead of her in several key markets (Freeman 1997c: 9). However, mainstream advertisers, including General Mills, Procter and Gamble, Kraft, and Warner Lambert were not advertising on the show. Thirty-second spot advertisements on the show were being sold for $11,000 to $16,000, about $10,000 to $15,000 less than what syndicators generally get from mainstream sponsors. One programming firm executive noted that "[the show is] about as exploitative as you can get, and it's working in terms of ratings" (Donovan 1997a: 42). The show's producer/distributor commented, "It's entertainment, pure and simple" (Donovan 1997a: 42). The show's popularity was attributed by those in the industry to its "racier content" and the increase in on-air fighting, which makes the show stand out from its competition, since many other shows have attempted to move more in *Oprah's* direction (Donovan 1997a: 42).

Syndicators and station representatives were characterized as thinking that the "shakeout" in talk shows over the prior two years benefited the surviving shows. With fourteen talk shows in syndication in fall 1997 (compared to seventeen in 1996), the shakeout had "effectively reduced competition and fattened the pie for incumbents," according to a syndication industry association executive director (Freeman 1997c: 9). Reflective of this, total daytime advertising revenue for syndication was expected to reach $296 million in 1998, a 22 percent increase from the 1997 season (Freeman 1997c: 9).

The forecast described in *Broadcasting and Cable's* December 1997 annual section on talk shows indicated that talk show offerings for fall 1998 would attempt to capitalize on *Rosie O'Don-nell's* success, casting "big names" (e.g., Roseanne, Howie Mandel, Marie and Donny Osmond) as hosts for proposed talk shows, of which there were now twice the number in development compared to the prior year (Donovan 1997b: 45).

In accounting for the success overall of talk shows as a genre attracting the valuable women aged 18–49 demographic, a station representative firm executive suggested why ratings for daytime dramas declined in the late 1980s: "Talk shows had taken away the vicarious thrill the soaps had offered for so long with storylines extended for weeks on end.... Talk offered viewers the same thrill in a single hour and promised another one tomorrow" (Plume 1997: 50). The only network-produced talk shows were *Leeza* and *The View* (which debuted in August 1997).

"The Only Wild Show Left": The Success of *Jerry Springer*

The cover story for the December 15, 1997, issue of *Broadcasting and Cable* was: "Jerry Springer: PUNCHING the Envelope" (with the word "punching" emphasized in a larger font size). The story emphasized *Springer's* being "on a roll," with ratings up 114 percent from the prior year. Nielsen ratings for the last week of November 1997 sweeps indicated that *Springer* achieved a 6.4 rating, beating *Oprah Winfrey's* 6.3. The article suggested that the fighting, which became the *Springer* show's signature, had propelled it in the ratings (Schlosser 1997b: 33).

In an interview, Springer suggested that the show's success might be attributable to its being "the only wild show left"

(Schlosser 1997b: 33). He commented that "I'll be the first to tell you it's totally outrageous in there [pointing to the show's studio]. There is no seriousness to it . . . Our show is nothing but fun, outrageous, total entertainment" (Schlosser 1997b: 33). With the rise in ratings, *Jerry Springer's* license fees rose substantially. For example, in Washington, D.C., considered a major market area, a local station agreed to pay up to $25,000 per week for the show, beginning in February 1999, up from the $8,000 per week that had been paid by the station running the show over the preceding three years (Freeman 1998b: 8). In addition, the show was reported to have been receiving time period upgrades to early fringe, for example in Detroit, where it aired in the 4–5 P.M. time period against Oprah, beating her with a 12.4 rating against Oprah's 10.1 (Freeman 1998b: 9).[7]

By January 1998, *Jerry Springer* was referred to in the industry press as "the biggest breakout hit of the 1997–98 syndicated TV season" (Freeman 1998a: 31). While new shows attempted to capitalize on *Rosie O'Donnell's* "advertiser-friendly, entertainment-based" talk show format, this contributed to the "thinning of ranks" among the "single-topic, confrontational shows," leaving shows like *Springer, Sally Jessy Raphael,* and *Jenny Jones* to grow (Freeman 1998a: 32). Major studios and independent syndicators still aimed to focus development on "advertiser-friendly" shows because major advertisers were reported to still shy away from *Springer's* type of show. In this vein, *The Roseanne Show* was being touted as "the most successful launch of any talk show ever, [with] the highest license fees and best time periods at launch of any take show launched," according to Roger King, chairman of King World Productions, the show's producer/syndicator (along with *Oprah Winfrey*). Roseanne was positioned as being "someone who easily related to people from middle America as she does with Hollywood stars" (Freeman 1998a: 32). In addition, while Roseanne's "off- screen relationship problems" and her "recent therapy for multiple-personality disorder" were framed as contributing an element of risk to the show, this element of unpredictability was also perceived as giving the show a "unique sort of edge. . . . It may have some risk [in terms of the show's cost], but it may also have an incredible upside" in terms of ratings, according to a programming executive (Freeman 1998a: 32).

By February 1998, *Adweek* reported that "the wall of resistance [was] breaking down," with respect to a willingness to advertise on *Jerry Springer,* given that the estimated cost of a thirty-second spot was reported to be at $30,000 compared to $85,000 on *Oprah* and $60,000 on *Rosie* (Brooke 1998: 17).

Springer continued his ascent in the ratings through 1998. By May his show was cited as the fastest-growing syndicated talk show in history and as having consistently beaten *Oprah Winfrey* for two months (Conlin 1998: 44). In the May sweeps, for example, Springer averaged an 8.1 household rating, against Oprah's 7.3 (McClellan 1998: 62). The show was estimated to generate as much as $100 million in 1998 (Conlin 1998: 44). In addition, Springer videos with titles including "Too Hot for TV," "Bad Boys and Naughty Girls," and "Wild Relationships" were reported among the top five hundred video rentals in the country (K. Johnson 1998). *The Jerry Springer Show* had become the paradigm of outrageousness, sex, and fighting such that a Springer-inspired spoof of the Clinton/Lewinsky sex scandal appeared on a late-night talk show and concerns that we are becoming a Jerry Springer-like country were voiced in the media as various legislators confessed their sexual indiscretions publicly.

Conclusion

Like it or not, talk shows have proven themselves a viable, low-cost daytime programming form. While strategizing to provide programming that will attract and keep specific audiences in an increasingly competitive business environment, the central aim of industry executives is to sell advertising time to sponsors who want to reach these audiences. Women who watch talk shows participate in the business of talk, whether or not this fact holds any personal significance for them. As is the case for all television viewers, they are the heart of the business, as it is their consuming potential as "audience share" that sponsors want to mobilize through their purchase of advertising time. In particular, women who watch talk shows constitute that "important female 18–34 demographic" upon which the success of daytime programming depends.

Having established their participation in the business of talk as viewers and consumer potential, we will now look at how this participation fits into the women's everyday lives.

3. Talk Shows and Everyday Life

I've never really been somebody that's been a slave to talk shows. Like, "Oh, I have to see it! I have to be home to see that!" You know, if I'm home and there's nothing else on I will watch it. You know. But, I've never really been, like, a "fan" fan, where, "Oh, my God!" you know, "I missed Oprah, I have to tape her!" I've never been like that.

(Chandra)

What I do is, after I finish watching Jerry—'Cause, I mean, I can sit home 'til two o'clock. They don't take attendance until the second class sometimes. And the first class is typing. But you're not really doing anything. If you need to catch up on some homework, that's the time to do it. That type of thing. So . . . You know, I'll stay home and I'll watch, and then I'll go to school.

(Jamie)

I used to have this little line-up when I was home with my daughter. I would start watching. I would change it around a little bit. But I used to watch *Jenny Jones*. Then I would watch *Jerry Springer*. Then I'd watch *Sally*. Then in the afternoon [laughing] I'd—it was terrible. I'm glad . . . I had to get off that rut, because you really—just like soap operas. You just, you get into it.

(Tina)

I watch, like, *Rosie* and *Ricki* and *Sally*, cause they're all in sync [laughs]. They're all at the same time so—pretty much, whatever is on. If it's on, I'll watch it [laughs]. If I have free time, I'm usually, like, turn on the TV. 'Cause, it's not like, they're just, they're easy 'cause you don't get hooked on them. Like you don't have to watch them in a series. And if you miss a day, it's not a big deal.

(Colleen)

The process of "making sense" occurs in the course of everyday life. Therefore, in trying to understand how the women I interviewed make sense of talk shows, I consider how watching talk shows fits into their everyday lives, in particular, how their practice of watching talk shows fits into the other routine practices of their everyday lives. Following Silverstone, I suggest that

> an inquiry into the audience should be an inquiry, not into a set of pre-constituted individuals or rigidly defined social groups, but into a set of daily practices and discourses within which the complex act of watching television is placed alongside others, and through which that complex act itself is constituted. (Silverstone 1994: 133)

To understand the ways in which watching talk shows fits into the women's lives one must consider when and where the shows are encountered, as well as the particular circumstance of those encounters. This understanding includes the different ways of watching television, how one pays attention to a program or the degree to which one pays attention to it. All this, in turn, can be understood against the institutional structures and practices that shape the contours of everyday life in contemporary American society.

The significance of the routine practice of watching talk shows varied among the women I interviewed.[1] However, the women consistently spoke about watching talk shows (and watching television more generally) as a habit—something each woman incorporated as a natural and self-evident aspect of her everyday life; for the most part, it was an unremarkable part, just done but not reflected upon. This quality of the practice being "routine" and "daily" and its varied significance are central to understanding how watching talk shows fits into the everyday lives of the women who watch them.

My analysis of the women's narratives also shows that their *experience* of time, their sense of temporality, is central to how they make sense of their practice of watching talk shows. Moreover, I show that each woman experiences herself in several distinctive but interconnected modes of temporality through which her sense of herself is constituted.

Everyday Life and Everyday Practices

What do I mean by the term *everyday life?* In the context of this study, everyday life is understood as the daily routines, practices, and structures that, for the most part, unproblematically order each day and our daily experience. This involves two interwoven and reciprocal dimensions. One dimension encompasses the material rituals, practices, and structures that we enact and in which we are involved on a routine basis. This includes, for example, getting up at a certain time, going to work, taking care of children, hygienic practices, the routines, practices, and organization of school, family, and work; ways of greeting others and interacting with others. The second dimension encompasses the modes of understanding, classifying, and categorizing that allow us to recognize and negotiate these material rituals, practices, and structures. The latter is referred to in phenomenological literature as "consciousness," with the important recognition that consciousness is always consciousness *of* something or directed *toward* something.[2]

Everyday life is historically, culturally, and geographically specific. That is to say, contents and routines of everyday life in the northeastern city in which I live are distinct from what they were 150 years ago. Similarly, the material everyday life of my middle-class urban existence is distinct from the material everyday life of, say, poor, rural Guatemala or, as a less dramatic example, rural

Nebraska. (Some factors, including media, for instance, may be similar across contexts.) Additionally, both how I am materially situated and how I discursively locate myself within my circumstances (my subjective experience) will also affect the way my everyday life is both constituted and experienced.

Temporality as a Key Dimension of Everyday Life

While the specificity of the substance and organization of everyday life in different historical, geographical, and cultural contexts varies, everyday life, as it is lived, is experienced in its dailiness as an immediate, up-close "vivid present" in which we find ourselves immersed and involved (Schutz, cited in Drotner 1994: 349). While the substance and organization of everyday life are distinct depending on a range of factors, their experiential quality of "dailiness" is consistent.

While it may be overstating the obvious, time is a key dimension of both the organization and experience of everyday life. Everyday experience occurs in time (and space), and how individuals make sense of this time and locate themselves in it has much bearing on how they understand themselves in relation to their own lives and society more generally.

Giddens (1986) takes seriously the constitutive role of temporality in social life in a manner I find useful to my analysis. He distinguishes three modalities in respect to the experience of time: the *durée of day-to-day experience*, the *time of the lifespan*, and the *longue durée* of institutional time. Distinguishing what he refers to as *the durée of day-to-day experience*, Giddens states:

> Whether or not time "as such" (whatever that would be) is reversible, the events and routines of daily life do not have a one-way flow to them. The terms "social reproduction," "recursiveness"

and so on indicate the repetitive character of day-to-day life, the routines of which are formed in terms of the intersection of the passing (but continual returning) days and seasons. Daily life has a duration, a flow, but it does not lead anywhere; the very adjective "day-to-day" and its synonyms indicate that time here is constituted only in repetition. (Giddens 1986: 35)

For the women I interviewed, the practice of watching talk shows has the repetitive character Giddens describes. The practice is something in which they engage with routine regularity, if not daily. Each viewing, though it is the enactment of an ongoing routine, is discrete and self-contained, even when the actual viewing includes "flipping around" between two or more shows, as was the case for several of the women I interviewed.[3] Additionally, some of the women talked about "getting into a rut," implying that they found themselves caught up in a repetitive routine they no longer wanted to continue but wanted to break.

Giddens contrasts this cyclical, repetitive time of the day-to-day (everyday life) to what he calls the lifespan of the individual. This time is "not only finite but irreversible, 'being towards death'" (Giddens 1986: 35). This time, he suggests, is "the time of the body. . . . Our lives 'pass away' in irreversible time with the passing away of the life of the organism" (Giddens 1986: 35).

The women I interviewed articulated varying senses of this lifetime as they shared how their routine of watching talk shows fit into their other everyday routines and through the differing values they explicitly and implicitly ascribed to these routines. The women's accounts of watching talk shows and how their routine of watching fit into their everyday life were generally informed by a usually implicit, although sometimes explicit, sense of a life trajectory. In their narratives, the women seemed to position themselves as being existentially located somewhere along a particular type of life trajectory that included a sense of their past, their present, and their imagined or assumed future. Some life-trajectory types included: locating oneself in a pre-career formative stage, assuming future upward mobility in a professional career; locating oneself as having completed one's career, having paid one's dues, so to speak, and now enjoying relaxing in the present; anticipating this for the future as well, locating oneself in a formative stage, moving back into employment after a temporary period of being unproductive (an atypical break in this life trajectory of honest work), anticipating a modestly successful career. An important dimension in each case was the mood in which each of the women spoke about her viewing practices and her everyday life more generally. Mood can be understood as being based in an assessment (usually not conscious or rational, in terms of "reasoned") of one's future possibilities.[4] Mood often served as a key to understanding how women located themselves in both their present circumstances and in relation to the future they imagined for themselves.

Giddens refers to a third dimension of temporality, the *longue durée* of institutional time. He conceptualizes this as a "supra-individual" temporality, involved with the "succession of generations," the time of institutions that is "both the condition and the outcome of the practices organized in the continuity of day-to-day life" (Giddens 1986: 36). This is the time of practices that may have come before and will likely continue after the individual lifetime of "everydays" is complete, but with which individuals are involved in the daily present of their everyday lives. These institutional practices are in many ways constitutive of individual everyday life. From this view, for example, the women I interviewed are not simply watching television programs as a cyclical, everyday, individual practice. Rather, through the routines of their own everyday lives they are simultaneously participating in, and in varying ways incorporating, institutional practices of the broadcasting industry, an industry with particular historical interests and practices. Morley points to what can be characterized as a reciprocal relationship:

[W]e need to be attentive on the one hand to the ways in which, at both micro and macro levels, the organization of broadcasting is influenced by pre-existing cultural orientations to time, within society at large, or within a particular sub-culture or family and, on the other hand, to the effect of broadcasting schedules themselves on the organization of time. Broadcasting and other technologies of communication must be seen both as entering into already constructed, historically specific divisions of time and space, and also as transforming those pre-existing divisions. (Morley 1992b: 266)

Scannell (1996) recognizes the complexity of time and broadcasting as they interweave with everyday life. He challenges critics who charge that both the press and broadcasting simply work to reproduce the status quo "of creating a frozen immediacy caught in an eternal present that obliterates the past and denies the future" (151). Scannell argues that "[n]othing could be further from the truth, for time runs to many rhythms in the structures of broadcasting, while always converging on the now" (152). He concurs with Morley that broadcasting participates in articulating our sense of time. Like Silverstone (who clearly incorporates a phenomenological orientation toward his analysis of temporality), he specifies (in the distinctive context of British broadcasting) the interplay of the industry's temporal practices and those of everyday life. Broadcasting, while delivering a daily service is always "being-ahead-of-itself. It is always already projected beyond the day that we and it are in, and, indeed it must be so in order to produce for us the day that we are in" (Scannell 1996: 152). The institutional practices of the broadcasting industry can be understood as simultaneously being involved in everyday practices as well as in practices more associated with the longue durée. Similarly, Scannell recognizes how individuals live in different types of time simultaneously. While we live in the immediacy of the cyclical, repetitive day to day, we also live in the "for the weekend," or "year to year for that one day of carnival when the world comes alive in it's fullness . . . or . . . long for Christmas Day or one's birthday as children do" (Scannell 1996: 153). That these different modalities of time converge in the women's everyday life is apparent in their narratives about their practice of watching talk shows.

Differing Temporal Organization/Differing Practices

My analysis begins with a focus on what the women had to say about how viewing fits into the organization of their day—when, where, and how they viewed the shows. I initially categorized the women's interviews into three distinctive viewing modes based on the way their viewing fit into the temporal organization of their day: "watching as a central daily practice," "watching as a 'break,'" and "watching as one activity among others." The women's narratives show that in order to understand how watching talk shows fits into their daily lives, simply tracking the temporal organization of their practice in relation to other routine daily activities is inadequate. The way each woman's day is organized must be considered as a complex of linked and overlapping activities and routines occurring in assorted, distinct physical spaces. Also important is the fact that the women assign varying degrees of significance to their activities and frame them within different temporal modes.

"All the Talk Shows, All Day Long": Watching as a Central Daily Practice

For Betty, Olivia, and Joan, watching talk shows is or was a *central* daily practice. While these three women shared a similar practice of watching television for many hours of the day, how they positioned their practice and how they articulated themselves as subjects varied considerably. The women's life circumstances also varied in substantial ways. For example, while two of the women did not work outside the home, even this circumstance was different in each case. What is consistent across all three cases is that all three women were available to watch daytime television, although each was home due to a specific circumstance.

Betty, a fifty-year-old black woman, was the full-time mother of a three-year-old adopted foster daughter (she also had a grown birth daughter). She had worked as a foster-care provider for several years after holding working-class jobs for over twenty years. She shared the following:

> Betty: Yes and I worked over 20 years. I worked eighteen years at the House of Giorgio as a stitcher for a bridal shop. And I worked five and a half years at Gillette. And I did the last—
>
> Julie: At Gillette, you said?
>
> Betty: Gillette. And the last seven years I did foster care in my home. And now I'm ready to, you know, leave it all alone.
>
> Julie: Yeah?
>
> Betty: Uhum. 'Cause I'm having a lot of trouble with my leg and my shoulder now. So, you know, I'm ready, you know, just stay home and raise my little girl. That's about it for me. I love to cook. I like to clean.

Betty's narrative makes it clear that she enjoys being at home, even though this development was precipitated by physical problems.

Betty was the only woman in my study to self-identify using the term "fan." When I asked her about the shows she watches, she explained:

Betty: Well . . . I like all the talk shows. I'm really, I'm really a
       Channel 5 fan. Any morning time. Oh, at nine o'clock I
       usually catch Rolanda. And then, if I don't watch her, if
       she don't have nothing on that I'm really interested in, I
       usually turn to Gordon.

Julie: Is he still on?

Betty: Yeah, he come on at nine now, in the morning. Channel
       4. And then, from nine to ten, I don't like the Rosie O'-
       Donnell show. I turn to Montel Williams on 25. That's at
       ten to eleven. And then, from ten, from ten, from eleven
       to twelve I catch *The Sally Raphael Show.* From twelve usu-
       ally, basically, I'm watching *Jerry Springer.* If I'm not with
       Jerry Springer, I'm on *Ricki Lake.* So that goes from twelve
       to one. . . . And then from one to two, that's *Jenny Jones.*
       From two, I usually change, you know, and watch a cou-
       ple of soap operas, if I'm not running around. 'Cause you
       know, they taken off about all the talk shows anyway, you
       know. Because they used to have shows 24 hours a day,
       you know. But they doesn't have that now. So, that's about
       the only one that stays on 'til two is *Jenny Jones.* And then,
       some time around—what time is *Geraldo,* come on some
       time around two-thirty, around three?—I may catch him
       some time. Cause I'm usually running through the
       house.

While all of the women talk about watching television as a
practice that spans the day (and night, for some) and share close
knowledge of daily programming flow, they vary with respect to
how they watch, both in terms of the attention they give it and
with respect to their valuation of the practice.

In my two interview sessions with Betty in her home (one conducted in the living room, the other in her bedroom), the television was on.[5] By Betty's account, her viewing practice entails her

watching by herself in her room, relatively uninterrupted, taking breaks to attend to her daughter.

> Julie: So, like, when you're watching them [talk shows], is it the kind of thing where you're mostly sitting here actually watching the whole show, or are you doing other stuff?
>
> Betty: Oh no. I'm going to sit down and watch my whole show. My kids are in here watching TV. [We were sitting in the living room, she watches in her bedroom.] Commercial come, I check and see what they're doing. 'Cause, see there's two of us here. [Referring to her sister, who shares the apartment and is a foster parent of a young boy.] So, at lunchtime, around—who come on at twelve? *Jerry Springer*. So I, you know, come in, see what they want or what they're doing. But I want them to, you know, they're running in and out. But, I'm sitting on the side of my bed. I sit in here sometime [referring to the living room], you know, with the kids. You know, but I don't sit around with the kids and we don't watch it together. They sit in here, and I'm in there. If they in there, I'm in here.
>
> Julie: Okay. And so, when are you watching when you have the kids here? Is that with the kids that you watch every day?
>
> Betty: Yes.
>
> Julie: I've got it. So, they're playing and you're . . .
>
> Betty: Yeah, on that visit, you know, lunch or anything. A commercial will come on, and either I fix it or my sister.

Betty's narrative is one about a day structured to allow her child-care responsibilities and television watching to weave together unproblematically. For the most part, she does not portray herself as a "distracted" viewer (Modleski 1983). Some of this orientation is present when she speaks about sometimes "catching" Geraldo, because she is usually "running through the house" at the time his show comes on. But, according to her account, this seems to be the exception. Betty speaks unapologetically about her television watching generally, and talk show viewing specifically.

Just like the other women for whom watching television is a practice spanning the day and who show a detailed knowledge of television programming flow, Betty speaks about "her" shows (e.g., "I'm going to sit down and watch my whole show"). This is a relational discourse, spoken with affinity, which, as I listened, evoked a sense of her pleasure and enjoyment.

Olivia, a twenty-three-year-old black woman, was the only woman of the three who was working outside the home at the time of the interview. She worked four days a week in an administrative job at a large hospital, with hours that allowed her to be at home during the daytime hours with some regularity. Olivia attended beauty school for several months, but was "terminated" for poor attendance and had been working since that time. At the time of our interview, Olivia was applying for another job. She was living in her mother's house in an inner-city Boston neighborhood, although prior to this she had had her own apartment. We spoke in the living room as her baby niece slept.

Olivia watches talk shows as part of her larger routine of watching television. Her schedule varies with her work schedule. She commented:

> I work like three to ten, five to ten. My hours are like that. Afternoon 'til the evening. So, if you have time to watch them, you can turn them on. You know what I mean? Like, sometimes I'll listen to music. But, the majority of the time there's nothing else to do. You just turn on the TV and just watch TV. So, that's the only thing you see between—if you're not into the stories, the only thing else there is to watch is talk shows.

Olivia shares her schedule, which, on her days off from work, is virtually filled with television:

> It's like I said, I have, let me tell you, I have, since I left school, I have a lot of free time on my hands. So, as I said, I work probably like four days out of the week. So, it's like if I have, I have a lot of time to watch talk shows. So it's a schedule. At home, if I don't work, and I'm at home the majority of the day, I get up probably around nine forty-five. I watch *Rosie* 'til eleven. And then, I watch *Sunset Beach*, the soap opera that comes on Channel 7. I watch that from eleven to twelve. And then from twelve to one I watching *Jerry*. And then from one to two, depending on what story's good that day, or whatever, I'll watch *Jenny Jones*. I might watch *Jenny*, and if I'm watching *Days of Our Lives*—'cause my mother and me are heavy *on Days of Our Lives*. So I turn to *Days of Our Lives* and I watch it until two. Mmm—two-thirty I watch *The Cosby Show*. Then from two- thirty to three, I watch [laughs] *Family Matters*. And then from three—now mind you, this is all TV. So this is, see how TV has an effect, right? Okay, so, from three to four I watch *General Hospital*. Then [laughs], this makes my life sound really boring. [Julie laughs] And then from four, from four to four-thirty, I watch *Oprah*. And from four-thirty to like five, I switch back and forth from *Oprah* to *Hard Copy*. Then at five, I watch *Ricki*. Then at six [laughs], at six—let's see where I was. At six, six is kind of my down time. I just kind of find something to do.

Continuing to describe her evening viewing schedule in detail, Olivia reflexively assesses what she has just shared with me

> My life sounds boring, right? No, I mean I don't have nothing to do now. Me and my boyfriend broke up so I don't call him. So, whatever.

Olivia talks about watching television because she has "nothing to do now." She has "a lot of time on her hands," given that she is working part time and has broken up with her boyfriend. She positions her television viewing as a way of filling time, by implication an activity by default. Olivia's account articulates a concern that her watching television as much as she does reflects negatively on her life (e.g., "My life sounds boring, right?"), indicating that she embodies certain standards, particular discourses of productivity, which she assesses herself as not measuring up to. In addition, Olivia repeatedly laughed as she spoke about her viewing. I sensed this as a laugh of self-conscious recognition of the automaticity of her routine, a routine she finds herself in because "the majority of the time there's nothing else to do." This raises the question of what underlies her having "nothing else to do." Is it that she is bored or otherwise psychologically unmotivated to "do something,"[6] or is it in at least some ways a function of lack of resources or access to opportunities? This is not clear, but is an important point in the context of understanding even apparently trivial everyday routines. Olivia does not speak about watching as a significant activity, although it fills much of her time. Rather, it is a way of filling time because there is nothing else significant to do.

Olivia's account is quite distinct from Betty's. Betty's practice of watching television is not *instead of* something else, but simply constitutive of her day. For Betty, watching television is not an activity by default, but rather a matter-of-fact, anticipated activity of her day. She does not articulate a self-conscious monitoring of herself as falling short of a prescribed standard. In retrospect, I speculate about why this might be the case. Perhaps Betty, having had a long career of work as a seamstress, a manufacturing worker, and foster-care provider, assesses herself as having led a productive and hard-working life and is now ready to "leave it all," while Olivia, in her twenties and speaking about herself as "'still going through the I don't know what I'm going to do with myself' phase," and "not really focused," understands herself as not yet fulfilling the criteria for a productive life. Olivia's comments about her having started school at a bad time are consistent with this. Her life story gives some insight into this. For example, in speaking with me about her academic career, Olivia shared the following:

Olivia: I graduated from Charlestown High. And—I don't know, I never really, I didn't go to college. I think that was a big mistake. I should have gone. I just wanted to take some time off. And then some time off led into more time off, then more time off, and then more time off [laughs]. I should've just went straight to college. 'Cause I would've been out [by now].

Julie: Do you think about going back now?

Olivia: Now I feel like I'm too old.

Additionally, Olivia shared with me her childhood experience of being raised for six years by a white family in a suburban section of Boston. She told me:

It's like two different experiences. Two different—believe me. But, I know when I first moved around here [Roxbury] I was sick for a week because I wasn't used to this. But, you know, I say once you get used to living a good life-style, you get used to living a good life-style. Once you get used to living a [pauses, then laughs] a shitty life-style, you get used to living a shitty life-style. You know what I mean? But, it's like I say—I try not to be a product of my environment. So, it's like I live like this, but, that's not where my mind is.

Olivia situates herself in a very complex way. While physically located in a particular environment and an associated "life-style," she distinguishes herself subjectively from it, identifying herself with the "good" life-style she has known versus the "shitty" one in which she finds herself now. She discursively places herself in a position superior to her current material circumstances, but is simultaneously frustrated in experiencing herself as unable to move out of these circumstances.

Olivia speaks about herself as not being a "typical young black woman." In speaking with me about the topics on *The Ricki Lake Show* and the audience to whom she thinks that show appeals, she shares:

I don't fit into the average stereotype of a young black girl in Roxbury [where she lives]. Because, first of all, I don't have any children [laughs]. You know what I mean? I'm not, I'm not on drugs. I'm not on welfare, or whatever. You know what I mean? I work, you know. So it's like—but [drawn out, then laughs] the overwhelming majority they have—about my age—out of all my friends—me—my friend, Shirelle—I only have like three friends that don't have children. And they're older. All my friends are like seven or six years older than me. Some even ten. So, but, I'd say the ones that I went to school with, that I grew up with, that we were friends all the way through like high school, up until high school . . . they have like—my friend Michelle, me and her are good friends since I was thirteen. She has a kid. And I have another girl, we grew up since like the age of like seven on up. She has two now. And it's like, "Oh, I'm going to start." Everybody has children. Everybody is on welfare. Everybody's you know—so, it's like, I can relate to some of the stuff that, like, some of the things people talk about on *Ricki.*

While she talks about herself as not having gotten "caught up in that situation," Olivia speaks with a sense of disappointment and defeat about her present circumstances. This sense is consistent with her talk about "filling time" with television viewing and with the self-monitoring she articulates in her responses to my questions. While she is positioned within a particular world, she speaks about being distinct from it but, at least to this point, being unsuccessful in moving out of it. Olivia's self-reflexive mood of disappointment is absent from Betty's account. While Olivia's account of her television viewing routines is communicated in a self-deprecating mood, Betty's account is communicated matter-of-factly. Olivia's account implicitly embodies a normalizing discourse of productivity and achievement. Her concern that I might negatively assess her life ("My life must sound boring.") illustrates her incorporating a discourse of what constitutes a "good" or "productive" day. Moreover, she assesses herself as not living up to the standard invoked by this discourse. Olivia speaks about her everyday life as routine and lacking a direction forward, a direction she seems to want. In contrast, Betty clearly articulates that her working days are behind her and seems content with the prospect of staying home to take care of her daughter and her home.

Joan, a thirty-year-old white woman from a working-class background, was completing beauty school at the time of the interview. She had been laid off from a supervisory job at a large insurance company and was unemployed during the three years she watched talk shows during the day.

Joan related to me that since she'd been at school, she had not been watching talk shows very much. However, this was very different from the three years before she started beauty school after having been laid off. She told me:

> And then when I got laid off, me and my cousin would wake up in the morning, we'd take her five-year-old to school. We'd go get our Burger King breakfast. Come home. Channel 4. Channel 5. Channel 7. All the talk shows, all day long [laughs]. At the time when I was watching them constantly, I would *make*

the time to do it. But now it's different. If it's there, it's there. Because what I found was, I always, me and my cousin both, would get so excited.

During this time, which she retrospectively speaks about with self-deprecation, Joan told me she watched talk shows with "full attention, all day long." She shared:

Joan: Usually full attention, all day long. That's all I did. In the summer time, I could be possibly laying out in the sun or something. And then I'd come in if the talk show was good enough, or something like that. But most of the time I'd be in front of the TV watching them. Full attention.

Julie: Just one after another?

Joan: Yes—got to run. Get my ice tea or something. Hurry up, you know. I don't have time to make food or something.

Similar to Olivia, Joan negatively assesses these viewing habits, but in contrast to Olivia, Joan distances herself from this practice. In Joan's case, that period of television viewing is clearly a past practice, while it is something in which Olivia and Betty still engage. Joan describes herself as now productively involved in other things. Her days of watching television as a central daily activity are over; she speaks about that time as a bracketed period of her life:

At the time when I was watching them constantly, I would make the time to do it. But, now, it's different. If it's there, it's there.

Not only had Joan been laid off from a job she had had for eight years, but she characterized her life as being in "turmoil." When I asked her about how she would describe her life, she responded:

Joan: Turmoil [laughs].

Julie: Really? In what way?

Joan: It just seems—oh everything! You, um, you come to a point in your life where everything is going really well. And then all of a sudden, everything goes haywire. And then you'll try to get yourself back on track. And sometimes it just takes a long time to do it.

Julie: So that's been kind of a path for you?

Joan: Oh, the past three years have been like that since—I was laid off from the company that I'd been working for quite a long time, eight years. . . . So, for a while, I was like, "Well, scrub them! I'm not going to let them put me down and make me feel depressed!" So I went and spent all my money [laughs]. Just like my mother did. It's almost like a thing. When you get depressed, and then saying, "Well, I'm going to take every bit of money that they can give me and I'm going to spend it."

The routine of this period is set against her sense of a longer lifespan time. She sees herself as having moved on. She describes her change of practice as "drastic":

And it was drastic, too. It wasn't just like—it happened over like four months or anything like that. I think it started, two years I didn't do anything. I didn't work. I didn't go to school or anything. So, I was constantly watching them. And then, on the third year, this was last year, I started to work part time. And then, of course, I'd come home, watch the talk shows. Do all this stuff. But then all of a sudden—I would say, I would say it took just about two weeks. I don't know, I kind of remember [said slowly] that it was just like the stupid show, like *Jerry* and who else. Oh, I forget who it was. Was it *Ricki Lake*—and someone else? I know, I had noticed it before. Like that would all have like the same type of show on in the same week. And it was strange. One might be like a day after each other. But it was about the same exact [said deliberately] thing.

When I asked Joan for clarification, she continued:

I don't even know what the talk shows were about, but it was like those three. And all of a sudden, I was just like—it made me sick to my stomach. Just listening to them like how everybody's so rude to each other.

The words she used to account for her reactions (including "disgusting" and "cruel," for example) prompted me to comment to her that her reaction seemed strong. She responded,

It was. That's why it shocks the heck out of me. Because I used to love them so much. Like I mean, you wouldn't understand how we couldn't wait to get home. We'd—step on the gas. Run in the house. It was, like, so gross. And then, all of a sudden, I actually, feel nauseous. I really just didn't like them any more. It's strange, I know. It's weird.

As a working-class high school graduate, Joan was now sorting out her career options. At the time of the interview, Joan was completing the eight-month program at beauty school and, in doing so, was taking the initial steps in fulfilling her current career plans to own a day spa. Her narratives portray her as someone moving out of a transitional period. Therefore, the daily routines and viewing practices Joan recounts were the norm only for this transitional period of time, thus accounting for her self-disparagement. Joan spoke, at the time of the interview, as a subject who was reentering the workforce, moving on with a goal-oriented life, versus the undirected experience of her three years of unemployment. She positions herself as moving toward a life less characterized by "turmoil."

While the cases of Betty, Olivia, and Joan are not exhaustive of the variations among the women I interviewed, they articulate some key distinctions within a particular mode of viewing practice. Even among those who have a regular practice of watching television as a central activity of everyday life, there are important differences, if not in the actual enactment of their practice, in how they make sense of it. Betty exemplifies a person for whom the practice is transparent, while Olivia and Joan exemplify those who are self-conscious that the practice may be problematic as they reflect on it. These varied orientations toward making sense of the practice can be read through the discourses explicitly and implicitly invoked by the women, through both language and structure of feeling. In articulating these orientations, the women subjectively situate themselves in particular ways. For example, each articulates herself in relation to a discourse of productivity. This is a normalizing discourse that embodies certain standards with respect to what one ought to do with one's life. Each woman locates herself differently within this discourse: Betty as having been productively employed and now shifting gears toward a productive domestic activity of rearing her adopted daughter, Olivia as falling short and being uncertain about moving forward, and Joan as having temporarily been in a slump and now moving on to productive activity. Each implicitly invokes a standard as to what is appropriate given her position in a lifespan trajectory. Within this discourse of productivity, what everyday routines mean varies depending on each woman's place in a particular idealized life trajectory as well as in relation to her expectation about who one ought to "be" at what point in life in the context of this trajectory. Therefore, the practice of watching television as a central activity of her day makes sense differently to each woman.

"Honestly, I Just Watch Them to Relax": Watching Talk Shows as a "Break"

Most of the young college women I spoke with describe their practice of watching talk shows as constituting a "break" from the other activities of their day. These women were currently attending college and either living in a dormitory or sharing an apartment with other students. Most of these women describe themselves as having grown up middle class. (Amanda was the only one who explicitly described herself as "upper.") All the young women who characterized watching talk shows as a "break" were white.

Responding to my question about how frequently she watches talk shows, Susan shared the following:

Susan: Well, I probably watch about, honestly, like during the week I watch maybe like a talk show a day. Because I have, like, I have time for lunch in the afternoon after my classes are done. So I just eat and watch, like, a talk show at the same time and just, like, relax for like an hour—before I do other stuff.

Julie: And for the most part that ends up being *Ricki* or *Jenny* [referring to shows she'd mentioned earlier]. I don't know when they're on.

Susan: Yeah. Yeah. Whatever's on, honestly.

She further explains:

So, like honestly, it has more to do with they're like the only thing on, really, that you can just start watching, and not have to know anything about what's going on. I mean, honestly, you know, I could watch CNN or something. But I don't. You know, I mean, it's like I want to relax.

Later in the interview she continued:

> It's more, for me, it's more just volume, honestly. It's just like
> what's on. So it's like—that's what I watch. Do you know what I
> mean? If I'm just relaxing, or whatever, like hanging out. Cause
> I'm really busy during the day. If I'm just like hanging out or
> whatever, if it's what's on, it's what I watch. . . . And it doesn't
> require much. I would never go out of my way to watch a spe-
> cific episode.

Even though this pastime is a "break" from the routine daily
activities, it is a break that itself constitutes a daily routine (at
least most weekdays). Susan is a twenty-one-year-old white college
student who grew up middle class in upstate New York. She is a
double major in accounting and finance and intends to become
a CPA and, after some work experience, to get an MBA. In
Susan's account, watching talk shows clearly constitutes "leisure."

But simply stating that watching talk shows is a leisure practice
is not precise enough to identify how this fits into Susan's life.
While she speaks about her practice as part of a "break" from her
other activities, a break she values as "down time" or a time to
relax, she devalues the actual viewing of talk shows. A sense of dis-
missiveness inflects Susan's speaking about this viewing practice.
The practice is positioned as a sort of "throw away" activity of little significance. In contrast to Olivia, Betty, or Joan, who knew
the details of daytime television programming and were quite
specific in the talk shows they preferred to watch, Susan's narrative communicates little such familiarity and intentionality.
Rather, she repeatedly states that she watches "whatever's on";
whatever *specific* show is "on" is incidental in her narrative. The
shows she watches fulfill her criteria of requiring little of her
(note her acknowledgment that she could be watching CNN),
thus permitting her to relax. In Susan's narrative, her intentional

(and primary) activity is relaxation. Viewing talk shows is a means to accomplish this, given that they "happen" to be on television at a time coinciding with her break.

Contrasting Susan's narrative to Betty's, for example, can see that both women point to certain kinds of pleasures in their practice of watching talk shows. Susan's dismissive discourse of watching "whatever's on," however, is distinct from Betty's familiar pleasure, which is articulated with a sense of affinity. Their distinctive discourses invoke differing relations with the shows they watch. In Susan's discourse the show is "there," and she encounters it as she takes her break. Her pleasure is in relaxation. (In a later chapter I will also examine another dimension of Susan's pleasure that I characterize as sadistic and voyeuristic.) By contrast, Betty represents herself as intentionally "sitting down" to watch *her* show. Simply saying that a person finds pleasure in her encounter with television is inadequate. Different articulations of pleasure position the subject differently. The individual's language and, importantly, the mood inflecting her discourse about pleasure are central to understanding the distinctiveness of each case.[7]

In Susan's account, the practice of viewing talk shows is unproductive in and of itself. The practice of watching talk shows as part of lunch is not just a break generally but, more specifically, constitutes a break from activities that Susan implicitly values as productive (attending classes and studying). By her account, most of Susan's day is structured by activities that are intended to move her toward the goal of taking a place in society as a professional. I suggest that Susan's narrative illustrates her sense of a lifespan trajectory distinctive from that of Betty, Olivia, or Joan. She articulates confidence in the probability of her achieving specific professional goals. Her break for lunch and relaxation allow her to gather her energy to move back into her productive activities. In this context she trivializes and denigrates both her practice of watching talk shows as well as the shows' content. As Susan accounts for her practice of viewing talk shows (e.g., "I would never go out of my way to view a particular episode"), she positions herself as distinct from those she imagines are *typical* viewers. In her narrative she is positioned at a distance from— above and better—what is represented on the shows as well as other imagined viewers.

Most other college women I interviewed gave similar accounts of their practice of watching talk shows. In each case, watching the talk shows is itself described as a routine practice, but generally, one that fits into other more valued routines. If not specifically positioned as a "break," talk show viewing consistently constitutes a leisure practice. More specifically, it is sort of a "filler" practice, filling in spaces not taken up by other, more "productive" and/or valued activities or practices. Amanda, for example, like Susan, told me that she watches "whatever ones are on when I'm around," specifying further that the extent of her viewing varies according to her schoolwork load.

> Julie: And how often do you watch these various . . .
>
> Amanda: Now? Like more than ever because I have no more classes. My roommate's away. So I'm alone. And so, I've read all my books I can read and so now I'm watching TV.
>
> Julie: Right. And when you're, like, during the semester, how would you—
>
> Amanda: Oh, a lot. Perhaps three [talk shows] a day. And sometimes—depending on the day and my work load, like three, four. Like I flip between them.

Another aspect of watching talk shows as relaxation often articulated by the young college women is the shows' serving as a "release" for them. Speaking about her experiences at boarding school, where she reports twenty girls would get together and watch Oprah every afternoon, Amanda shared:

> It just affects them. I don't know. It's a good release, I think. You come home from work and school work. And like college is not easy. And it's—anyway, you can release—I gather people like releasing by drinking, drugs, you know, whatever. But for some people, like, this is a healthy release.

Similarly, when I asked Karen, another young college woman, what talk shows she watched, she began:

> Karen: We usually watch them together. And we usually—
> Julie: Who's the "we"?
> Karen: Like me and Pam.
> Julie: And how often do you tend to watch?
> Karen: I did a lot more, I watched a lot more last semester. Like I watched almost one a day. And this semester maybe once a week.
> Julie: And why is that?
> Karen: I just have more stuff to do.

For Karen, as with several of the other college women I interviewed, an important dimension of watching talk shows was that it was a group practice. When I asked her how watching talk shows fit into her day, she explained,

> Karen: I guess it's like after I go to my classes, like, and I'm kind of stressed. And I go to the library and I get stressed. And I'll come home, and I'll just laugh at the TV for like and hour before I do my work.
> Julie: And that's the context in which you watch?

Karen: Like, it kind of just like relieves everything. And then I can, like—

Julie: That's interesting. Some other people have talked to me about this. And would you say that doing, watching it as a group is part of that? I mean, is everyone kind of doing the same thing?

Karen: It's much more fun when you do it in a group, too.

Julie: Tell me about that.

Karen: Because like, when I'm watching it by myself, who am I going to comment to? It's like, "Oh, I had a really good joke there for someone."

Julie: So there's something about the conversation that occurs?

Karen: I think that's like half of it. And it's just like the time to to-tally—because if you watch like another serious show in an hour, you're just going to like not really get rid of the stress. Like it's just like a time of total relaxation, not thinking. And just doing nothing.

Julie: I have my shows for that, too. I have the shows I do that with. So, what other TV do you watch, if you do?

Karen: We watch, we have a set schedule now. We finally got our stuff down this semester, like when we do our work. Like, we'll go to the library all day on Sunday and be back by eight to watch—

Julie: How many people? Is this just you and Pam? Or others?

Karen: It's just pretty much me and Pam now. And at eight, we'll watch *X Files*. And that I think is really a—that's just like you actually have to think. It's very intriguing.

This interchange illustrates two dimensions relevant to my analytic focus. First, Karen contrasts her watching talk shows to her watching another program, *The X Files*. Watching talk shows requires "nothing," while *X Files* requires that "you actually have to think." While watching both shows constitutes a leisure practice, Karen classifies them quite differently. Second, she comments that watching is "much more fun as a group." That viewing is done as a group, and that this is constitutive of the viewing practice itself, challenges notions of the isolated, atomized television viewer, which emphasizes viewers longing for absent community for which the parasocial television relation acts as a substitute. For Karen, as well as other college women, watching as a group is a key aspect of the pleasure derived from watching the shows and has a ritualistic quality. This is particularly the case with respect to the conversation among those watching the show together. The women's accounts of their group's conversations were consistent through the interviews. My interview with Karen was typical:

Julie: So let me ask you a little bit about, just about this thing that you said. Like you watch with friends—so when you're watching, do you actually tend to watch the whole show," or do you click around, or do—

Karen: I like to watch the whole show.

Julie: And are these half-hour or an hour?

Karen: Hour.

Julie: And while it's going on, are you guys kind of just sitting and watching and being quiet? Or are you talking?

Karen: We'll comment through the whole thing.

Julie: I'm really interested in that.

Karen: Like if it's me, Pam and Francine, it's always, I make jokes through the entire thing, because I'm a very sarcastic person. And I feel like I have to make fun of everyone on the show. And then like, if the husband comes back, I'm the one that's like, I'm very loud, or whatever. And I'll be like, "Oh get him out of here!" or whatever.

Julie: So, you're actually commenting about the show.

Karen: Yes. Like I feel like I can talk to the people.

The practice of watching as a group and its accompanying conversation positions these women in a particular relation to the shows they watch together. Their conversation is generally a commentary on what they are watching. This commentary is spoken from a position of superiority in relation to that which is being commented upon. Here, perceived difference is not simply difference, but difference construed along a hierarchical scale on which those making commentary speak from a position of superiority.

In each case, the young white college women's discourse about the way talk shows fit into their lives is related to relaxation or the relieving of stress due to the other activities of their day. They speak about watching talk shows as a bracketed time. While valued for the function it serves, the young women's discourse consistently devalues the practice of watching talk shows in terms of its productive value. It is "time out," a sort of "nonactivity," "doing nothing." The women consistently cite the shows' format and content as contributing factors in their being able to enjoy the shows in this way. There is no plot to follow, no work they must do in their encounter with the shows. They are not compelled to engage seriously in the shows by virtue of the substantive issues and people featured, as well as the form of interaction on the shows themselves. Understanding how it is that watching these shows so consistently serves as a source of relaxation and stress relief is addressed more fully in chapter 5. There I discuss watching talk shows as "entertainment," as well as the particular character of the shows that seems to attract people even as they devalue them.

Watching Talk Shows as One Activity among Others

Jamie also watches talk shows as part of her daily routine. Her narrative is characteristic of those of the other women who included watching talk shows as a regular but not central part of their day. Generally, these women include the practice of watching talk shows as part of their daily routines, but do not organize their day around this practice.

Jamie is eighteen years old and had been graduated from high school a year earlier when we spoke. She was attending a technical school, training as a medical assistant. Jamie is black and grew up both in Boston and in Florida in a middle-class family. She was now living with her mother in a predominantly black neighborhood of Boston. As we spoke, Jamie described a schedule in which she watches several talk shows each day. These include *Jerry Springer, Jenny Jones, Sally Jessy Raphael,* "sometimes" *Montel Williams* and *Maury Povich,* and "occasionally" *Oprah Winfrey.* As with the women for whom watching television constituted a key dimension of their day, Jamie's account shows a regular daily viewing schedule that fits into her school schedule. She told me:

Jamie: *Sally* comes on first. And then *Jerry*—

Julie: Is that during the day or evening or—

Jamie: It goes from the morning to the afternoon. *Sally* comes on at eleven. *Jerry* comes on at twelve. And *Jenny* comes on at one.

Julie: So how do you manage that with school? I'm just wondering.

Jamie: Well, it's like thirty minutes away from here [laughs].

Julie: What's your school-day schedule like?

Jamie: Well, what I do is after I finish watching *Jerry*—'cause I mean I can sit home 'til two o'clock. They don't take attendance until the second class, sometimes. And the first class is typing. But you're really not doing anything. If you need to catch up on some homework, that's the time to do it. That type of thing. So, you know, I'll stay home and I'll watch . . . and then I'll go to school.

Julie: I got it.

Jamie: Yeah. And then, I get out of school. They let us out at five-thirty. After that I go straight to the gym and work out there. And then I go home. That's what my day is like, pretty much.

When I asked Jamie about how she started watching talk shows, she discussed her television viewing routine in more detail:

Jamie: I watch *Ricki* also, whenever I get a chance. I watch Ricki.

Julie: She's on in the afternoon, though, right?

Jamie: Yeah. She's on in the afternoon. And if *Jerry Springer* has a repeat, she comes on at twelve o'clock, same time. So that I flip over to see her.

Julie: I get it, you switch.

Jamie: [Laughs] Right. Normally the twelve one's a repeat. But the ones at, I think she comes on at five, is it? So, if I'm home, then I'll watch it. Like if there's no school—then I'll watch *Ricki Lake*.

From Jamie's account it is clear that she chooses to watch certain shows. This extends to include those (like *Ricki Lake*) that do not figure as part of the daily schedule she describes, but that she says she will watch "whenever she gets a chance." It is not clear whether Jamie organizes her day around being able to watch talk shows in the morning, before going to school, or her schedule simply accommodates her being able to do so. Her level of intentionality about watching certain shows is not clear based on reading her narrative. What is clear is that while Jamie does speak about "getting information from talk shows" (something that will be explored in the next chapter), watching talk shows is a leisure practice for her. For example, distinguishing between those shows she watches and those she is less compelled to watch, Jamie shares about *Montel Williams*:

Jamie: [Montel Williams] comes on in the morning. And he also comes on in the afternoon. But while he's on I'm watching something else. So that's why I don't watch him. But, he has mostly serious topics, um—and—the way he deals with them. Another thing is, a good talk show host is what makes the talk show.

Julie: Right. So tell me about this. What is a good talk show host, in your opinion?

Jamie: With Jerry [Springer], he makes jokes.

Julie: Yeah?

Jamie: Yeah—a lot of jokes. Jenny, she's funny. Ricki Lake? Ricki Lake cracks me up sometimes.

For Jamie, if it's not fun, it's not worth watching. Like Betty, she makes no negative self-assessment of her television viewing generally, and her watching talk shows in particular. Jamie describes herself as a focused viewer. She shared:

Jamie: When I'm watching it, no, I don't flip around. It depends. If I have something that I have to do, make phone calls or something, I'll call on commercials. If somebody calls me, then I'll talk to them a little while, 5 minutes. And I'll say, "Well, I've got to go!" You know.

Julie: You want to get back to your show?

Jamie: Yeah. 'Cause normally, I'm the type of TV watcher that would sit there. And I like to watch the whole thing without being interrupted. So, I would like the light off, no talking [laughs]. So, I'm the same way with the movies. It's, like, just all quiet.

Julie: So, do you mostly watch by yourself, or are there other people? I don't know your living situation.

Jamie: Well, my mother, she goes to school in the morning. So, I'm normally watching it myself. I tape her soaps for her [laughs]. But I normally watch it by myself.

As with Betty, Jamie's account of her viewing shows her as unabashedly enjoying the shows she watches, incorporating her viewing unproblematically as a routine activity of her day. In her narrative, she positions herself as having affinity for the shows she watches. She does not seem to value the shows any differently than other practices or routines of her daily life. This contrasts with the young college women who speak about their watching the shows as "mindless," "relaxing" in the sense of requiring no effort, and as a practice generally less valued than the other activities of their day. Related to this, Jamie does not situate herself as distanced from the shows (as the college women did); rather, she positions herself as proximate to them. The enjoyment she articulates through her account illustrates this. She engages with the talk shows as entertainment, and while she articulates amazement at some of what she sees on the shows, she does not denigrate them. This dimension of how Jamie and the other women I interviewed make sense of the talk shows, and in particular, how their narratives position them in relation to the shows, is explored further in the next chapter. Much of what accounts for this positioning has to do with viewers' assessments of the substantive content of the shows as "legitimate" and/or as "entertainment.

Conclusion

In this chapter, I have explored women's accounts describing how watching talk shows fits into their lives. What became clear in this analysis is that in trying sort out how a mundane daily practice fits into everyday life, I had to get a sense of each woman's everyday life more generally, understanding the routines and practices that constitute her day. Getting a sense of the activities that filled each woman's day and how she negotiated these activities through her day (including the significance these various activities held) made clear the extent to which the everyday, far from being mundane or self-evident, is a convergence of many factors. Through her narrative, each woman situated herself (explicitly or implicitly) with respect to convergences of age, class, race, gender, as well as material and discursive institutional structures, including, for example, the domains of work, family, and education.

Another dimension important to the women's accounts is that of temporality. While their accounts are of a current (or recent) everyday practice, the women make it clear that they implicitly understand their practice not just in the context of their current everyday life (as discussed above), but within a larger time frame. Through the way the women value or devalue their practice of watching talk shows, they implicitly, and sometimes explicitly, articulate a particular life trajectory. The meaning that the practice of watching talk shows has for each woman varies depending on the kind of life trajectory in which she imagines herself to be involved. Where each woman currently positions herself in her life trajectory also makes a difference with respect to how she understands and values talk shows and to her sense of subjectivity more generally. In the starkest contrast, for example, Betty, the middle-aged black adoptive mother who has had a substantial working-class career, gives an account of unabashedly enjoying the shows as part of her daily routine. In contrast, Susan, a white college student on a professional trajectory, trivializes and is dismissive of her own practice of viewing. Giddens's distinctions of temporality (*everyday, lifespan,* and *longue durée*) are useful in this kind of analysis and help to articulate the simultaneity of times and spaces in which we live.

The women make sense of their circumstances and discursively situate themselves in these circumstances through culturally available discursive repertoires. In analyzing the women's accounts, a discourse of productivity consistently informed their assessments of their everyday practice and subjectivity. As an example, Joan's negative assessment of her watching talk shows during the three years after she was laid off and was unemployed (a period from which she has now moved on) contrasts with Olivia's self-conscious concern that, given the amount of television she watches, her life might sound boring to me. This discourse operates as a normalizing discourse. In their accounts, they implicitly or explicitly evaluate themselves (and others) against a standard of productivity. Generally, the mood inflecting their speaking is an indicator of the extent to which they assess themselves as measuring up to the standard. The women can be understood as articulating themselves as subjects through this discourse.

Giddens's distinctions of temporality are again useful for analysis here. The normalizing discourse of productivity must be understood as historical and thereby connected with particular material and discursive practices (for example, the idea and practice of a regular workday, career, steady income, goals that are set and achieved, which in different historical and cultural settings have different form). The women's invoking this discourse can be seen as making present the *longue durée* Giddens refers to.

The *longue durée* is also evident with respect to material practices. The range of the women's viewing choices is determined by television industry management practices. These practices have a specific history and are part of the continually developing media business. Therefore, women's individual practices can be understood as intersecting with institutional practices. These institutional practices, while enacted by individuals in present time, are part of an ongoing, developing institution (the television industry) in which they play an integral part by virtue of their viewership.

Before even beginning to examine the actual substantive content of talk shows, the women's discourse about their practices of watching reveals much about how these women make sense of the shows and discursively construct themselves as subjects. That individuals on the face of things share a common practice (i.e., watching talk shows on a regular basis) does not mean that the practice fits similarly into their lives, nor that the practice has the same meaning for all. The apparently mundane practice of watching talk shows can be unpacked and shown as historical and complex.

4. Making Sense of the Shows

Discerning "Legitimate" Discourse

Making Sense of Experience

In reading this chapter, it is important to remember the insights gained from the previous chapter. Watching talk shows should be understood as a practice, organized differently and having varied significance in each woman's life. How the women make sense of the shows occurs as a dimension of this situated practice. Therefore, I speak about how the women "encounter" the shows in order to emphasize that, rather than being an *after-the-fact* assessment of a show, "sense-making" is a process whereby women constitute their experience of the shows. I explicitly refer to "making sense" rather than "experience" in order to problematize "experience" as something unmediated and direct. Furthermore, "encounter" is meant to connote something more complex than "watching" or "viewing"—a more complexly textured experience encompassing the sensorial, affective, cognitive, aesthetic, and psychic, all of which are constitutive of intelligibility.

I asked the women I interviewed questions that were intended to provoke them to describe, categorize, and evaluate various talk shows. I explored the extent to which each woman felt the shows were similar or different. While I explicitly questioned some women about this, how they distinguish between shows often flowed directly out of the discussion about their watching habits. I was interested to know which shows they enjoyed and why. What constituted a "good" show for them? A "good" topic? A "bad" show? A "bad" topic? What, if anything, did they think was the point of talk shows? My focus was to discern the distinctions or systems of classification the women used in making sense of the shows.

The women's responses were rich and detailed. They made clear that the mainstream discourse that conflates talk shows into a singular genre misses some important distinctions, which were fairly consistent across the women's accounts. More specifically, the distinction "trash talk," used unproblematically and pejoratively in mainstream discourse by both public critics and media to designate certain shows as particularly vulgar, glosses over other distinctions made by many of the women. The conflation of shows within a single classification ("trash"), and the mood or tone in which this classification is made as an epithet, illustrates how speakers position themselves in a particular way, in an assumed superior (often moral) position. This view *was* shared by some but clearly not all of the women I interviewed.

Through the women did not always use the same words in classifying talk shows, they did consistently invoke similar classificatory categories. For example, they spoke about certain shows as "having an impact," "being meaningful," "making a difference," all of which I categorized as distinguishing certain shows as "serious" or "legitimate" versus those referred to as "fun," "garbage," "having no purpose" (which seemed to distinguish shows as "entertainment"). While the women with whom I spoke did consistently articulate similar classificatory categories, these categories were not always used in the same way. For example, while all the women categorized some shows as "entertainment" and other shows as more "serious," the particular shows and/or specific topics they referred to within these classifications varied. Given my interest in "sense-making" or intelligibility, this was particularly important and informs the structure of this chapter.

"Making sense" or intelligibility can be understood, following Foucault (1984a, 1984b) and Butler (1993), as attempts to "fix" representation and privilege certain understandings as unproblematically "true." Foucault's work makes it clear how power is implicated in the construction of knowledge through the privileging or devaluing of the terms through which experience can be understood or represented. In particular, and of relevance to this study, Foucault emphasizes "[k]nowledge which fixes the normal" (Clegg 1989: 152). This phenomenon is evident in the narratives of the women I interviewed by virtue of the classifications they employ in speaking about the shows, which serve to distinguish a standard, that which is "normal" (and therefore "legitimate") from that which is not, what Foucault would call "normalizing discourses." These normalizing discourses, while deployed differently by different women, provide a consistent repertoire of terms for how a show *can* be understood. Language, particularly classificatory systems, are never neutral in this view. Classifying the shows in one way rather than another is a function of the discourses available. The discourses provide the terms through which one can "make sense," organize what gets called (usually unproblematically or uncritically) "experience," and determine the value assigned to this experience. So, while I select particular women's narratives for discussion, I do so with the view that the means by which each woman can say what she says is constituted by particular culturally available vocabularies that are socially constructed and embody a legacy of particular relationships of power. By "relations of power" I refer to the issue of who gets to say "what" is "legitimate" in the mainstream of society, and, conversely, whose discernments of legitimacy are minimized, overlooked, or rarely come into play at all. Therefore, analyzing how different women employ similar classifications differently is central to my concerns.

As in the previous chapter, I have paid attention not just to how each woman categorized and described the shows, but also to *how* they spoke about the shows—the affective dimension or emotional tone of their talk. This was important to me since in speaking with people informally even before beginning formal interviews for this project, I noticed they commonly articulated their views about talk shows with remarkable emotional force, especially when these views were negative.[1] I was interested in trying to gain insight into this aspect of people's response to the shows.

The question "Who, if anyone, engages with talk shows as legitimate public discourse?" drives the focus of my analysis in this chapter. Therefore, the issues of how the women discern "legitimacy" and the dimensions that appear salient to making this discernment (as well as what they counter to) are central to my concerns. In order to focus my discussion, I have selected interviews with three women, each of whom is oriented differently toward talk shows as "legitimate discourse." The women also differ with respect to their life experiences and current situation, with race, class, and age figuring among these differences. Michelle engages with the shows she watches as *both* entertainment and as something more "meaningful." Sandi watches *only* those shows she classifies as legitimate public discourse. Susan, while conceding the possibility that some shows might constitute legitimate public discourse, in the end engages with them *only* as entertainment.

I have also included one other women, Janice. Janice is unique in that she is the only woman I interviewed who classified *The Jerry Springer Show* as a forum of legitimate public discourse. I was particularly interested to find that even in Janice's case, the criteria she invoked for classifying the show were consistent with those used by the other women. This was significant, given that the *Springer* show is generally regarded as an exemplar of "trash talk" by both the women I interviewed and in mainstream discourse. My interest, then, is in understanding how Janice used these criteria in discerning *The Jerry Springer Show* as legitimate discourse.

What's Meaningful/What's Fun: Talk Shows as Legitimate Discourse and Entertainment

I met Michelle as a student in a class I taught. I did not interview her until almost a year later. I was especially interested in Michelle's account because she occupies a complex and multi-faceted position in society. She crosses a variety of boundaries by virtue of being involved in several "worlds." Michelle is a twenty-year-old black woman who grew up middle class in a predominantly black urban community. She participated in a program in which children from inner-city neighborhoods attended school in predominantly white suburban communities and traveled to school by bus each day. She shared that after her second year of high school she decided to switch to a Boston public school because she wanted a more diverse environment. At the time of our interview, Michelle was a sophomore at a mid- sized predominantly white, Catholic university, and was planning a career in law. While she lived at home during her first year of school, she now lived on campus. We spoke in my office as she ate her lunch. After asking her which talk show she watched, I asked, "Do you see the shows as all the same, or do you distinguish between the different shows in any way?" She responded:

> Michelle: Well, honestly, the only show that I feel has like a good
> purpose is . . . what did I say? I said that I watched *Ricki
> Lake, Monte—*

Julie: *Jerry.*

Michelle: Jenny Jones—

Julie: *Geraldo, Montel, Jenny*—

Michelle: Like out of all those shows, I think *Montel* is the most meaningful show because he—on his show, he brings people that, you know, can't find their family member. Touching things emotionally, you know. And sometimes he helps poor people or people who are less fortunate than others. His show usually has like a purpose. And the rest of the shows I watch—because it's funny, and I like to see stuff like that. But most of them, they fight. But then, sometimes the show—I mean I watch them to just learn how people are out there and just—it helps me to realize that there are ignorant people out there. Because the last time I watched *Jerry*, the Ku Klux Klan was on it and, like, people who really hated black people. People that were white supremacists, they were on the show. And they were like—they were sitting on one side and then you had some black people on the other side on the stage, and they were going back and forth, and they almost fought. And they were like, "Yeah! You guys are monkeys!" So, stuff like that. I like to watch stuff like that because, although it makes me angry when I watch it, I still know there still are people out there like that. I may not have encountered them, but they're still there. And *Ricki Lake*, sometimes her show—*Ricki Lake*, her show, I love her show. I don't know why because all—I think it's just garbage. Like people come on the show—"You slept with my man!"—and she wants to tell her baby's father that she was having sex with someone else and stuff like that. And I don't know if I just need a laugh, but I watch those things. But it's not meaningful. It doesn't teach me anything.

Julie: Right. But when you were talking about Montel—when you say it's meaningful, what—

Michelle: It's meaningful because it helps me. Like one time when I watched—I don't know, this might not—this might be totally irrelevant. But I watched *Montel* one day and it just got me—it just got me thinking more, just thinking about how fortunate I am, you know. Because [on] one show he had this girl, she couldn't find either of her parents. And it just made me think, you know, my parents are here. And it just made me more appreciative of—and then, another show was about helping teens that don't have homes, helping them find a home. And he was, you know, "I'm going to put you here. I'm going to give you this money"—Whatever. And he helped them. And stuff like that will make me go downtown the next day and drop a quarter in the homeless person's thing. So it just allows those emotions—I mean, I don't look at the people, the guests on his show as being ignorant. Some of them really have good stories to tell. Whereas the rest of the shows, it's mostly like—I don't even know sometimes—sometimes I think they just do it to get—gain, you know, publicity. Because I don't understand how some of the people go on the show and, like, fight their own friends. So, those shows I just watch for fun, I guess.

Michelle distinguishes what is "emotionally touching," "helping," "learning," "having a purpose," "meaningful," contrasting this with "garbage," "what's funny," and "needing a laugh." Fundamentally, I understand her as distinguishing a *degree of seriousness*. The shows she classifies as "emotionally touching," "helping," "learning," and so on are understood as being more serious than those classified as "garbage" or "funny," which she does not consider serious at all. Michelle also clearly enjoys that which is "just for a laugh" but places greater value on that which is "meaningful" or more serious, something made evident by not just what she said, but the affect with which she spoke.

If this distinction between "fun" and "meaningful" or "serious" is a key classificatory distinction, what criteria does Michelle use to distinguish something "serious" from something that is not? While this may seem *just* a matter of semantics,[2] I point out that, historically, certain matters, actions, and modes of discourse have been taken seriously and others are trivialized. Classification is central to constructing knowledge, in which certain knowledge is taken as "true." As an example, feminist scholars have shown that issues of concern for women or about women have historically been considered "private" matters, not properly discussed in the public sphere. These issues have included, for example, spousal and child abuse and rape.[3] This secrecy has meant that because these are private matters, a perpetrator could not be prosecuted publicly. A linguistic classification ("private" in this case) therefore has had real material consequences.[4] Similarly, worker safety was for much of our country's history considered an internal institutional matter. Furthermore, there is the insidious use in everyday language of terms such as "dark" or "black," commonly used to denote that which is bad or evil. Foucault has analyzed the emergence of certain classificatory schema and accompanying practices as working to establish "the normal" in institutional practices such as medicine and psychiatry (1973b). His work, as well as that of others who analyze the exclusionary and marginalizing character of classificatory systems, illustrates that these systems, constituted in relations of power, have material effects. Therefore, it is important for us to grasp that what gets considered "serious" in common discourse has consequences and is not *just* a matter of words.

Michelle articulates several distinctions as she differentiates between that which is "meaningful" and that which is "for fun." Her categorizations are based on the extent to which a substantive issue and its presentation or particular behaviors or appearances are encountered as violating cultural norms of appropriateness and civility. Like Michelle, all of the women with whom I spoke used words such as "outrageousness," "outlandishness," the "bizarre," the "extreme," "funny," "silly," "stupid," and "foolishness" when distinguishing the shows they recognized as entertainment. All these classifications indicate that what the women observed on the shows was seen by them as the trivialization or transgression of the dominant social norm:

The people are stupid, and what they're doing is ridiculous. (Natasha)

Oh, like, usually people will sit there and only watch like, the sex ones. 'Cause those are, like, usually the ones that are going to get like the craziest. (Colleen)

Jerry Springer was the one that I watch for fun. 'Cause he has stupid topics on, with stupid people on there that are just out of their minds. And I watch that. And *Ricki* sometimes had that on, too. But she also had some regular things on, too. (Joy)

I just like watching to see what bizarre questions people are going to ask and—I think they're pretty funny. (Karen)

To be honest, I think [I watch *Ricki Lake*] to see what foolishness Ricki is gonna come up with. (Tina)

Like, I think *Jerry Springer* is like the really weird one. Like the really crazy one. Which is why, I mean, I guess it's kind of fun to watch. But, like [laughs], you know, I'm in college, like I don't care—you know what I mean, I just watch them for the fun of it, really. (Susan)

While in this chapter I focus on the classifications the women employ in distinguishing entertainment from more serious fare, the women's *attraction* to watching shows they themselves often refer to as "garbage" or "trash" will be explored in chapter 5. Suffice it for now to say that the women's narratives indicate that the elements of transgression and excess (in relation to mainstream cultural norms of appropriateness and civility) seem to "draw" the women in and keep their attention. Even though most of the women suspect or claim to know (for a "fact") that this display of transgression is orchestrated by the shows' producers, it appears to operate on them nonetheless.

For some of the women I interviewed, the distinction between entertainment and more serious matters was not always so clear. For example, while Michelle distinguishes between shows that are meaningful and shows she watches for fun, it is apparent that the shows she generally categorized as "fun" can also feature topics that are more serious. Michelle shares:

I must give them some credit, because sometimes Ricki Lake and Jenny Jones, and, you know, sometimes—Jerry Springer, sometimes they do bring on shows that do—they do make sense. Shows like a girl, she's very overweight and she's made fun of all the time. And then there's the bully that always beats her up. Like this show, for instance, the bully would be the one that I'd refer to as ignorant. But I mean, shows like that let me—they also teach me, too. So, I should have mentioned that earlier because they teach me that there are people out there still acting that way. . . . Stuff like that, it arouses emotions in me, too. So, I must add that sometimes they bring on shows as such. But the rest of the show was fighting with boyfriend versus girlfriend or whatever. And sometimes they put on funny shows—so they showed a lot of shows like that. But most of them to me were mostly fighting. And I'm guessing because that's what the public likes.

Still, while these shows will sometimes feature topics that Michelle says "teach" her or "arouse emotions" in her, she characterizes certain shows (*Ricki Lake, Jenny Jones, Jerry Springer*) as "mostly fighting." Therefore, the more "serious" topics are seen as inserted into a context of entertainment. My point here is that "entertainment" and more "serious" matters are sometimes intelligible as overlapping or existing side by side, an issue of context I explore later in this chapter.

Michelle's criteria in discerning seriousness were consistent across the women's interviews more generally. In our conversation, Michelle distinguished *Montel Williams* as the only show that had "a good purpose," describing it as "the most meaningful show." When I asked what she meant by "meaningful," she said, "It's meaningful because it helps me." She distinguished this show from *Ricki Lake*, noting that, while she loves *The Ricki Lake Show*, "it doesn't teach me anything." Moreover, Michelle shared that after seeing a particular *Montel* episode on which he helped a homeless teenager by finding her a place to stay and giving her some money, she was compelled to "go downtown the next day and drop a quarter in the homeless person's thing." These distinctions point to a key criterion I identify as a *concern for efficacy*. Shows that are intelligible as serious are seen as producing some positive benefit for guests, studio audience members, or viewers. Importantly, as well, Michelle emphasized that a show is "meaningful" when "it helps me." As with most of the women interviewed, shows that are encountered as producing at least the possibility of some positive benefit are classified as more serious, in comparison to those that are encountered as pure display, with no discernable attempt at facilitating change or improvement. In her now dated analysis, Masciarotte (1991) emphasized this point.[5] Contrasting *The Phil Donahue Show* to *The Oprah Winfrey Show*, she describes Donahue as facilitating a discussion in which rationality and reason are invoked, consensus is at least attempted, and resolution is accomplished. Masciarotte frames Donahue as enacting an orthodox model of the public sphere, a mode of discourse grounded in male norms made invisible and universal. She contrasts this approach to Winfrey, whom she characterizes as being interested in the "pure display of narrative" (Masciarotte 1991), with no pretense of resolution.

Related to this, Michelle spoke about guests on "the rest of the shows" and wondered:

Sometimes I think they just do it to get—gain, you know, publicity, because I don't understand how some of the people go on the show and, like, fight their own friends.

Here, Michelle makes several more distinctions relevant to understanding what constitutes something as "serious." First, in questioning whether guests appear on a show just to gain publicity, Michelle articulates a *concern for authenticity*. Are the guests "real," are they who they say they are, and do they *really* have the issues they claim to have?[6] In addition, Michelle speaks of some guests' behavior disapprovingly, of not understanding how the guests can fight the way they do on these shows. Here, I suggest Michelle articulates a *concern for appropriateness*.

Michelle also describes a recent *Jerry Springer* show that featured white supremacists "sitting on one side" and "some black people on the other side." She recounts the interchange in which the white supremacists yelled insults at the black people, reflecting that

I like to watch stuff like that because although it makes me angry when I watch it, I still know there still are people out there like that. I may not have encountered them, but they're still there.

Michelle encounters this issue as not just a "real" (authentic) issue, but as an issue that bears relevance for her life, thus reflecting a *concern for relevance* in discerning talk shows as legitimate.

For Michelle, talk shows are not encountered in just one way. Rather, she has an ambivalent relationship to the shows, encountering some as legitimate discourse and others "just for fun." I suggest that this ambivalence is related to both Michelle's materially multifaceted social location, in which she negotiates several distinctive but intersecting worlds, and how she locates herself subjectively in the process of this negotiation.

"I Think in Order for Us to Get Along . . . We Got to Care about Each Other": Talk Shows as Legitimate Discourse

Sandi is a twenty-five-year-old single (and she emphasized, "more importantly, available!") black woman with two young children. She completed three years of undergraduate study at a local state university and shared with me that she intended to return to school unless financial difficulties got in her way. I met Sandi while she was a student at a local beauty school during the summer. She shared with me that she was working on getting her beautician's license as part of a financial backup plan for herself. Sandi's professional goal was to become a lawyer, however. Her feisty and articulate character left me thinking that she would be well suited to the practice of law.

Sandi's concern for the authenticity, relevance, appropriateness, and efficacy of talk shows was woven through most of my interview with her. When I asked which shows she watched, she said:

Sandi: Well—I used to watch, I liked to watch *Ricki Lake.* I used to watch her before. You know, 'cause at UMass I only had classes on certain days. I used to watch her faithfully every day [said slowly and deliberately].

Julie: 5 o'clock?

Sandi: 5 o'clock show. *But!* She was getting kind of boring to me because she started—I don't know, she just started like really—degrading women and certain things they go through in their lives—I don't know. She just kind of turned me off. But I watched *Maury Povich* since—God knows how long. I've always watched *Maury.*

Julie: Can you tell me a little about the differences for you between the two shows?

Sandi: *Maury Povich*, to me he's more sensitive. No, he's not a fake, thank you! [Said in response to a negative comment by a fellow student listening to our conversation.] There, now, you have a lot of people are fake. But to me, Maury is more sensitive, whether it's on certain issues—when it comes to *Ricki*—he has a sense of caring about his— [guests] on his shows. And he really does.

Sandi emphasized the extent to which she felt Ricki Lake "put people down." I asked her what she saw Ricki doing that made her feel that way. She responded by enacting Ricki's interaction with a teenage mother:

Like, say, for instance, a teenage girl, right—say she's got three kids, okay. She's still living with her mother. Whatever. And, for instance, on her show, she's like, you know, "Are you gonna go to school? Are you gonna do this? What are your plans for the future?" [Said with the affect of an interrogation.] You know. And then a child says, you know, "Well—right now I'm not going to school. I'm, quote, unquote, "taking care of my children" or whatever—. If they say, "Why, I do plan—" [Ricki says,] "Well are you going to have more kids?" And they may say, "Yeah, I wanna. I may. I plan to have more kids," or something or other. And it's like, she [Ricki] feels like that's a big no-no. You know, like, it's degrading for you to have children. It's degrading for you to have three kids, unmarried.

Sandi began to contrast this with how she thought Maury would interact, but continued with her critique of Ricki Lake:

Sandi: She [Ricki] doesn't influence positively. It's like anything negative that's going on in her [the guests] life, instead of making it better, she's going to make it worse. She's going to cover all the—come out with all kinds of negative, you know, scenarios that—you know, "You shouldn't have done this." Or she loves to say this, "I didn't get married until I was so-and-so!" [Mimicking Ricki's tone of chastising a guest.] "Well, I didn't have sex—." We don't know what she did. You know what I'm saying. So, it's like, you know, "Well, are you better than me because I had sex when I was 15?"

Julie: It's a whole lot of different life circumstances.

Sandi: Yeah! Exactly! And, as I say, everybody's life experience is different. [Shanelle, a woman listening close by as we talk, adds, "Instead of highlighting that the child has three kids, instead they're saying, 'Well, you know, I do have— after the show would you like to get more information about jobs?'"] He's [Maury] always offering help. He's always offering. Even with, like, I say, I call them "children who've been abused." You know, in their childhood, whatever. But, they're adults now. You know, they're still struggling with the ghosts. You know what I'm saying? And it's like he's always offering help to them. He's even paid for certain things—people to get therapy. You know what I'm saying? And you never see that with Ricki Lake [said slowly and deliberately]. Even Jenny Jones, she's offered help. I love Jenny Jones. I love Maury Povich.

Sandi legitimizes certain shows (*Maury Povich, Jenny Jones*) over others (*Ricki Lake*). Her account shows that not only is she concerned with the shows' efficacy, but that the efficacy is bound up with concerns for authenticity and relevance:

Sandi: I guess why—the reason I watch and why I started watching talk shows, I don't know. It's interesting to me to see what other people go through. I know what my struggles are in life. It's interesting for me to see what other people go through. And like, you know how you have those bad days or those bad moments? You know what I mean? And so, like for me, I wonder, I wonder, do they, do other people go through this, or do other women have these problems? So, that kind of thing. A comparison thing. Like, I get a reality check. I'm not the only one that has things such and such. I'm not the only one that's going through this and that. Because everybody has their own struggles. And they may be different in the manner in which they're happening, you know. But, in reality, everybody, the struggle is sort of similar. So, I think that's one of the reasons I watch a lot of the talk shows. And the rest of it, TV is basically entertainment for me.

Julie: So these are a little bit different in that way, you're saying? These shows are, perhaps, there's something a little bit different about them that you can identify?

Sandi: Yeah, I can identify. Like when you're watching basic TV, you know. A lot of the shows that come on TV, the movies or whatever, a lot of them you may be able to relate to or you may see some realism in them. But sitcoms and stuff, it's just not realistic for me. You know what I mean? The family structure's so torn down. So for me to look at *Family Matters* and see how close the family is, you know, a lot is really not like that for me as far as the family structure. I don't see it. Other than that—there's just not a lot of shows. You just don't see the realism in it, you know, unless you have a movie that's coming on, you know, that's based on a true story. So you can see the realism there. But, for the most part, it's just entertainment.

Julie: So when you see the guests on the talk shows, it sometimes feels to you like—

Sandi: Yeah, I can relate to a lot of issues on the talk shows. I mean from child abuse to, you know, to having a boyfriend cheat on you. So a lot I can relate to. People on drugs. So, I can relate to a lot of issues that are being brought up. So, I can sit down, and I can watch that. And I can be, you know, I can believe that. You know, this isn't a setup. You know what I mean? Cause a lot of times talk shows, I used to think that, you know, they rehearsed it for the night and they tell you what to say. But because I can relate to it, you know, it's more real for me.

Sandi's personal connection with the issues she sees presented on the shows is the basis upon which she talks about the issues as "real" issues. While she appears aware of production practices (i.e., wondering if guests rehearse, whether the show is a "setup"), the familiarity and relevance of the issues featured on the shows she watches convince her that the shows are "real." This particular dimension of authenticity, a concern for whether or not the guests and/or issues are "real" is distinctive to the talk show form. Research on soap operas and prime-time drama deals with the issue of the realism of representation.[7] This research describes and explains the extent to which some viewers find certain representations more "realistic" than others. Research on more orthodox public affairs programming or on news deals with issues such as "bias" and "framing"[8] in representing issues assumed to be "real." A distinctive problem with talk shows is that viewers consistently seem to question whether or not the guests who appear *are* actually who they (and the hosts) claim they are, and whether the issues they claim to have are actually *real* issues. As consistently articulated by the women I interviewed, this issue indicates a strong concern for authenticity as a key component of legitimacy.

Sandi's critique of Ricki Lake arises in the context of legitimacy. To Sandi, Ricki's way of relating to guests as well as the discussion she facilitates are inappropriate. Sandi clarifies what she considers an appropriate relationship between host and guest largely through her critique of Ricki Lake. She distinguishes several dimensions in which concerns for appropriateness, authenticity, efficacy, and relevance are interwoven.

Sandi charges that Ricki "degrades" her guests, providing the specific example of a discussion between Ricki and a teenage single mother. More specifically, Sandi is concerned that Ricki assumes an unwarranted position of superiority: what she sees as Ricki's lack of experience with and understanding of the complicated day-to-day reality confronting many of the guests on the show. In Sandi's view, Ricki degrades not just the women per se, but the circumstances of their lives as well. Ricki demonstrates her superior positioning through her suggestions that issues can be dealt with in a rational and clear-cut manner and through the often incredulous mood in which these suggestions are made. Sandi shared:

> She [Ricki] makes it seem like women, you know, like we're naive when it comes to men. And, you know, because your man cheated on you, you should dump him. You know what I mean? Things that are happening in life that you have no control of. You understand? And a lot of times when you do have control, it's your choice. You know what I mean? I just—I struggle with that stuff.

In Sandi's view, Ricki embodies and enacts indignation toward those whose lives and sensibilities don't conform to an implicit, idealized, rational middle-class norm. This is an idealized norm within which things are black or white, that certain things are just not permissible and appropriate action toward resolution is clearly apparent. In contrast, Sandi makes the point that sometimes one just *doesn't* have control over circumstances and, furthermore, one must be granted "choice" with respect to possible action. Given this disconnection with Ricki, Sandi concludes that

> [s]he's not like a person I could sit down and listen [to] or take advice from. Because she's not sensitive. She's not sincere about what she's saying, you know. That's how I perceive her.

Sandi contrasts Ricki with Maury Povich, whom she sees as having a more respectful relationship with guests, a respect grounded in the kind of sensitivity and caring Sandi alleges Ricki lacks. For example, Sandi charges that Ricki does not *really* care about guests, something evidenced in her not making offers of help to them. (Ricki, Sandi shares, is "just into the 'grit.'"). Moreover, "instead of making it better, she's going to make it worse." In contrast, Sandi repeatedly referred to Maury's and Jenny's offers of help to their guests, offers Sandi accepts as authentic and facilitating a positive benefit for the guests. Sandi shared:

> You know, there's a better way. You may, like with Jenny and Maury, you may, be stuck in this mold right now. But, let me tell you, there's always something better. You can—there's always something to look forward to. But Ricki [she enacts Ricki], "You may be stuck in this mold, but I really think you need to do—." She doesn't give them an alternative to what they're doing now. It's like there's not an alternative on her show. Everything, like I say, is degrading. She makes it seem like, you know, women, like we're naive when it comes to men. And, you know, because your man cheated on you, you should dump him. "Oh girl, [you] shouldn't take him back!"

In the logic of Sandi's narrative, an appropriately and authentically respectful and caring relationship with guests manifests itself in making certain kinds of offers of help to them. These are sincere offers that make viable alternatives available and indicate the host's respect for the guests' ability to make choices that affect their lives. This kind of offer is held in contrast to Ricki's authoritative pronouncements about what a guest ought to do.

While Sandi and a fellow student, Shanelle, object to what they perceive as Ricki's authoritative and morally superior positioning, they refer to another type of authoritative positioning they *do* find acceptable when speaking favorably about Montel Williams:

> Shanelle: And I like his show because he takes control of the show.
> Sandi: He really does. I do like that about him.

Shanelle: He really takes control of the show. You can hear what
           each individual is saying.

The host's "taking control" is acceptable when it is understood
as being in the service of creating a respectful forum for guests.

For Sandi, another way in which a host's sincerity or authentic
caring is evidenced is by having "updates" on former guests:

> With Maury Povich and Jenny, you know how they, they always
> do updates on different scenarios that they have on the show.
> They always do updates. So, it's like I said, it's a sense of caring,
> like they really care about this person.

This sense of authentic caring is more than just an interpersonal issue for Sandi. It is something she articulates as a larger social concern:

> So that's the kind of stuff I'm talking about. A sense of caring
> about people. Because this is America. And I think in order for
> us to get along and to—for us to take care and do what we need
> to do, we've got to care about each other.

For Sandi, legitimate talk shows represent a forum in which an
important dimension of American society can be expressed and
fulfilled.

"I Guess the Whole Concept Is Kind of Pointless": Talk Shows as Entertainment

I introduced Susan in chapter 3. In order to understand how she
makes sense of talk shows it is important to remember that she
watched talk shows as part of her lunch break and repeatedly ar-

ticulated that she watched "whatever's on." That Susan's practice of viewing of talk shows does not hold much significance for her is apparent in how she makes sense of the shows substantively.

For Susan, the way an issue was handled on a show, in particular the interaction between the host and guests, was central to whether or not she encountered an issue as "legitimate." Susan's concerns echoed Sandi's, though they were articulated very differently. Susan began by talking about *Jerry Springer*, whom she described as "being probably the sleaziest of all of 'em." When I asked her what she meant by "sleazy," Susan explained,

> Honestly, that's what I think of it. Because he tends to have more—he'll always have like strippers on, or, like, women with like really big breasts. Do you know what I mean? It seems a lot more like sexploitative type of stuff than the other ones that might actually have like real, like actual topics. Whereas this was more like he'll just have a lot of exhibitionists on and that type of thing.

Interested in her reference to "real . . . actual topics," I asked Susan what she meant:

> Susan: Well, it can vary a lot, honestly. Like I was thinking about it the other day, when I found out I was doing this. And it can—no seriously—it can vary a lot. Because every once in a while you know they'll have something on that's pretty much, you know, pretty exploitative in the sense that it's, you know—a lesbian whose husband is dating [said with emphasis in a sing-songy cadence] like, some—you know what I mean? Like, they can have these really whacked, far-out topics. Like someone dating a thirteen-year-old or something like that. But then every once in a while they'll have an episode where it's like, you know, they're trying to

find missing and exploited children and things that, you know, are more legitimate.

Julie: Uh hmm—

Susan: And that type of thing. Or like, they'll reunite lost relatives and stuff like that. And, so that the topics can vary like a lot between them.

Julie: Hmm—

Susan: But pretty much *Jerry Springer* [laughs] is the one that stands out in my mind as just being a lot different than the other ones. Like *Jenny Jones*, like you can tell she's trying, like being legit, legitimate in the sense of a real person trying to cover, you know, legitimate topics. But at the same time she still has the same elements as *Ricki Lake* and the other shows like that, that tend to deal with more just— like, they just bring 'em on so they can start fi—at least that's the way I perceive it. Like they bring 'em on so they can start fighting,

Julie: On Ricki in particular?

Susan: Yeah. Yeah. I mean, I guess I'm a little biased about that, too, because I've read stories about, about talk shows too—about how they do encourage them before the show. And it makes you look at it differently. When you're watching it you're like, "They're kind of encouraging that." And they try to pretend not to encourage it. Like they'll call their security guards and stuff like that. But, in reality, they're probably like, "Ratings!" You know what I mean? So, that's how I perceive it.

I was struck by Susan's explicit use of the term "legitimate" and how it operated as a "slippery" distinction in her accounts. She commented several times that shows can "vary a lot" with respect to the kinds of topics they feature. What is "legitimate" for Susan seems connected with what she discerns as "real . . . actual topics." She describes shows like *Ricki Lake* and *Jerry Springer* as featuring topics and behaviors that fall outside dominant norms of appropriateness (e.g., "whacked, far-out" topics and fighting). In addition, she assesses these shows as having no real efficacy but being oriented toward the kind of outrageous display that primarily serves the purpose of drawing high ratings. There is, however, a group of shows that she categorizes as having a more ambiguous status. For example, Jenny Jones slides back and forth. While "trying to be" legitimate, Jenny Jones still displays some of the "exploitative" characteristics of Ricki Lake.

When I asked Susan to talk a bit more about her characterizing Jenny Jones as "real," she used Oprah Winfrey as an example of a talk show host who has successfully made the move from "sleazy" to legitimate:

Susan: Well, you get the sense that maybe like—for example, *Oprah Winfrey* I guess is a good example. She went way back when I think that she used to cover more of the topics that you consider on normal talk shows today. She would have more racy type topics. You know what I mean? Like incest, or just random—like the really far-out types, do you know what I mean? Sort of the far-out types of topics that, you know, people watch for shock value, too.

Julie: That's the kind of stuff when you were talking about *Jerry Springer* and those kind—

Susan: Yeah, exactly. Exactly. But, I know that, for example, Oprah—what I was gonna say was she went more from that type of typical where she only has topics and shows about things to do with like family. Like how to childproof your home. Or she'll have celebrity interviews. So she's become, tried to be, more like a news sort of informative type of thing. And that's sort of—like you get the sense of maybe *Jenny Jones*, for example, is trying to sort of copy

that sort of style. Like she's maybe trying to move more towards that. But she still has the more exploitative type of
stories on, too.[9]

It is important to pay attention to how Susan categorizes "incest" as an example of a "racy," "far-out," or "random" topic. This
indicates that not only is this a topic removed from her everyday
experience ("random" and "far-out," an issue of relevance), but
that it also occupies a questionable status with respect to appropriateness (by being characterized as "racy"). This runs in contrast to Sandi, for example, for whom the issues featured are both
relevant and appropriate. (Remember that for Sandi, the problem was the way the host interacts with the guests about the issue,
not the issue itself.) The topics Susan seems able to connect with
are those that fall within the bounds of an *idealized* middle-class
life-style (given the fact that statistics indicate incest is by no
means an issue confined to marginalized groups). In this, it is apparent that what is intelligible as "appropriate" to Susan is tempered by both how she is materially situated in her everyday life,
as well as how she locates herself as a "normal" subject. Susan's
concern for appropriateness is a concern embodying dominant
cultural norms.

Like Sandi, Susan identifies *Montel Williams* and *Maury Povich*
as shows where

they try to have more topics on that could really, genuinely
help people. They seem to treat their guests with more respect
than Jerry Springer or Ricki Lake, where you sometimes get
the sense that they're just inviting them on so they can rip on
them.

However, Susan also voices concern that the talk shows seem
to "feed off" certain kinds of people:

Susan: [The show] feeds off it in the sense that they know pretty much where these people are coming from. I mean, I personally perceive that a lot of them are very vulnerable. They've had certain things happen to them.

Julie: Can you give me an example of one that you've seen or— you know—

Susan: I don't know. I think a good one would be maybe like— like rape victims or something like that. Where they go on—but, it always winds up, at least you always wind up getting the sense that it's not like the talk show is solving anything. And what is really being accomplished by having them on talking? So, that, I think, would sort of be an example of it. Or things where it's a family, family type of issues. Where it, where it would be, like, a parent cheating on another parent. Or things like that. I mean, sometimes they do it in the name of getting issues out in the open. Like spousal abuse, for example. But, I really don't buy that argument. Because I don't think that people watch these shows thinking, "Oh well. I'm going to go out and join—you know, like, work for a battered women's shelter." Or something like that. So, I think their motives are thinly concealed. But . . . just in the name of ratings.

Julie: Right. They try to make it sound noble.

Susan: Exactly. Exactly. Like, you know, "We're having these battered women on so they can tell their story and this and that. But, I have trouble buying that. I really do. I guess the whole concept in itself is kind of pointless. But, yet, they're so popular. I mean, you can't argue with the numbers.

Julie: Do you think there's no point to them? Do you think they're trying to—

Susan: Honestly, no [laughs]. I really don't. I think that's, maybe that's a little too harsh. Because I think sometimes some good does come of them. When they're on—if for certain topics and things where they are, I think, genuinely trying. But, overall, it doesn't balance out. Like I think all the sort of trash [laughs] sort of more than covers the other.

Here, Susan's concern for efficacy is interwoven with a concern for authenticity. As Susan sees it, nothing gets "resolved" or "accomplished" through the guests talking on talk shows, guests she characterizes as "vulnerable." Susan can be seen as assuming a superior positioning in the way she characterizes guests. She expresses concern for those seen as "less" than herself, a relation based more in "taking pity *on*" than "empathy *with*." This contrasts, for example, with Sandi, who speaks about "everyone's struggle being sort of similar," even if specific issues are different. Sandi positions herself in an equal and empathetic relation to guests. Also, in contrast to Michelle and Sandi, who cite some specific ways in which certain shows impact them, Susan doubts that viewers are affected positively at all by the talk shows they watch. Susan is highly skeptical of producers' "thinly concealed motives" to do good by getting certain issues "out in the open." While Michelle and Sandi both show some awareness regarding production and media industry practices, they continue to find the public presentation of certain issues both legitimate and valuable. Susan's dismissive stance about the possibility of the show's efficacy and, therefore, its legitimacy is amplified by her finding neither the people on the shows nor the issues they discuss relevant to her life. She distinguishes herself both in terms of her material social location as a white, middle-class, college- educated woman on track to fulfill her professional aspirations, and in terms of how she locates herself subjectively in society—as an aspiring professional.

"It's a Reality": Jerry Springer as Legitimate Discourse

Janice is a forty-three-year-old black woman. She shared with me that she grew up middle class, completed junior college, and worked for about ten years at a community health center, where she moved up the ranks from receptionist to counselor. She left work when she gave birth to her second child (now in high school) and held assorted jobs upon returning to work, including telemarketing as well as helping her older daughter operate a beauty salon. At the time of my first interview with Janice, she was attending beauty school with the intent of getting her license so that she could open up her own shop. By the time we met for a second interview, a couple of months after the first, Janice was no longer attending school due to health issues (panic attacks) that necessitated her frequent absences. She was, however, strategizing about her return to school. Janice was engaged and living with her teenage daughter, her fiancé, and his son in a predominantly black, lower-income and working-class neighborhood in Boston. She commented to me that she was looking into moving, since she preferred a more diverse neighborhood, like the one she lived in previously. She noted, in particular, some problems with a neighbor's son, who had gotten into trouble with the police and how that had shaken her up.

I was compelled to include Janice's interview because Janice was one of the few women I interviewed who did not classify *Jerry Springer* as *just* entertainment. That is to say, that while she does speak about watching *Jerry Springer* as entertainment (and does so with a delight I discuss in the next chapter), this is not the *only* way in which she encounters the show. Janice often (and, as her narrative indicates, usually) encounters the *Springer* show as being a more serious and legitimate discourse than the other talk shows she enjoys watching.

Some research would tend not to focus on an exceptional case, considering it interesting, but an aberration in terms of identifying patterns and/or trends. I include this distinctive case since a central analytic focus of my inquiry concerns how "legitimacy" is discerned. It is analytically important to include Janice's case precisely because she is the only one among the thirty women I interviewed who classified the *Springer* show as legitimate discourse at least a good portion of the time. Moreover, she does so in the face of the shows being considered an exemplar of "trash talk" in mainstream discourse. Trying to understand why Janice finds the *Springer* show intelligible contributes to an understanding of how individuals make discernments of legitimacy more generally, because Janice employs criteria that are consistent with those used by the other women.

When I asked Janice to characterize the various shows she watched and the extent to which she found them similar or different, she made some clear distinctions between them, with each show addressing a different domain or scope of life:

Sally, she relates to a lot of teenage problems—children. Her shows are geared for teenage problems—parents that are having problems with children, which I relate to because I have a teen myself. So, I could find that I can get things from watching her show. Jerry I like overall because he touches every part of life, and it's more of a reality with his show with things that are going on everyday, and everyday life. Jenny, I found that her show is sort of, I guess, more on the—love basis. If you're in, you know, marriage, boyfriend-type problems, you can watch her show and get something from that aspect. Geraldo is basically—he covers everything that's going on in the world, from shootings, gangs, you know, anything that you might want to pick up there. I did like him a lot.

It was apparent through much of what Janice talked about that she regards the shows as representing not only "real" issues, but issues that are relevant to her everyday life, which demonstrates (in my analytic terms) a concern for relevance. The issues she sees presented are not marginal or "far-out" in her view, a stark contrast with Susan's account of "whacked, far-out topics." Noting that Janice characterized *The Jerry Springer Show* as being "more of a reality . . . with things that are going on everyday, and everyday life," I asked Janice to talk a bit more about this.

Janice: I like Jerry's show because he touches on—you might and I like hearing so many problems with say, the gay community. And Jerry does a lot of shows on gays. And I think it's been a lot of informative shows. I mean, you have young teens that are coming out and gay. And I've noticed at school that we had a lot of younger ones that were into hair. But maybe really weren't sure what direction they would go into. And then, when you, I went home and I watched Jerry and I said, "Gee," I was telling my daughter, "And I noticed the kid at school that I was talking to today and he's going through the same thing." So to me, it's sort of like when I turn Jerry on there might be a topic that we've talked about all day in school. Husbands cheating or, you know, the girls may talk about their boyfriends. "I know he has another woman," or whatever. Then when I go home, boom, there's Jerry, he's done the same topic.

Julie: So there are issues—

Janice: So there are issues that, you know, I can look at and I think, "Gee, we talked about that this morning," or my own personal—I mean I was in a relationship where I thought my boyfriend was cheating on me. And I found that when I listened to Jerry, I got different pointers. You know, different people saying, "Well, look for this. You do this." You know. Or—one part that was really good was when—that made me think, "Oh, gee. Do I want out of this relationship?" It's really not sometimes one person that has everything for another. We might have to have or you might go through two or three relationships within one in order to get whatever you're looking for. You know, through different people, different avenues. So, when I watched that, it, it opened my mind up, you know, to say, "Well, gee, maybe you just don't have everything that this person is looking for. And that's not to say that I had to settle for that relationship. But in watching Jerry, that one show, it opened up a lot of things in my mind. So I watch some that's sort of like—Jerry's shows are a little crazy, as you know [laughs]. But basically with him I know there's something that I'll get from his show that really relates to my life or a person at school or coworker or whatever.

Not only are the issues Janice sees represented on the shows encountered as authentic ("real") and relevant, but the shows are also seen as being efficacious with respect to these issues. This includes even those issues that are dismissed in mainstream discourse as topics of legitimate public discussion by virtue of either their outrageousness (relegated to "*just* entertainment" status at best) or their classification as a "private" issue. Janice's inclusion of these kinds of issues as legitimate topics for public discourse was apparent in her response to a piece by William Bennett that I asked her to read.[10] In the piece he expresses moral outrage at talk shows featuring topics such as "a thirteen-year-old who claims to have slept with over one hundred men." She responded:

Basically, he seems to be upset with [shows] that will show a teenager expressing how many men she slept with and the ones that she slept with. To me—my daughter has been home on a vacation, my youngest, thirteen at the time. And, it helped her. Because she saw this girl on there talking about how many men, boys she slept with. And she said, "Mommy, gee, at that age, she's already having sex? I don't even like boys, you know. And if I did, I wouldn't do that." And to me, it might be for, maybe there are some people out there that don't want to deal with that issue. But it's a reality. And I think for them to come on and express that, and there are other kids at home. I mean there might be a child sitting at home that has done the same thing, but can't talk about it. Or feels that maybe she's the only person out there that does. Or has done it. And she's feeling low and bad about herself. But I feel if she turns on the TV, there's somebody else out there. Not that it makes it okay. But at least she will know, "I am not the only person." Because a lot of times kids really concentrate and get into suicide. Because they've been made to feel—well, after it's over the guy dogs them and they don't want to be bothered. And they think maybe in their community—they can live in a small community where there aren't many teens or whatever. And it depresses them. But I think that if it's exposed, if it's out there, they can turn on the TV and find something that touches their life. It helps.

Janice, however, is not approving of *all* issues featured on talk shows. Speaking about *The Ricki Lake Show*, a show she feels is geared "basically more to the younger set," she comments that "[s]ometimes I get a little aggravated."

Sometimes the guests are a little—sometimes I look at the shows and I'm like, "She really should not even have them on there." And they're like a total disgrace, or "Where does she get these people?" How could they come on TV and embarrass themselves like that?" You know?

In particular, Janice shared her concern about young black girls who appear on the shows:

> Ricki tends to have a lot younger—she seems to have a lot of young black girls which I find most of them to be immature, on the ignorant side of life, not well educated. Actually a lot of her guests seem to really hate themselves, I feel. Or really make fools or mockery of themselves. And that's what basically really started turning me away from her shows. Because it's like—I guess, you would say it was like she was going out getting—you know, I don't really believe in ghettos—I would have to say to the ghetto-style of life. You know, just young girls that are—low self-esteem and you bring them on the show and they don't really know how to phrase what they're saying, or, you know, they're just straight out. They are themselves and this is their everyday life. But, still if you come on a talk show and you want to talk about certain things in your life, you should sort of compose it a little bit more. You don't want people to look at you and say, "Oh, she's pathetic." You would like to have people look at you and say, "Oh, I can sympathize or understand what she's going through."

Janice's concern is with how the young women present themselves, a concern for appropriate public behavior, in other words, behavior that will allow one to be taken seriously as a speaker. Appropriately "composing" what one says facilitates one's engagement in legitimate discourse, rather than allowing one to be dismissed as "pathetic." To evoke sympathy rather than pity or, perhaps, disgust, one must present oneself as a certain kind of speaker, a speaker whose experience is deemed worth listening to according to the standards of the dominant culture.

Janice shows awareness about television production and the orchestration of talk shows when she wonders whether Ricki actually "goes out looking" for a certain "ghetto-type" young black woman, although, like many of the women I interviewed, she is uncertain if this is actually the case.

Janice also indicates concern about some of the issues the young black women discuss on *Ricki Lake*.

> I mean this is just everyday simple stuff, you know. Your girl-friend is sleeping with your boyfriend and you know it. Then that ends your friendship. You don't really come on *Ricki Lake* to discuss that. You should have done that at home. So some of the topics I feel that they didn't really have to be aired. I mean, yeah, it's nice to know that, you know, for the world to see that this does happen. But [by] the same token, in everyday life, you know, these things do happen, I don't feel that—like one week she just focused on that every show, every day. With some-thing similar to that. And then it just became monotonous. I was like, "I'm not watching this."

Janice is ambivalent about the appropriateness of these kinds of issues being featured on talk shows. While these are topics she thinks are more appropriately discussed "at home," she also rec-ognizes that they are part of everyday life and worth making pub-lic. However, what Janet finds most problematic is the repetition of such topics. This contrasts with Susan's account, in which she found most of the issues discussed on the shows marginal and "whacked, far-out." Janice's concern is that, if anything, these is-sues are too mundane for broadcast and do not warrant being re-peated on the various talk shows.

Another salient dimension of Janice's interview was her dis-cussion of the proper relationship between host and guests. As with Sandi, Janice's standards for how a host ought to be oriented and act focused on issues of respect. Geraldo Rivera, for exam-ple, used to be her favorite, but, she noted, "he sort of changed himself in the last couple of years."

It's like he's gotten more—um—cynical. He's—it's like he's the talk show, but that people come on his show, he ridicules them and he sort of doesn't really give them a chance to say why they're there before he breaks them down and comes with his own theory about anything. Well, he's sort of like—people on the show, it's sort of like he condemns them, or he'll get angry and he'll say, "Oh, well, you're nothing but a piece of this." You know, and you don't do that to people, like, or no one likes to come on the show, even if they say something outrageous or ridiculous. You're the host, you should give that person respect.

Similar to Sandi's concerns about Ricki Lake's assuming a position superior to her guests, Janice is troubled that Geraldo is apparently more interested in his own "theory" than in what the guests have to say. This is distinct from Susan's concern about host's exploitative behavior. She is concerned that a host "feeds" off people who are vulnerable and have "deep-seated problems." Susan's account identifies an unequal relation in which the host (empowered by virtue of her position) takes advantage of the (disempowered) guests. It is important to note that in her interview Susan clearly identifies guests as being from marginalized positions in society, such that class and race are coded into her account on this topic. She generally dismisses the value of what guests have to say, given the context of the media industry in which the speaking occurs and in which ratings (and by implication, profits through advertising revenues) are the imperative. On the other hand, Janice's concern (and Sandi's, as well, for that matter) is that guests be allowed to speak and be listened to respectfully. She is concerned that the guests' speaking from their experience be privileged over the "theoretical" pronouncements of the host.

In speaking further about the mode of discourse on talk shows, Janice comments on several other hosts—Sally, Jenny, and

Jerry—pointing out their strengths and weaknesses against her implicit standard. In Janice's view, Jenny sometimes "brings up a topic and sometimes she's not able to handle it." Importantly, "she's not sometimes in control of her show." Janice shared that

> [s]ometimes her show can really get out of hand where like, "Jenny, why don't you," you know, "This is your show. Tell them to stop or tell them," you know. I find myself getting upset and I'm like yelling through the TV, "Jenny, stop a minute! Jenny, get control!"

About Sally, Janice commented:

> Sally, on the other hand—Sally stays in control of her show. Because one thing I like about her, she'll tell them, "See, I'm not going to go for this, and you *will not* do this on my show." She's gone through a lot, you know—and she's really into teens and, and helping people as a whole. So she's tougher, Sally's real tough. And a lot of times she gets overbearing. Sometimes I'm like, "Oh, Sally should have let that go. She didn't have to come off like that, you know."

Janice discusses Jerry Springer as the most skillful of the hosts:

> I'll say that Jerry handles himself well. He doesn't, he doesn't get himself—like Geraldo will snap back at a person. Where Jerry, you know, sort of does it in a playful way. He might say, "Oh, all right. So, you think everybody should stick nails in their head." He has a sense of humor and doesn't get upset. He very seldom throws anybody off his show. So overall, I think he handles himself very good—and how he can mellow things out when the show gets too crazy. He'll go, "OK. All right. Let's take a break." You know, so he keeps everything in perspective.

Janice used the same general vocabulary and criteria as most of the other women I interviewed in terms of their standards for a "good host"—the ability to keep perspective, to be nonjudgmental, facilitative, respectful, listening, caring, and appropriately in control. But her finding Jerry Springer a "good," even exemplary, host against these standards stands in stark contrast to the views of the other women. Given this, I asked Janice what she thought Jerry Springer was trying to do on his show. Her response was consistent with her positive views about Springer as a host:

> I think for the most part it's to—I mean Jerry pretty much likes to let the world know that there are things out there. I guess we shouldn't be so judgmental because people go through all kinds of changes and have all kinds of problems in life. And who are we to sit back and say this person is wrong for doing this? Or, you know—his way through life may not have been like ours. Or, maybe because—and then—he totally—where these rich people have come on that look certain ways and do certain things. And you really can't condemn them because they have lots of money and they live the way they want to live. You know? So, I think his outlook is just to let people know that there's all avenues in life. And there are reasons why people do things. And society as a whole shouldn't be so quick to judge and condemn. And that's basically what I get from most of his shows.

Janice clearly finds *The Jerry Springer Show* (as well as the other talk shows she watches) a legitimate forum for public discourse at least some of the time: authentic (even when outrageous), efficacious, appropriate (in terms of Springer's relation to guests), and relevant to her life. By Janice's account, the show is not *just* entertainment (although she does talk about his crazy shows as "fun"), but provides a service in exposing viewers to "all avenues of life." While she does not focus here on the show's efficacy in terms of the benefit accruing to guests, as Sandi does, Janice articulates at least a potential broader societal benefit from the show.

Who's the "Other"?

Who each woman identifies with or against on the talk shows correlates with what she discerns as "legitimate." The more a woman explicitly or implicitly situates herself as being different from, better than, and/or more morally virtuous than the guests or others she sees on the shows, the less likely she is to engage with a show as legitimate. Conversely, the degree to which a woman identifies with a show's guests, or at least sees herself as having the same status, the more likely she is to find a show legitimate. In addition, women who find themselves feeling identified as "the other" by a show's host (as in the case of Ricki Lake) also have difficulty with engaging that show as legitimate discourse. This is the case even when they find the substantive issues legitimate and empathize with the guests on the show. This is generally a matter of degree for the women, rather than simply an issue of whether a show is "legitimate" or not.

For example, Michelle, who gives the most ambivalent account presented in this chapter, clearly identifies with many of the people she sees, as well as the issues that are presented, on the talk shows she finds legitimate. This is evident in the fact that she actually knows people who've appeared on some of the shows. In addition, Michelle talks about being encouraged by those who seem able to be bold in their stand against experiences of racism. Moreover, even when she talks about shows that fall into her "mostly fighting" category (e.g., *Ricki Lake, Jerry Springer*), she shares that doesn't "understand how some of the people go on the show, and, like, fight their own friends." Here, Michelle shows concern about the guests' behavior. But the mood in which she voices this concern indicates that, while she does not condone the behavior she sees, she does not seem to position herself as superior to these people. Michelle does not strongly identify *against* the guests or the audience on shows she considers as having legitimate discourse. For Michelle, there is not a strongly articulated "other."

In contrast, Susan, who dismisses any possibility that talk shows may constitute legitimate public discourse, identifies herself against both the people and the issues she sees on the shows. The people Susan sees on talk shows are, by and large, "vulnerable" and open to exploitation by the hosts, in her view. The shows' producers, she suggests,

> try to segment a certain part of the population that's just so out there sometimes that you can look at them and say, "Well at least I'm normal." You know what I mean? Like, "At least I'm normal, relative to them."

Susan's assumed superior status as "normal" is communicated in how she speaks as well as in the words themselves. Furthermore, Susan generally classifies the issues these people present as "whacked out," thereby discursively marginalizing both the people and their issues. The people who appear on talk shows who are "just so out there" remain an abstract and pathetic segment of the population, not having an existence as distinct individuals. Susan positions herself with those who, like herself, represent the "voice of reason" against this population she objectifies as being deviant. Susan's pity of "them" reenforces her sense of superior status.

Susan's positioning stands in contrast to Sandi's. Sandi empathizes with guests and their issues on the talk shows she finds legitimate. For Sandi, "everybody has their own struggles. And they may be different in the manner in which they're happening. But, in reality, the struggle is sort of similar." Sandi shows a sense of compassion, which reflects her sense of being "like" those she watches, even if their particular issues may be different.

Sandi also identifies with and against certain audiences and hosts. For example, she "loves" *Jenny Jones* and *Maury Povich*, but in comparison only "likes" Sally:

> Sandi: She's okay. But she's not my kind of girl. She's like, for a different type of audience from me. You know, she's up there with Oprah. I don't watch Oprah, either.
>
> Julie: What's the difference do you think?
>
> Sandi: For me, I'm not trying to be stereotypical. But, uh, like Sally, you know, if you look in her audience, like, people, they look like really successful people who've got . . . you know what I mean? But when I look at Jenny or I look at Maury . . . I can relate with people in the audience 'cause they look like they're on my level.

[Another woman working next to Sandi and listening to our interview comments,"Ordinary people."]

> Sandi: Yeah! You know, not people who are way up here and, like, looking at me way down here.

Sandi's comments show that she positions herself as having an inferior social status compared to the audiences she sees on *Sally Jessy Raphael*. Similarly, Sandi's view of Ricki Lake as "degrading women" and always relating issues to her own life appears to be connected to Sandi's concern about being looked down on by someone assuming a superior status. For Sandi, this assumption of superior status correlates with Ricki's lack of understanding of people and issues, with whom Sandi identifies. Importantly, the superior status that Sandi feels Ricki Lake assumes is not necessarily related to an actual social-structural location. This is evidenced by Sandi's accounts of Maury Povich and Jenny Jones as good hosts, for example. While clearly Maury Povich and Jenny Jones occupy a more advantaged social location than Sandi and the guests on the shows she watches, Sandi suggests that these hosts do not position themselves as morally superior but, rather, respect their guests.

While Janice identifies with guests on the shows, she distinguishes herself from the young black women she sees on the show. However, it is specifically how the women present themselves on the shows that she finds problematic. In Janice's view, these girls represent "the ghetto side of life." In her account, Janice distances herself from this "side of life" and implies her lifestyle is superior. (For example, Janice emphasized to me that she preferred living in more "mixed" neighborhoods.)

When distinguishing herself from "young black girls," however, Janice's superior positioning is inflected with empathy rather than contempt or pity. She feels, for example, that many of Rick Lake's guests "seem to really hate themselves" and suffer from low self-esteem. The young women don't "compose themselves" properly on the show, and thus viewers are likely to react to them as "pathetic" rather than empathize with them. Here, distinct from Susan, for example, Janice distinguishes herself against certain behaviors, not against the girls themselves. Likewise, it is not the issues per se that Janice finds problematic, but the way the girls present them. Janice seems concerned that the girls' "straight-out" presentation of themselves and their issues gets in the way of their being taken seriously. I suggest that Janice's identification in some ways with these young black girls and their issues accounts for this mixed positioning of herself in relation to them.

While the actual words they used varied, the women were consistent in the kinds of concerns they articulated and the criteria they invoked in making their discernments of legitimacy. However, exactly *what* they discerned as legitimate varied, in some cases quite substantially. The point I make here is both similar to and distinct from Fiske's (1987, 1989a, 1989b) notion of the "openness" or "polysemic" character of media texts. Fiske argues that differently situated people may have differing interpretations of the same media representations. He understands that how a representation makes sense to an individual can occur within a matrix of discourses coming from multiple sites (including other media sources) in society. However, in general he tends to celebrate that alternative readings *do* occur and takes this as an indicator of individuals' agency in the face of dominant systems of representation. Fiske inadequately examines the implications of the terms or systems of classification through which dominant or alternative readings *can* occur.[11] In contrast, while I note alternative readings, I also attempt to look more specifically at the character of the discourse employed by those encountering a particular media form (in this case talk shows). I have focused both on the kinds of classifications used and how they are used.

To be sure, material life circumstances and social location make a difference in what each woman considers legitimate. But these differences cannot be reduced to these sociological factors. That is to say, one's material life circumstances and social location certainly *do* matter in terms of the various discursive repertoires to which one has access and is likely to invoke, but there is more at play. Another dimension operating in the women's narratives is how they locate themselves as subjects both in the discourses they invoke and in their material circumstances. Here, a key question I ask in analyzing each woman's account is, "What kind of subject would encounter the shows in this particular way?" For example, Susan is materially situated as a white, middle-class college student and aspiring professional. In addition to her material social location, she subjectively locates herself firmly within the bounds of the "normal" as opposed to the marginalized "segments of the population" she sees on talk shows and characterizes as "just so far out there."

Michelle is situated in a more complex way. A young black woman from the inner city, she attends a predominantly white, suburban university. Coming from a lower middle class background, she aspires to be a professional. She situates herself more ambivalently in relation to the shows. While she sees some of the guests as ignorant, she also clearly relates to others. In addition, she admits that she is affected by some of the shows she sees. I am suggesting that Michelle locates herself as a subject in a more multifaceted, "double" way, akin to the "double consciousness" invoked by Dubois (1989) and theorized further in the contemporary scene by Gilroy (1993). In her narrative she negotiates a subjectivity in which she locates herself in at least two sometimes simultaneous, worlds that traverse race and class. She is comfortable in both discourses.

In Sandi's account as well, we see evidence of a more complex relation. Sandi does not watch talk shows for entertainment. Rather, she watches only those shows she discerns as legitimate discourse. But what she considers "legitimate discourse" is clearly broader than what is encompassed in the orthodox liberal definition of "rational-critical debate." In answering my question, "What kind of subject would find the shows intelligible this way?," Sandi seems less anchored in an idealized notion of "the normal," based in dominant cultural standards. Rather, she recognizes the contingency and quirkiness of people's everyday lives. Both the material and discursive dimensions of Sandi's experiences of race, gender, and class undergird the way she finds the world intelligible.

Consistent Criteria Applied Differently: Historical Discourses Meet Everyday Life

Even when they applied them differently, the women I spoke with consistently invoked similar criteria when discerning the degree to which a talk show was legitimate. I emphasize that though they did not necessarily use the same words, they brought similar concerns or standards to their process of discernment. Why is this the case? Here I appeal to Foucault's work, in which he discusses the terms through which knowledge is produced, experience, truth and falsity are understood, certain experiences are legitimated over others, and particular types of subjectivity are possible or at least more likely than others. While they may be deployed differently by different institutions or individuals, discourses provide the vocabulary through which we encounter and make sense of the world. Importantly, Foucault shows how these discursive repertoires or discourses are historical in that they arose in particular circumstances in particular moments in the context of particular power relationships. Therefore, the terms by which we organize our experience are never "neutral" but (at least) carry the legacy of this history. In his genealogical approach, Foucault is interested in

> not the chronological process of what happened in time, but the historical record, the narrative account of what happened in time . . . the way people record, narrate and explain their own past [and present, I argue] and evaluating the effects of various types of historical narration upon life. (Mahon, cited in Gatens 1996: 76)

I focus on two distinctive discourses—what I will call a "discourse of rationality and reason" and a "therapeutic discourse." Together these discourses seem to supply a good portion of the women's discursive repertoire, the terms through which the women discern the degree to which a show is encountered as legitimate discourse. These discourses are used and interwoven in numerous permutations with both each other and with other discourses.

Rationality and Reason:
The Bourgeois Imaginary and the Public Sphere

The criteria of appropriateness, authenticity, relevance, and efficacy so present in the accounts of the women I interviewed draw on a clustering of discourses that Stewart (1996) refers to as the "bourgeois imaginary." She suggests this imaginary emerged in late eighteenth century western European civic republicanism. Stewart describes the bourgeois imaginary as

> [a] set of precise, strategically deployed discourses of modernization, transcendent rationality and self-control . . . writ large as a naturalized, universalized order of things. A cultural diacritics rooted in difference and social conflict was displaced by an internalized struggle for self-discipline, discerning judgment and good taste. (Stewart 1996: 117)

The emergence of the "bourgeois imaginary" was tied to the important reorganization of social and physical spaces that were hallmarks in the development of the modern city. These included

> the creation of a clean space in which rational organization attempts to eliminate all physical, mental and political pollution . . . the displacement of particularized traditions by a totalizing classificatory order; and . . . the creation of a universal and impersonal subject. (Stewart 1996: 117)

Three key interrelated dimensions of this "bourgeois imaginary" are relevant to the accounts of the women with whom I
spoke: *impartial reason, the public/private distinction,* and the idea of
respectability (Young 1990). The discourses of the bourgeois imaginary were embodied in the discursive practices of a particular
kind of "public sphere" in which "private persons joined together
to exercise their reason in a public fashion" (Landes 1995: 99).
Feminist scholars, in particular, across a range of disciplines (history, philosophy, political theory, sociology, literature),[12] have
documented and critiqued this "bourgeois imaginary" and the
public sphere associated with it as being fundamentally based in
exclusions. That which was actually particularistically white,
male, and bourgeois was passing as universal.

Consistent with Stewart's characterization of the bourgeois
imaginary, Young (1990) traces the emergence of the bourgeois
public sphere in western Europe. Before the hegemony of republican philosophy in the late eighteenth century, the developing urban centers of western Europe fostered the intermingling
of people of different classes in shared public spaces, which en-
gendered a "unique public life" (Young 1990: 108). Through an
array of institutions, including coffeehouses, newspapers, salons,
theaters, and reading societies, bourgeois men to some extent
men of other classes, aristocrats, and even bourgeois women participated in public discussion. As Young characterizes it,

> Public life in this period appears to have been wild, playful and
> sexy. The theater was a social center, a forum where wit and
> satire challenged the state and predominant mores. This un-
> bridled public mixed sexes and classes to some degree, mixed
> serious discourse with play, and mixed the aesthetic with the
> political. (Young 1990: 108)

Young suggests that republican philosophy suppressed the
rich public culture of the eighteenth century. The newer

conception of the civic public was "the universal and impartial point of view of reason, standing opposed to and expelling desire, sentiment and the particularity of needs and interest" (Young 1990: 108). While not negating the role of the particularistic dimensions of emotion, need, and desire of human beings, these dimensions of being human were to find expression in the *private* sphere of domestic life. In this idealization, the model citizen (member of the public) was the "rational man" (literally) who operates impartially and impersonally in the public sphere, "detached from any particular interests at stake, weighing all 'interests' equally" (Young 1990: 96). In other words, the model citizen was a detached, dispassionate subject who reserved emotionality and desire for the private haven of the family.

Feminist scholars have challenged the privileging of this ideal as universal. For example, Young notes that

the ideal of the civic public as expressing the general interest, the impartial point of view of reason, itself results in exclusion. By assuming that reason stands opposed to desire, affectivity, and the body, this conception of the civic public excludes bodily and affective aspects of human existence. In practice this assumption forces homogeneity upon the civic public, excluding from the public those individuals and groups that do not fit the model of the rational citizen capable of transcending body and sentiment. (Young 1990: 109)

Women and other groups who have historically been identified with emotion, the body, nature, and the particularistic in western European societies were excluded from the mainstream public sphere in which reason prevailed. Young notes the view that "[a]llowing appeals to desires and bodily needs to move public debates would undermine public deliberation by fragmenting its unity" (Young 1990: 109). Moreover, Young continues,

The impartiality and rationality of the state depend on containing need and desire in the private realm of the family. The public realm of citizens achieves unity and universality only by defining the civil individual in position to the disorder of womanly nature, which embraces feeling, sexuality, birth and death, the attributes that concretely distinguish persons form one another. . . . Modern normative reason and its political expression in the idea of the civic public, then, attain unity and coherence through the expulsion and confinement of everything that would threaten to invade the polity with differentiation: the specificity of women's bodies and desire, differences of race and culture, the variability and heterogeneity of needs, the goals and desires of individuals, the ambiguity and changeability of feelings. (Young 1990: 110)

In contrast to a "wild, playful, sexy," heterogeneous, and polyvocal public, a discourse privileging *impartial reason* came to prominence, privileging those who demonstrated or were deemed to demonstrate the capacity for operating in this detached, abstract, and dispassionate mode. This issue of *whose* common concerns come to represent the "public's" common concerns must be raised here, as well. Feminist scholars point out not only the exclusionary constitution of this "public," but also the lack of acknowledgment (in Habermas's seminal account, for example)[13] of the other less dominant "publics" with which it co-existed, even if overpowering them with respect to actual influence.

Nonetheless, this concept of impartial reason, which lies at the heart of this notion of the public sphere, serves as a discursive resource for the women in making sense of talk shows as well as a discourse that they resist. For example, while Susan's account of talk shows holds close to a privileging of impartial reason, Janice's and Sandi's cases are more complex.

Janice and Sandi both note that certain characteristics of impartiality are desirable. For example, both women speak positively about a host having "control," although this "control" is distinguished by degree. (Recall Janice's discussion of Sally as being *too* overbearing at times.) In Janice's and Sandi's accounts, "control" is recognized as the facilitation of a guest speaking and being listened to, rather than the use of the show as a platform from which the host makes pronouncements and judgments about guests and issues. Janice and Sandi also demand that guests be respected regardless of their situation. They feel that respect is not something the guests should have to earn, but rather is a given, a place from which the host ought to begin interacting with the guests. This reflects certain aspects of the model of impartial reasoning—that in the public sphere differences are "bracketed" and citizens engage in discourse about issues on common ground without regard for their differences. In the idealized public sphere, citizens engage as equals, irrespective of their differences in status in other domains. For example, in her discussion of Jerry Springer as an exemplary host, Janice emphasizes his ability to "keep things in perspective" and not get upset. Both women value at least some degree of proceduralism and dispassion.

On the other hand, Sandi's and Janice's accounts indicate their resistance to some aspects of the ideal of impartial reason. For example, Sandi's objections to Ricki Lake and Janice's to Geraldo echo Young's theoretical concerns about impartial reason. Sandi objects to Ricki's applying certain moral rules universally to situations that she feels need to be considered in their particularity. This problematic behavior is manifested in Ricki's pronouncements to the guests about what they *ought* to do. Moreover, Sandi objects to Ricki's assuming a superior position, a positioning that can be read as that of a "transcendent reasoning subject." Janice's concerns that Geraldo is more interested in his own "theory" than in what his guests have to say also reflects this concern and is an objection to the impartial and dispassionate reasoning subject. In contrast to the positioning of the hosts, both women speak from a position of knowing and empathizing with the talk show guests and their situations. They situate themselves similarly to the guests in a relation of equality. This is a positioning in which they recognize the complexities, "quirks," and contingencies of everyday life *as it is lived*. Janice and Sandi are concerned that what certain hosts present as impartial, "commonsense" reasoning is actually (and problematically for them) speaking from a particular position. This is a transcendent position that the hosts value as superior to the more situated, particularistic subjectivity of the guests. Both Janice and Sandi sense this. Conversely, the hosts Janice and Sandi cite as exemplary (Montel, Maury, and, in Janice's case, Jerry Springer) are characterized as attending to the particularities of each guest and his or her situation. I suggest that here Janice and Sandi invoke other, less hegemonic and often devalued or marginalized discourses, including those generally associated with women's discursive practices and African American cultural practices.

Susan's viewing stance is clearly more distanced and dispassionate than both Sandi's and Janice's. She deploys a discourse of rationality and reason in a fairly orthodox manner and speaks from a solidly bourgeois position in society. While, like Janice and Sandi, she refers to certain hosts (Montel and Maury) as "definitely respecting their guests more" than, say, Ricki Lake, Susan focuses more on the issue of a host's or a show's exploitation of people who are "vulnerable." Susan's stance is one in which she cannot see an equal relationship between host and guests. The weak could be helped, perhaps, rather than exploited, but the show would still not constitute a discussion among equals, and thereby cannot qualify as legitimate public discourse.

The public sphere constituted through impartial reasoning and the rational, transcendent subject had the effect of producing clear distinctions between issues classified as appropriately public or private in mainstream discourse. Issues classified as public were deemed worthy of such consideration according to standards of impartial and dispassionate reason. Issues classified as appropriately *private*, issues pertaining to emotion, desire, and particularity were to be dealt with in the context of the family. While in contemporary society there is currently a higher degree of ambiguity and more openness with respect to what is construed as appropriately public versus private issues in mainstream discourse, these distinctions continue to be key terms or categories through which discernments of "legitimacy" are made. The women I interviewed invoked these distinctions in making sense of the shows, in particular through their concerns for what constitutes an appropriate talk show topic, appropriate behavior, and an appropriate mode of discourse on the shows. For example, when I asked Chandra (a twenty-three- year-old single black woman with one child, holding an Associate's Degree and working toward her beautician's license) whether there were things that "just shouldn't be put on TV," she answered:

> Absolutely. 'Cause I don't [care] about someone who's sleeping with her boyfriend's sister or brother. I don't care. I mean, personally, I don't think it's happening. But if it is happening, then, you deal with that. But I would, like, know how to identify a pedophile. You know, someone who's going to molest children. What to look at if your child is molested, and how they'll act differently.

Many issues formerly considered private are now squarely situated as public in contemporary society. These issues include child abuse, sexual harassment, domestic violence, and worker safety. The kinds of issues for which we've seen this shift illustrate the link between a group's degree of power in society and the classification of issues that reflect *their* "common concerns" as "private" or "public" in mainstream discourse. Classificatory systems, then, can be understood as being enmeshed in the power relations of a society rather than their being simply and impartially descriptive. They are part of a process through which issues come to have existence as legitimately public (or not), and thereby even make it onto the mainstream public agenda.[14] While the boundary distinguishing "public" from "private" has shifted over time, the women I interviewed still consider talk shows *through* the *categories* of public and private.[15] This distinction of "public/private" seems to hold even in light of the feminist movement's injunction that "the personal is political" (read "public"), making the boundary between the two sides of the classification fuzzy and permeable. Notably, almost all of what is considered inappropriate by the women interviewed concerns issues historically placed in the private sphere as delineated by the orthodox liberal model of the public sphere. While the boundary is not so clearly fixed, the women's accounts show that, indeed, there *is* still a boundary that, when crossed, has the result that an issue is no longer classified as public discourse; it may be classified as "entertainment" (in which case it can be enjoyed on its own terms) or simply as inappropriate. As I show in the next chapter on "the lure" of the shows, this boundary varies among the women I interviewed.

The notion of *respectability* is closely related to both the public/private distinction and the privileging of impartial reason, and it is also present as a concern in the accounts of the women I interviewed. Young gives a useful definition of the term in the context of the bourgeois imaginary:

> Respectability consists in conforming to norms that repress sexuality, bodily functions and emotional expression. It is linked to an idea of order: the respectable person is chaster,

modest, does not express lustful desires, passion, spontaneity, or exuberance, is frugal, clean, gently spoken and well mannered. The orderliness of respectability and things are under control, everything is in its place, not crossing borders. (Young 1990: 137)

Standards of respectability, that which is respected as legitimate public behavior, is constituted through norms historically grounded in the bourgeois imaginary. This is apparent, for example, in Janice's concern that young black women need to "compose themselves" if they want viewers and studio audience members to sympathize with them rather than view them as "pathetic." Janice implies that to be taken seriously as a speaker one must demonstrate behaviors of comportment akin to the dispassionate citizen of the bourgeois public sphere. Chandra voiced similar concerns about the conduct of members of "the underclass." Talking about the "newer" talk shows, like *Ricki Lake*, she shared that

young people, when they get on these talk shows, they get worse. It's not like they're getting on these talk shows to get information—you know, they would straighten up their act. It's a way for them to have fun. You know. And that's a waste of a TV station. . . . That is something that, like the new talk shows, they feed off of that. You know, the underclass. And the black people. You know what I'm saying? Like, young—it's not even black. I don't even want to use color because they have a lot of underprivileged, you know—Latinos, Caucasians, blacks. All that. They feed off that—how do you say, their misfortune, I guess. You know what I'm saying? Because they don't really have a clue of how to, say, conduct themselves or to act in certain ways. And that's why I say it's the hostess's responsibility to guide these people and—you want to tell people, "Okay well, we have some regulations we need to follow, you know."

For Chandra, it is the job of the host to guide people in appropriate behavior that conforms to norms of mainstream respectability. In particular, she specifies "underprivileged" people as "not having a clue" about "how to conduct themselves in certain ways." People, including usually marginalized individuals, may speak, but they must do so on the terms of the dominant culture if they are to be taken seriously as "legitimate" speaking subjects. A "good" host is one who demonstrates these behaviors and fosters them in guests and studio audience members.

Habermas (1991) as well as others (e.g., Sennett 1992, Postman 1985, Putnam 1995) lament the decline of the public sphere grounded in principles of rationality and reason, the ascent of the consumer over the citizen, and the prevalence of radical individualism over concern for the common good. However, to a large extent, ironically, the women I interviewed drew on standards of rationality and reason to make sense of talk shows. The women I interviewed understand themselves in relation to the "bourgeois imaginary," something that can be seen in terms of who they discern to be a legitimate speaker as well as the modes of discourse and issues they find legitimate. Some women solidly embody this discourse of the "bourgeois imaginary." Others more fluidly deploy some, but not all, dimensions of this dominant discourse by incorporating, for example, the particularism, empathy, and passion characteristic of discourses more often associated with women's discursive practices, or as African American cultural practice. With respect to the latter, West points to practices and styles that are rooted in the specificity of black Americans' history of enslavement. He suggests that

the concrete everyday response to institutional terrorism was to deploy weapons of kinetic orality, passionate physicality, and combative spirituality to survive and dream of freedom.

By kinetic orality, I mean dynamic, repetitive and energetic rhetorical styles that form communities, e.g., antiphonal styles and linguistic innovations that accent fluid, improvisational identities and that promote survival at almost any cost. By passionate physicality, I mean bodily stylizations of the world, syncopations, polyrhythms that assert one's somebodiness in a society in which one's body has no public worth, only economic value as a laboring metabolism. And by combatitive spirituality, I mean a style of historical patience, subversive joy and daily perseverance in an apparently hopeless and meaningless historical situation. . . . Black cultural practices emerge out of acknowledgment of a reality they cannot not know . . . a reality historically constructed by white supremacist practices in North America during the age of Europe. These ragged edges—of not being able to eat, not to have shelter, not to have health care—all this is infused into the strategies and styles of black cultural practices. (West 1988: 42)

These cultural practices appear in present-day society as "style." However, West emphasizes that they evolved from the African appropriation of Euro-American Christianity. Blacks' attraction to "dissenting Protestant Christianity provided many black slaves with a sense of somebodiness, a personal and egalitarian God who gave them an identity and dignity not found in American society" (West 1999: 436). In addition, West suggests that a particular conception of "existential freedom" infuses Afro-American Christianity, one that "embodies an ecstatic celebration of human existence without affirming prevailing reality . . . a rejoicing in the mere fact of being alive" (West 1999: 436). According to West, this sense of celebratory freedom "flows from the kinetic orality and affective physicality inherited from West African cultures and religions. This full-fledged acceptance of the body deems human existence a source of joy and gaiety" (West 1999: 436). West argues that the robust, bodily, and expressive participation characteristic of this sense of freedom are "weapons of struggle and survival. They not only release pressures and desperation, they also constitute bonds of solidarity and sources of individuality"(West 1999: 436).

While material conditions in which these African American cultural practices emerged have changed over the past several hundred years, I am suggesting that the discourses of these practices and the sensibilities they embody live as discursive repertoires which African Americans access in making sense of their contemporary circumstances.[16] Theses practices come to operate this way by virtue of their being enacted over time, thereby becoming interwoven in the everyday commonsense of the community. (This is distinct from, although intertwined with, the commodified appropriation of black cultural practices and sensibilities in mainstream culture.) These less dominant and culturally specific discourses and the sensibilities they embody interact with more hegemonic discourses and inflect them in distinctive ways. The way these particular discursive resources inflect each woman's account varies with respect to how she locates herself within these discourses and within more hegemonic discourses. The way that Janice, Sandi, and Michelle (all African American women) make sense of certain shows as legitimate is indeed inflected through these less hegemonic discourses, for example.

Important variations are clearly present in the women's accounts of talk shows. However, a discourse of rationality and reason and the standards constituting this discourse pervade contemporary cultural "common sense" and seem consistently to provide the criteria through which the women discern the degree to which a talk show is "legitimate."

Therapeutic Discourse: The Appropriately Emotional Subject

The bourgeois imaginary with its centerpiece of the exemplary rational subject is not the only discourse that pervades the women's accounts of talk shows. A "therapeutic discourse" also provides a distinctive discursive repertoire upon which many of the women draw. Whereas a discourse of rationality and reason privileges detachment, dispassion, and the abstract, the therapeutic discourse privileges feeling, the personal, and the particularistic.

Lears (1983) points to the historical moment in which a therapeutic discourse (or what he calls "ethos") emerged in the United States:

> The therapeutic ethos was rooted in reaction against the rationalization of culture—the growing effort, first described by Max Weber, to exert systematic control over man's external environment and ultimately over his inner life as well. By the turn of the century, the iron cage of bureaucratic "rationality" had begun subtly to affect even the educated and the affluent. Many began to sense that their familiar sense of autonomy was being undermined, and that they had been cut off from intense psychical, emotional or spiritual experience. The therapeutic ethos promised to heal the wounds inflicted by rationalization, to release the cramped energies of a fretful bourgeoisie. (Lears 1983: 17)

Lears (1983) focuses on the close relationship between the emergent therapeutic ethos and its appropriations by advertisers in service of the developing industrial corporate system. This was a key process through which a therapeutic ethos has been incorporated into mainstream cultural terms of intelligibility in everyday life. Lear's analysis makes it apparent that this ethos emerged in a particular historical moment:

The bourgeois ethos had enjoined perpetual work, compulsive saving, civic responsibility, and a rigid morality of self- denial. By the early twentieth century that outlook had begun to give way to a new set of values sanctioning a periodic leisure, compulsive spending, apolitical passivity, and an apparently permissive (but subtly coercive) morality of individual fulfillment. The older culture was suited to a production-oriented society of small entrepreneurs; the new culture epitomized a consumption-oriented society dominated by bureaucratic corporations. (Lears 1983: 3)

Lears argues that while "people have always been preoccupied by their own emotional and physical well-being," the concern emergent among the bourgeois classes in the late nineteenth century United States was distinctive (Lears 1983: 4). He suggests that while in earlier times and places concerns for health were tied to "larger communal, ethical or religious frameworks of meaning" (Lears 1983: 4), the late nineteenth century American concern occurred within a context in which these "frameworks were eroding . . . [and] the quest for health was becoming an entirely secular and self-referential project, rooted in peculiarly modern emotional needs—above all the need to renew a sense of selfhood that had grown fragmented, diffuse and somehow "unreal" (Lears 1983: 4).

Lears traces the technological change that made "modern conveniences" (e.g., prepackaged foods, indoor plumbing, central heating) more widely available but also served to distance individuals from "primary experience" and the "interdependent national market economy." Lears suggests that this distancing contributed to individuals' having a diminished sense of autonomous selfhood. Awareness of the insights of psychoanalysis and psychology, more generally, in which the unconscious or inherited drives constrain individual choice also contributed to this diminished sense of autonomy (Lears 1983: 8). Lears suggests that this lay at the core of a sense of "unreality" experienced by many of the bourgeois class. Further, "[s]elf-control became merely a tool for secular achievement; success began to occur in a moral and spiritual void" (Lears 1983: 10). In this historical context, Lears notes a shift in therapeutic discourse from one advocating conservation and self-control to an "abundance" therapy that emphasized the potential of human life.

In addition to the more general therapeutic ethos traced by Lears, the aspect of therapeutic practice that most apparently operates as a discursive resource for women in making sense of talk shows draws on the "talking cure" of Freud's accounts. The talking cure is the name given by Anna O. to the process of her "free associating" speech that allowed for the unconscious and repressed to emerge and through which she is relieved of her symptoms. Feminist critiques of Freud have pointed to the centrality of the relationship within which such speaking occurs. This relationship is characterized as a hierarchical relationship of power between patient and therapist, in which it is not just through the patient's speaking, but the patient's speaking in the context of her relation to the therapist that the cure occurs. Both Shattuc (1997) and M. White (1992) reference Foucault's theorization of "the confessional" as central to an understanding of a therapeutic discourse. "The analyst or therapist becomes the 'authority who requires the confession, perceives and appreciates it and intervenes in order to judge, punish, forgive, console and reconcile; a ritual in which the truth is corroborated by the obstacles it has surmounted in order to be formulated" (Foucault cited in Shattuc 1997: 112). At the same time, they note the differences inherent in the construction of talk shows, differences Shattuc traces in her summary of the development of twentieth-century American clinical psychology.

While appearing to counter the "rational subject" of impartial reason with characteristics historically identified as feminine (e.g., feeling, emotion, etc.), the ego psychology that became popular in American clinical practice emphasizes the subject as inherently rational. Shattuc notes that proponents of ego psychology (e.g., Erikson, Hartmann, Kroeber) claim that the ego "develops a measure of independence from the unconscious and the id," that it is "a rational agency responsible for individuals' intellectual and social actions" (Shattuc 1997: 114). This echoes Adler's argument that "personality was determined by *conscious* elements—social and interpersonal factors—rather than by a controlling *unconscious* to which only the therapist had access" (Shattuc 1997: 114, emphasis mine).

Shattuc outlines a development of therapeutic practice grounded in this perspective: Horney's emphasis on "self- esteem" in the 1930s; Erich Fromm's rejection of Freud's notion of "innate, undesirable human traits" in the 1960s; George Miller's 1969 injunction to "give psychology away to the people" in humanist therapy of the 1960s and '70s, grounded in "a belief of an inherent tendency toward self-actualization, growth and enhancement"; and, finally rational emotive therapy, the "most influential of these self-actualization revisions and a source for the recent self help movements," in which man is placed "squarely in the center of his universe and of his emotional fate" and is given almost "full responsibility for choosing to make or not make himself seriously disturbed" (Shattuc 1997: 114–20). Shattuc (1997) and White (1992) argue that while in this more apparently democratic theorization the formal hierarchical power relationship of therapist and patient is deemphasized, one can also understand this therapeutic as one that actually enforces a more insidious "self-policing" or self- monitoring by the patient.

Running through these more contemporary American revisions of Freudian psychoanalysis and through the therapeutic ethos more generally is the characteristically American individualism grounded in liberal humanism. This is a conception of what Foucault calls "the sovereign subject," a notion of the subject as unique and self-authoring. Here, the link between the therapeutic and rational discourses becomes apparent. Sandi incorporates this link in her account. When discussing her problem with Ricki Lake's pronouncements and assumed authority, Sandi emphasizes the need to recognize the guest's capacity for personal choice as a matter of respect. In her view, the job of the host is to make alternatives available rather than to tell guests what they *ought* to do. Janice demonstrates this self-reflexive monitoring in her talk about what she had learned from the shows with respect to relationships and other issues.

In the distinctively American therapeutic discourse, the authority of the analyst is downplayed and professional expertise—knowledge based on scientific method—is displaced by the authority of lived experience, which emphasizes particularity and the legitimacy of emotion (Carpignano et al. 1993; Shattuc 1997; Masciarotte 1991). This discourse is apparent in the women's narratives in their emphasis on "caring," "helping," "listening," "sensitivity," etc.

However, while most of the women speak about authenticity of feeling and having the space to speak and be listened to, they also make it clear that certain displays of emotion or talk about certain issues are *not* appropriate. While on the one hand, the therapeutic discourse legitimates (and for its distinctiveness relies on) emotionality and self-disclosure, the women I interviewed indicate that there are limits to this if a person, topic, or show is to be taken seriously. While emotionality and/or self-disclosure are taken as indicators of *authenticity*, this is only the case *up to a point*, beyond which such enactments become *inappropriate*. This "point" varies among the women.[17]

Mimi White suggests that "[c]onfesssion and therapy are engaged toward finding one's 'proper place' as an individual and social subject, even as they are mediated through the apparatus of television" (M. White 1992: 19). The women I interviewed clearly articulated a sense of the "proper" subject. The point of the therapeutic encounter is to return one to a rational state. If not a "dispassionate" or "detached" subject, at least a finally "rational" subject is incorporated into standards of appropriateness the women articulate in their accounts. While, on the face of it, the therapeutic discourse and the discourse of rationality and reason may appear to be two sides of a binary, this illustrates the extent to which standards of rationality and reason interweave the therapeutic discourse.

The women's concern for *efficacy* is also complicated in this regard. While this concern is grounded in a rational and utilitarian discourse focused on the useful, impersonal, and geared toward action, a concern for efficacy is also evident in the therapeutic discourse. In the accounts of the women I interviewed, emotionality and self-disclosure are generally positioned as being in service of returning the guest to his or her position as a properly rational and reasonable subject, a subject "in control." The point of being "given alternatives," having hosts make offers of help, and Ricki's and Geraldo's pronouncements or "theories" is the guest's return to such a normative state. Furthermore, Shattuc (1997: 98) suggests, "Through the discourses of Protestantism, liberalism, and the therapeutic, the shows reproduce the dominant ideology of 'self- contained individualism' in which change is synonymous with individual change versus more structural, system change" (Shattuc 1997: 98). This, too, is apparent in the accounts of the women I interviewed. The subject is now not *just* the rational, sovereign subject, but also an *appropriately* emotive and self-disclosing subject. The emotive and self-disclosing dimensions of this subject do not challenge the discourse of the subject as a fundamentally rational individual, but rather construct the subject as more multifaceted. While all the women privilege the "rational" subject to a large degree, what actually constitutes this normative rational subject varies among the women. This variation is influenced by the extent to which viewers encounter a particular issue as legitimate and how they locate themselves in relation to those discussing the issues. A key factor in this regard is a woman's material social location. Similar to my discussion of "respectability" in the previous section, the issue of what constitutes the normative rational subject (who is "respectable") is also inflected through the discursive repertoires and sensibilities of the traditions of cultural practices within which the different women are grounded.

Conclusion

While the women I interviewed are situated differently in society and bring a varying mix of understandings and experiences to their viewing of talk shows, the criteria they invoke in discerning certain shows as "legitimate" are grounded in several distinctive cultural discourses that provide the terms through which they organize their "experience" in this regard. The range of discourses that cross-cut the distinctive rational and therapeutic discourses give rise to the women's articulating hybridized vocabularies that are sometimes contradictory and/or paradoxical. It is all of this that results in the women's deploying consistent criteria (efficacy, appropriateness, relevance, and authenticity) in different ways. While the criteria are consistent across women's accounts in respect to discerning legitimacy, what substantively actually counts as legitimate varies. Using the same criteria, we can still see the world quite differently.

5. THE LURE OF THE SHOW

Talk Shows as Entertainment

There are a lot of shows that are, like, information. And then there's shows that you just watch for entertainment. . . . Like, with the juicy ones on *Jerry Springer.* That's for entertainment. And you know, he has people on there that are Siamese twins. You know, that type of thing. I think he's having two Siamese twins tomorrow that are joined at the stomach.

(Jamie)

Jerry Springer's my favorite. I don't know, he just seems, like he has off-the-wall—just different kinds of topics which you—sometimes he seems like—it seems like it's not real. (Tina)

It's all—it's like a monkey show! (Chandra)

It's just like watching to see what bizarre questions people are going to ask and—I think they're pretty funny. (Karen)

I don't know. I kind of sit back and have to think to myself, "Do people really do this type of thing?" It's more like a curiosity thing, to see do people really—you know—act that way or do those things? It's kind of more like a disbelief. I can't believe it. You know? Did it really happen? A whole lot of curiosity. I'm wondering to myself, "They can't really be talking seriously about this. This can't be serious." (Gina)

Jerry—Jerry always wants to see a fight. He's always, like, sleazy. You know what I mean? He never—he doesn't—I don't think he tries to make his guests feel comfortable. I think he tries to make them fight and get them, like, frustrated. I think Jerry is more sleazy and Rosie is more nice. You know, like she tries to make her guests feel comfortable. I think Jerry is just a freak. (Olivia)

Just about all the women who acknowledged watching talk shows as entertainment consistently referred to the shows and guests as "weird," "bizarre," "crazy," "wild," "strange," "freaky," a vocabulary clearly situating what they watch as not "normal." They also consistently spoke about their attraction to these shows, characterizing this attraction as being "lured," "pulled in," "fascinated," or having their attention "grabbed." Moreover, in mainstream popular and television industry discourse, *The Jerry Springer Show*, to which the women refer in the opening quotes of this chapter, is generally identified as being an exemplar of "trash talk" (usually informally ranked with *Ricki Lake*), while simultaneously being rated as the most watched daytime television talk show, recently surpassing *Oprah Winfrey* (the long-standing ratings leader).[1] I consider the shows as a contemporary embodiment of *symbolic inversion* and, more specifically, the *carnivalesque*, a particular type of violation of mainstream cultural norms.

I am interested in getting beyond the "cultural common-sense" in which the shows are characterized as "trash," illustrated, for example, in the analysis of Abt and Mustazza (1997). Even those who situate the shows as potential sites of "oppositional discursive practice" (Masciarotte 1991; Carpignano et al. 1993; E. Willis 1996) still analyze or theorize the talk shows in the context of their viability as legitimate public discourse, albeit a discourse that adheres to standards other than those of orthodox rational critical debate. I aim to shift the terms of discussion for understanding what these talk shows "are" and for understanding their place in contemporary American culture. This requires shifting focus from the shows as "talk" to the shows as "performance."

"An Hour of Outrageousness":
Who's Calling It "Talk"?

In an interview with Larry King, Jerry Springer makes it clear that his show ought not to be categorized as a "talk show."[2]

> I don't do a talk show. There is no talking on my show. People are yelling and, you know, they're going wild. It's not talking. (*Larry King Live!* 5/8/98)

> I've become a cliche for crazy, outrageous, on-the-edge television. . . . [O]ur show is as silly, crazy, outrageous, sometimes it's as stupid as you can get. (*Larry King Live!* 5/8/98)

The women I interviewed shared Springer's sentiments. It is clearly not the talking per se that features prominently in their enjoyment:

> I like seeing the arguments and the fighting. I think it's funny. I get a kick out of it. I really do. Like when they have, okay, "I have this one, I'm having an affair with this one." And, "I'm having an affair with, like, my brother's sister's mother." You know what I mean? "My brother-in-law's sister's mother," whatever. And they all get caught because they have so many, you know, affairs going on. I just think it's funny that they all get caught and how they react when they all get caught. I think it's funny. And then, when you find out that your mate is gay. I think it's hilarious. I just think it's funny as anything to see how people act. (Joy)

> When you have good issues, you have action. When you have action, you have lots of arguments and punches. That's a good show—like when they're fighting. When they're fighting over men. That gets me. They look like idiots—oh, and when they

have the paternity tests. Those are the funniest—when they find out that they ain't the daddy or they're the daddy. Oh, that can be funny! (Natasha)

He has "I want to be a stripper," "This is my fantasy to be a stripper." "I'm a male prostitute." He had something—like yesterday he had a show on Satan churches, "I worship Satan." And then another time, he had a show, "My boyfriend used to be a woman" [laughs]. He had another show on today. The topic is, "I'm going to tell my mate I want to be a stripper." And then, let me see—another one he had—he had another topic about this girl who had sex with three hundred men within a three-hour period or an eight-hour period, or something like that, to break the world's record. And then, he had another [laughs]—let me see another one he had that was weird—he has a lot of weird ones. I don't know. I think the weirdest one was the one where the girl had sex with three hundred men in like three hours or something. And then he had one about this man who married this fourteen-year-old girl, and he's already married to eight other women. It's weird stuff like that. You know what I mean? He always has something weird. I watch it because I just like to see people get on there and make fools of themselves. (Olivia)

In describing the shows, the women cite issues that are classified as "personal" by prevailing mainstream cultural standards. These shows prominently feature interpersonal and intimate relations and specifically focus on sex and sexuality. The women frequently referred to the "fighting," seeing the guests "look like fools" or "idiots" and the level of "action," and they emphasized the active, performed, and visual mode through which these usually personal and therefore private issues are made public. Moreover, this violation in which the private is made public is vivid, hyperexpressive, flagrant, and unapologetic. This is apparent in the extent to which the women's accounts focus on the display of the show rather than the discussion per se. Many of the women enacted portions of specific episodes for me, rather than simply talking about them.

An emphasis on what is *seen, performed, revealed,* or *made apparent* is central to the women's accounts of *The Springer Show.* Their accounts are full of details outlining, for example, the "twists and turns" of complicated situations, in which secrets are made public, mistaken identities (usually with respect to gender) unmasked, wrongs publicly confronted, and betrayals revealed. These characteristics of excess and vividness pervade the substantive topics featured on the shows—in guest demeanor and appearance as well as in the character of the actual talk itself. This display is central to the pleasure the women say they derive in watching the shows.

The Jerry Springer Show is intentionally constructed as transgressing mainstream cultural standards by its producers and is encountered this way by viewers. This transgression, which millions seem to enjoy (and many others find disgusting and/or morally reprehensible), has a distinctive character, constituting more than a simple violation of norms. Its character as *excessive* and *performative*—intentionally, flagrantly, unabashedly, and actively privileging that which is generally devalued in mainstream culture—compels me to consider the show as a contemporary enactment of *symbolic inversion,* in particular, the *carnivalesque.*

"All the Things That Society Don't Care for Very Much": Talk Shows as Symbolic Inversion

And with Jerry Springer. Oh God! He has everybody [laughs], everybody on there. Most of his shows are about homosexuals, gays and lesbians and strippers, and all the things that society don't care for very much. And that's what makes it most attractive, cause everybody watches it, you know. There are people sitting in the audience that have, like, a million questions. And then they also have where they tell everybody what to do. "Do you know, you shouldn't do that!" And [laughs], it just goes on and on. With Jerry Springer, he does those kinds of shows. His shows are more wild [laughs].   (Jamie)

The people are stupid, and what they're doing is ridiculous.
(Natasha)

I was hired to be a ringleader of a circus. I am hosting a show about outrageousness. Most of the subjects that we, perhaps you and I [speaking to Larry King] are interested in, or maybe a lot of your viewers are interested in, are not outrageous. We do represent, in the way we live, probably mainstream America. But our show is about that which is not mainstream.
(Jerry Springer in interview on *Larry King Live!* 5/8/98)

The women I interviewed as well as Springer himself characterize *The Springer Show* as consistently featuring people, topics, and behaviors that are flagrantly, excessively, and unapologetically enacting a *symbolic inversion* of prevailing cultural hierarchies, the classificatory systems and practices that comprise the mainstream common sense discussed in the previous chapter. Symbolic inversion can be understood as a cultural process through which "any act of expressive behavior . . . inverts, contradicts, abrogates, or in some fashion presents an alternative to commonly held cultural codes, values and norms be they linguistic, artistic, religious, social or political" (Stallybrass and White 1986: 13).

The Springer Show and similar ones turn "commonly held cultural codes, values" upside down. These shows not only privilege that which is ordinarily marginalized and/or devalued, but put it onto the television screen, making it accessible to more than ninety million American homes at least five days each week. A sampling of topics makes apparent the symbolic inversion *The Springer Show* enacts on the air:[3]

- "A Mother Who Ran Off with Her Daughter's Fiancé"
- "Women Discuss Their Sex Lives with Their Mothers"
- "My Daughter is Living as a Boy"
- "Nude-Dancing Daughters"
- "I'm Marrying a 14-Year-Old Boy"
- "A 17-year old married to her 71-year-old foster father . . . they first had sex when she was 14. They have four children."
- "A male guest admits to sleeping with his girlfriend's mother."
- "Now that I've slept with him, he treats me like dirt!"
- "A woman who claims she got pregnant while making a pornographic movie."
- "You're too fat to dress so sexy!"
- "Drag queen pageant."

Even while distributed on mainstream television, in mainstream popular discourse the show is generally devalued. It is precisely because of this devaluation that the show constitutes a useful site of study for the construction of cultural order. Babcock notes:

Far from being a residual category of experience, [symbolic inversion] is its very opposite. What is socially peripheral is often symbolically central, and if we ignore or minimize inversion and other forms of cultural negation, we often fail to understand dynamics of symbolic cultural processes generally. (Babcock, cited in Stallybrass and White 1986: 20)

According to Stallybrass and White (1986), symbolic inversion is based in a cultural classificatory schema grounded in an opposition of "high" versus "low," a "binaryism" through which the "high" (or dominant) constructs itself *against* the "low." Understanding the construction of the "low," then, is central to understanding a culture and the classificatory systems through which it is constituted. Stalleybrass and White suggest that this kind of binary schema has been foundationally operative in European cultures since the Renaissance. Talk shows like *The Jerry Springer Show* can be understood as a contemporary case of the "low," a radically visible and accessible site through which the "low" is constructed and encountered by viewers. This "lowness" is not just a matter of the substantive topics featured, but also the mode of behavior, people featured, and geographical siting. Springer himself notes as much, commenting:

> I think people are often upset with our show not because it's violent, compared to guns and muggings you see on the news and what you see on soap operas and primetime television. It's nothing like what you see on our show. They wrestle. But, I don't think they like the people who are on our show. (Jerry Springer from interview on *Larry King Live!* 5/8/98)

> I honestly believe there is an elitist mode. American television has historically been from an upper-white-middle- class perspective. . . . Think about it. African American shows nowadays are put on the WB network, are put on UPN. If you are black and on American mainstream television, you have to dress white, talk white. I'm not saying that there is anything wrong with that perspective. It's part of who I am. But it is wrong if that's the only thing that we have on American television. What is wrong to have one show like mine that is so crazy and outrageous and nuts? It shouldn't be. We should see it all. Not just upper-middle-class whites. (Jerry Springer from interview on *Larry King Live!* 5/8/98)

Springer's comments resonate with Douglas's (1985) conceptualization of "matters out of place" in her study of pollution, taboo, and their relationship to the construction and maintenance of social order. In Douglas's analysis, that which is intelligible as "dirt" and "filth" in a society is associated with the "low" in society and is that against which the norm is constructed. Therefore, when the dirty or filthy is found "out of place," it is disorienting and disturbing to those of the dominant culture. I am suggesting this kind of dynamic is at play with respect to the "place" or "siting" of talk shows in contemporary American society.[4]

The "low," historically constituted as that which is opposed to dominant cultural practices and against which the dominant or mainstream identifies itself, must be understood more specifically as implicitly gendered, classed, and racialized. At least in western European cultures (and those like our own which are derived from them), who and what is designated as "low" corresponds to that which stands opposed to the discourse of the rational, autonomous individual, a discourse, as shown in the previous chapter, that privileges that which is white, male, and of the privileged (bourgeois) class. In the contemporary case, we may find ourselves unreflectively encountering certain phenomena featured on talk shows as "low, demonstrating the extent to which we find the world intelligible through particular historical cultural discourses. Phenomenologically, however, what we experience appears to be simply and objectively "the way it is." Springer makes this point explicit in his analysis of his own show.

Symbolic Inversion and the Carnivalesque

More specifically, *The Jerry Springer Show* can be understood as a particular type of symbolic inversion characterized as *carnivalesque*.

Following Stallybrass and White (1986), the concept "carnivalesque" is a way of characterizing a category of symbolic practices,
images, and discourses that manifest an inversion of dominant
cultural norms. Remembering the ways in which the women I interviewed characterized *The Springer Show*, consider Stallybrass
and White's description of "carnival":

> Carnival in its widest, most general sense embraced ritual spec-
> tacles such as fairs, popular feasts, wakes, processions and com-
> petitions, comic shows, mummery and dancing, open-air
> amusements with costumes and masks, giants, dwarfs, mon-
> sters, trained animals and so forth; it included verbal composi-
> tions (oral and written) such as parodies, travesties and vulgar
> farce; and it included various genres of "Billingsgate," by which
> Bakhtin designated curses, oaths, slang, humour, popular
> tricks and jokes, scatological forms, in fact, all the "low" and
> "dirty" sorts of folk humour. Carnival presented by Bakhtin was
> a world of topsy-turvy, of heteroglot exuberance, of ceaseless
> overrunning and excess, where all is mixed, hybrid, ritually de-
> graded and defiled. (Stallybrass and White 1986: 8)

Clearly the women I interviewed encountered *The Springer
Show* as carnivalesque. This is evidenced in their frequent references to "ridiculousness," "silliness," "wildness," and "craziness,"
their finding the shows "funny," their suggesting that "nobody
takes them seriously," the guests fighting or being provoked to
fight (instead of engaging in "rational/reasonable" discourse),
the guests swearing, and the women mentioning "all the different kinds of people" found on the show. Moreover, the concern
voiced by some of the women (and many with whom I have spoken informally) that the shows are "exploitative," "disgusting," or
"trash" is consistent with the morally tinged rhetoric of members
of dominant classes in various historical moments. The domi-

nant class's commentary on carnivalesque cultural forms, rang-
ing from medieval fairs and carnivals to Shakespeare, from popular theater in the late nineteenth century to burlesque in the
twentieth (both examples in the American context), makes use
of a vocabulary that consistently marginalizes and devalues these
various carnivalesque forms.

As Susan commented in her account in the previous chapter,
the shows are "pointless." Encountered as entertainment, *The
Springer Show* is not "productive" in the sense of accomplishing either closure or a "useful" outcome. It is about consumption,
about excess, about an unfolding story with its twists, turns, and
surprises.[5] It is "useless." It is pure entertainment. It violates the
boundaries of legitimate discourse while simultaneously being
positioned as public "talk" (given its designation as a "talk show"
by television industry management). It begins with the appearance of being a forum for "talk," then always violates the rules.
And its viewers, much as with public theater historically,[6] begin
their viewing by anticipating that this violation will occur. This
anticipation contributes to the ritualistic dimension of the practice of watching talk shows, as noted in the previous chapter.
Knowing what's going to happen is a big part of the fun. Most of
the women anticipate their reaction of amazement, amusement,
or shock. (I explore this issue of "anticipation" and "predictability" later in this chapter.)

Carnivalesque forms are characterized by robust participation
consistent with what many of the women displayed in their accounts of watching talk shows. The women's accounts indicate
that far from being passive viewers, many find themselves compelled to interact with show.

Sometimes her show [*Jenny Jones*] can really get out of hand
where, like, "Jenny, why don't you," you know, "This is your
show. Tell them to stop or tell them . . ." you know. I find

myself getting upset and like I'm yelling through the TV, "Jenny, stop for a minute? Jenny, get control!" (Janice)

Many women also shared that when they watched talk shows with other women, the group's conversation figured as central:

I watch it with my friends and we make fun of people that are in the audience or the guests. I watch with my friends and we just laugh at what people say or what they're wearing or something. I'll watch with a group of people and just make fun of them. That's basically how I watch talk show. I always watch it with a friend sitting on the other line saying, "Do you believe she said that?" (Joy)

It's much more fun when you do it in a group. . . . Because, like, when I'm watching it by myself, like, who am I going to comment to? It's like, "Oh, I had a really good joke there for someone." (Karen)

Even among women who generally watched talk shows alone, many indicated that often they were compelled to call a friend or close relative on the telephone during the show or that someone else who was watching called them:[7]

It's like you want to have someone to react with about it. You know what I mean? Because you have the audience going crazy with each other, high-fiving each other and doing "hummas." And you want to be able to say to somebody, "Oh, my God! Did you hear that?" And have their opinion and see if they felt the same way you did—oh, God. Every time it got exciting, or someone did something stupid on the show, or crazy. Or something that was, like, so shocking. And, you call them right up. "Oh, my God!" If it was, like, so exciting that we couldn't stand it, we would just stay on the phone so we wouldn't have to keep calling each other back. (Joanie)

If I'm home, I have two or three people call me watching the same show, wanting to know if I'm watching. We really get on the phone and it's, like, "That's crazy! Did you see the show, so and so was on?" and, "Did you see the one where the drag queens were on and they started fighting and he snatched the wig off?" You know, we really get into detail about it. You know, it's an everyday thing . . . I love it. (Janice)

Sometimes, if it's good, we'll call each other and we're like, "Girl, did you see that?" Yeah, we do. When something special . . . definitely, definitely when someone we know is on there, everybody calls everybody. I mean you get excited. . . . Call somebody up and make them excited, too. (Tina)

The substantive issues featured on the shows, as well as the shows' imagery and mode of interaction, embody the carnivalesque. For the most part these shows fail to enact rational discourse, discussion moving toward resolution, or, at least, to inform. This runs against dominant cultural standards in which talk about issues ought to have a point (Masciarotte 1991).

Mobile Transgression: The Talk Show as "Displaced" Carnival

As a distinctive form of symbolic inversion, carnival is a specific historically situated ritual practice. Understanding its history, then, at least in brief, is useful to situating *The Jerry Springer Show*, and the other shows women consistently watch "for fun," as contemporary "carnivalesque" forms, forms embodying traces of characteristics originating in the ritual of "carnival" itself. I aim to show, however, that the carnivalesque embodied in talk shows is distinctive given the historical circumstances in which and through which it exists, and that this distinctiveness makes a difference in terms of its impact on society.

Summarizing the history of carnival and carnival's suppression in European cultures, Stallybrass and White note that, historically, carnival was positioned before Lent as a celebration of physical and emotional *excess* prior to the Lenten period of fasting and abstinence. Etymologically, the word "carnival" likely has its origins in the phrase *"Carne Levares,"* the roasting and taking up of meat, which was characteristic of carnival celebrations (Stallybrass and White 1986: 184). This illustrates the ritual practice as materially situated within a matrix of social and cultural practices.[8] As Europe became modernized, the ritual calendar associated with the rural, agrarian-based population was eliminated, replaced by the work week structured by the imperatives of developing industrial capitalism. The "elimination" of carnival as a specific ritual form is viewed by many historians as "simply one of the many casualties in the movement toward an urban, industrial society" (Stallybrass and White 1986: 177). Stallybrass and White argue, however, that, in fact, carnival was *not* eliminated. Rather, they suggest, it was suppressed and displaced through four different processes: fragmentation, marginalization, sublimation, and repression.

During the long and uneven process of suppression (we often found that a carnival is banned over and over again, only to re-emerge each time in a slightly altered fashion), there was a tendency for the basic mixture to break down, certain elements becoming separated from others. Feasting became separated from performance, spectacle from procession: the grotesque body was fragmented. At the same time it began to be marginalized both in terms of social class and geographical location. It is important to note that even as late as the nineteenth century, in some places, carnival remained a ritual involving most classes and sections of a community—the disengaging of the middle class from it was a slow and uneven matter. Part of that process was, as we have seen, the "disowning" of carnival and its symbolic resources, a gradual reconstruction of the idea of carnival as the culture of the Other. This act of disavowal on the part of the emergent bourgeoisie with its sentimentalism and its disgust, *made* carnival into the festival of the Other. It encoded all that which the proper bourgeois must strive *not to be* in order to preserve a stable and "correct" sense of self. (Stallybrass and White 1986: 178)

The displacements of carnival constitute a dispersal of transgression across a variety of "artistic and psychic domains" in which the fragmented carnivalesque "formed unstable discursive compounds, sometimes disruptive, sometimes therapeutic, within the very constitution of bourgeois subjectivity" (Stallybrass and White 1986: 182). This analysis correlates the fragmentation and negating of the ritual practices of carnival and festivals (rituals that emphasized period enactments of excess, consumption, and inversion of hegemonic norms), with the emergence of scientific discourse and the rise of a bourgeois class in western Europe in the eighteenth and nineteenth centuries. Carnival was suppressed, sometimes transformed into official and, in particular, military celebrations and state pageantry, in these cases voiding the carnivalesque of its constitutive function of symbolic inversion in favor of celebrating the status quo. Stallybrass and White note that this transformation provoked a change in the "structures of symbolic activity in Europe." With the displacement of carnival from a central symbolic role, which included the disengagement of the middle classes from participation, carnival gradually became "the festival of the Other" (Stallybrass and White 1986: 176–78).

Stallybrass and White track some of the displacements of carnival through western European history, including, for example, the enactments of hysterics in the early twentieth century which, they suggest, drew on a carnivalesque repertoire of images, gestures, and other behaviors repressed in the dominant culture.

In this context, *The Jerry Springer Show* (and other talk shows encountered similarly by viewers) represents a contemporary displacement of the carnivalesque. As a displacement, talk shows like *The Jerry Springer Show* do not replicate "carnival" per se. Rather, the show acts as a site of symbolic inversion by enacting certain carnivalesque elements in some distinctive ways. Since the dimensions of "when" (time) and "where" (geographical siting) have historically been central to the existence and repression of carnival, I focus on these two dimensions in examining talk shows as a contemporary embodiment of the carnivalesque.

Fragmented Temporality:
The Symbolically Cyclical to the Daily Mundane

With the imposition of the work week of modern capitalism, the carnivalesque was no longer temporally grounded. The wholeness of carnival as a clustering of symbolic practices was fragmented from the context of a larger matrix of social/cultural practices within which it had been situated, particularly from its symbolic calendrical or seasonal positioning. This temporal fragmentation, Stallybrass and White suggest, contributed to a sense of "unpredictability in the moment of surface of emergence" of the carnivalesque, contributing to its evoking a sense of danger (Stallybrass and White 1986: 181). Talk shows like *The*

Jerry Springer Show present a distinctive contemporary case in this regard.

The *Jerry Springer Show*, while not pinned to a calendrical or seasonal cycle, *is* pinned to the daily programming cycle of television, which, in turn constitutes a dimension of daily practice for millions of people. The issue of "dailiness" is central here. First, *The Springer Show* occurs each day, sometimes (depending on the channel's programming) with two airings (although often not the same show on both airings). It can be argued that the oscillation between production and consumption, which Stallybrass and White point to as a defining dimension of carnival, is, in fact, occurring, but in a simultaneously constrained and vastly accelerated fashion. (I think of Susan, for example, who watches talk shows as a "break" from the activities she values as more productive.) Even granting this analysis, this daily cycle makes the talk show a distinctive embodiment of the carnivalesque by virtue of its providing a vastly greater frequency (at least potentially) of encounters with the "low other" and the aesthetic of the grotesque. Second, whereas Stallybrass and White suggest that dissociation of the carnivalesque from the calendar "involved a degree of unpredictability with respect to moment and surface of emergence," by virtue of its production and distribution within a matrix of television industry programming practices, The *Jerry Springer Show* is *fully* predictable in terms of its being consistently aired at certain times each day, and it involves a predictable duration as well. Moreover, within this predictable hour or half-hour, the show is predictably broken into segments designed to accommodate commercial breaks, which further demonstrates the show's ties to contemporary production and distribution practices. In fact, as I noted in the previous chapter, many of the women I interviewed were aware that the outrageousness of the show was organized around the imperative of generating high ratings in order to attract advertising revenues. This practice demonstrates the rational and productive use of the carnivalesque to forward the aims of television industry management. The "uselessness" of the carnivalesque is thereby put to use. That which originated as a break from production is now actually produced through the matrix of rational work practices. This, I suggest, transforms the symbolic, ritual character of the transgressive.

Most of the women I spoke with emphasized the predictability of the outrageous displays on *The Jerry Springer Show* and similar shows, often noting their repetitive character.

> Like at the beginning, like I said, it was funny. "Oh, my God! Did you see that person jump up and scream?" "Oh yeah! Give it to him!" If it was like a jerk or husbands being rude to their wives or something, I'd be like, "Yeah, yeah, yeah!" But now it's just all tiresome. It's all just . . . that's when it became too—everything was too repetitive. (Joanie)

> I mean this is just everyday simple stuff, you know. Your girlfriend is sleeping with your boyfriend and you know it. That ends your friendship. You really don't have to come on *Ricki Lake* to discuss that. You should have done that at home. I mean, yeah, it's nice to know that, you know, for the world to see that this does happen. But at the same token, in everyday life, you know these things do happen. . . . Like one week she just focused on that every show, everyday with something similar to that. And then, it just became monotonous. I was, like, "I'm not watching this." (Janice)

In fact, many of the women indicated that it was precisely this repetition that began to "turn them off" or bore them. What is initially encountered as "shocking" begins to lose its edge. For example, Mary shared:

Like some of the guests they have on the show, you just want to say, "Don't you see!" I mean, like, honestly, it's almost the standpoint to where you see enough of the talk shows that you look at them like people to an extent. But then, it's like you become so cynical about it, I'm like, "Well, what can really be done for them?" And this and that. So, it's not like I actually, like I don't react. Maybe when I first started watching, I might have reacted emotionally about it. Like, "Oh, well doesn't she see what this is . . . !" But now it's just, "Eh." 'Cause you see it so much it's like—you know—it's commonplace. You don't even think about it anymore. (Mary)

Perhaps, echoing Baudrillard's (1988) notion of the *hyperreal*, talk shows can be understood as "hypercarnivalesque." What originated as a disruption or "break" from production (the ritual of carnival), set off from "everyday life" yet ritualistically incorporated into a larger matrix of social practice, has become almost constantly available. For most of the women with whom I spoke, the talk show is encountered as a mundane daily occurrence. Following Baudrillard's (1988) concern that representations in contemporary society are devoid of meaning, referencing only themselves, talk shows like *The Jerry Springer Show* can be understood as a carnivalesque spectacle evoking emotional intensity but disaggregated from any meaningful connection to social practice.

"Matters Out of Place" Writ Large: Geography and "Dispersed" Transgression

Geographic location figures centrally in Stallybrass and White's analysis of the displacements of carnival. In their analysis, geographic locations are understood as sites of cultural practice, with certain sites being associated with certain practices that are classified according to the "high/low" opposition that Stallybrass and White suggest is fundamental to the ordering of western European society. For example, they suggest that "the slum" has historically been taken to connote the "low" in a way currently signified by the "inner city." The identification of certain geographic locations as "low" includes (implicitly, although sometimes explicitly) the people who inhabit that location. In the contemporary example, this group is disproportionately poor and lower-income people of color, which shows how the "low" is coded both racially and with respect to class.

Stallybrass and White summarize the actual geographical marginalization of the carnivalesque in western Europe, which includes, for example, the confinement of such practices (including fairs, carnivals) to specific bounded areas within a town as these rituals are being pushed out of well-to-do neighborhoods. In England, carnivals were pushed to the seaside, literally the country's geographic margins. (Stallybrass and White 1986: 178–79)

Geographical marginalization has also operated in American forms of the carnivalesque. For example, Levine's (1988) histories of Shakespearean plays and opera in the United States show that initially these forms included many characteristics of the carnivalesque in contrast to the contemporary regard of these forms as "high culture." People from a range of social classes attended Shakespearean and operatic performances, although even in this case, seating was generally by class, with the bourgeoisie sitting in contained boxes and the lower economic classes in the "pit" and galleries (which accommodated prostitutes doing business as the shows went on). The performances were in the tradition of "popular theater," with substantial interaction between audience and performers. Audience members were participatory rather than passive spectators. They registered their approval and disapproval of the performance vocally, sometimes by throwing objects onto the stage and insisting that a particular song or speech be repeated. A farce or parody might be inserted in between acts of Shakespeare, a nonoperatic song inserted into an opera. Gradually, through the course of the nineteenth century, the bourgeois classes began to build their own theaters, distancing themselves from the raucous participatory events, where they adopted a more passive, polite stance as audience members. Burlesque and saloons were also attacked as undesirable and morally reprehensible. Burlesque theaters and saloons were confined to particular areas of towns and cities and, in some cases, were forced to close. (Allen 1991; Rosenzweig 1983)

Another relevant and distinctive dimension in examining the suppression of carnivalesque practices in the American context is the domain of African American cultural practice, especially given the viewership of talk shows as well as the overrepresentation of African Americans on certain shows. In the context of tracing the histories of rock-and-roll and jazz, Ventura (1985) notes that in the nineteenth-century American South, whites, connecting the practice of voodoo with the successful revolt of slaves in Haiti, prohibited the congregation of slaves, concerned that their collective spiritual practice might precipitate local revolt. Ventura characterizes the spiritual practices of voodoo as "embodied" practices in which music, singing, and dancing were central and in which there were no "spectators," with everyone participating. These rituals embodied characteristics of the carnivalesque in respect to being bodily, hyperexpressive, collective, and violating mainstream (white) cultural norms. In New Orleans, in one manifestation of the prohibition on the assembly of slaves, white slave owners organized Sunday dances for slaves in Congo Square, providing a sanctioned assembly that operated as a social control. Ventura suggests that here, dance and music were disembedded from the spiritual practices of which they had historically been an integral part.[9] He suggests that the Congo Square dances were also an occasion through which whites became spectators of a cultural form that had been not only an exclusively black practice, but exclusively participatory as well. Dance and music were allowable on the terms of dominant whites, in a way in which they felt assured that the music's and dance's subversive potential was dissipated (Ventura 1985). These practices shared with European carnival rituals the process of being geographically and temporally contained by a dominant class and, by virtue of this, disembedded from the larger matrix of social practice in which they originated and had been an integral part.

The carnivalesque, I argue, continues to find expression in American culture currently, for example, not only in talk shows, but in other ("low") cultural forms such as World Federation Wrestling and, as Ventura (1985) suggests, in rock-and-roll, jazz, and, more recently, rap and hip-hop culture.

Unlike earlier geographic sitebound forms of the carnivalesque, however, the talk show is potentially "everywhere" by virtue of the technology through which it is produced and distributed. At the same time, it is at no one "place," given its mode of distribution through cable and airwaves. The talk show is literally a mobile image performing the carnivalesque, encountered across dispersed (national and international) geography. This dispersion operates through a disembedding of the carnivalesque "low other" from a specific temporal and spatial context, a particular context of situated practice.

The carnivalesque depends on its reference to social structure to be intelligible as such. That is, in order to be intelligible as "low," it must be defined against the dominant standard of the "high." Furthermore, the aesthetic embodied in the carnivalesque is constituted through its social-structural reference. Those characteristics that constitute the carnivalesque—the grotesque body, hyperexpressivity, extreme emotionality, and its sheer uselessness—are not just visual representations and behaviors. Rather, they embody a particular sensibility that stands in contrast to bourgeois standards of "economy of utterance" (Stallybrass and White 1986) such as, civility, appropriateness, or modesty.[10]

The historically unprecedented disembedding of the carnivalesque and its embodiment of the "low-other" from a geographic location are clearly problematic for talk show critics like William Bennett. His concerns, while paralleling those of critics in earlier historical moments, are situated in a distinctive postmodern context.[11] In an opinion editorial published in the *Los Angeles Times* and also distributed over the Internet at the Empower America Website, Bennett discusses "trash" talk shows:[12]

> Almost every society has its red-light districts. That is part of reality, and we all understand that. A free society can tolerate such districts. But society should also do what we can to discourage them and contain them. And so, too, with the popular culture version of red-light districts. They ought to remain on the periphery, away from Main Street, our living room, our schoolyards. (Bennett 1996)

Responding to Larry King's question about why guests go on *The Jerry Springer Show* to say "I'm sleeping with your friend," the kind of topic Bennett and other critics find reprehensible and hope to see banned, Springer stated:

> Princess Diana was on international television a year and a half ago saying that she had been unfaithful in her marriage, that she had bulimia, that she had contemplated suicide. The most intimate, personal, sometimes humiliating things you can talk about. And there wasn't a person on Earth who

said, "How dare she go on television and talk about that." As crazy as it sounds, the guests on my show often talk about the same things—cheating in their marriage, dysfunctions, suicide, the same things. But they don't speak the Queen's English. (Jerry Springer from interview on *Larry King Live!* 5/8/98)

Springer's response makes apparent the way in which social structure pervades Bennett's concerns, which have surfaced due to the ever-growing network of communication and information structures that extend nationally and globally.[13] While containment and marginalization have historically been strategies for suppressing or controlling the carnivalesque, in its contemporary displacement in the form of the talk show such control is near impossible. This frustrated concern is registered in the moral outrage expressed by William Bennett in his campaign to get talk shows to "tone down" the "salacious" topics they feature. Bennett's rhetorical metaphors are geographical. Talk shows like *The Jerry Springer Show* (a show high on his list of worst offenders) need to be "contained" and "marginalized," the same types of strategies advocated and executed in the eighteenth and nineteenth centuries. Bennett's moral outrage is, I suggest, further evidence for the argument that while information and communication structures allow for hypermobility of signs (that is, images, representations, knowledge) (Lash and Urry 1994), social structure continues to play a formative role in both the production and distribution of these signs, as well as with respect to how they are encountered.

Bennett's outrage also illustrates the centrally symbolic role of that which is considered dirt, filth, and taboo in constructing and maintaining social order in a society. Consider Bennett's framing of talk shows as "cultural rot" (Bennett 1996: B9). He asserts,

We are witnessing the pollution of the human environment. Cleaning out our cultural air ducts won't happen by itself; it requires concerted effort and specific action. . . . What we are seeing, here and elsewhere, is the shock of recognition that in too many places, not just in back alleys but in the main thoroughfares, America has been cheapened. We, the American people, have allowed this desecration to occur. It's past time that we do something about it. (Bennett 1996: B9)

Douglas asserts that "ideas about separating, purifying, demarcating and punishing transgressions have as their main function to impose system on an inherently untidy experience" (Douglas 1995: 4). Therefore, "contacts which are thought dangerous also carry a symbolic load" (Douglas 1995: 3). In the contemporary world where images, knowledge, information, and other forms of representation evade boundaries by virtue of technology and are complicated by an increasingly multicultural population, contact with ideas, images, and people considered "impure" is inevitable. These "impure" entities are potentially everywhere. The force of Bennett's concern, with its explicitly moral tone, can easily be understood as an attempt to preserve a particular social order in an increasingly "untidy" world.

Transgression on One's Own Terms

By virtue of the frequency and scope of their broadcast via television, talk shows provide dispersion of and access to the carnivalesque on an unprecedented scale. However, in contrast to historically earlier carnivalesque forms, those who engage with this televisual form do not encounter the carnivalesque directly, "in the flesh." This distancing is important in that it alters the character of the carnivalesque. It becomes possible to experience a hot, fleshy, and sensual form from a distance. For example, while a viewer may see and hear the volatile exchange among guests, they can't smell them, feel their breathing, or get splattered with their spit. The viewers are always at a safe distance and therefore can encounter the carnivalesque on their own terms.

Furthermore, those who watch the shows do, in fact, have control over their engagement with them. In addition to the shows' being bounded within a commodified form, viewers can also at any moment turn off the television, flip to another channel, mute the TV, or choose not to watch it at all. Fundamentally, those who watch the shows have a choice about whether or not, or to what degree, they will engage with them, rather than their being involved in a ritual practice within a larger community. How is it, then, that even with such control, many of the women I spoke with feel pulled or compelled to watch the shows, even against their own "better" judgment in some cases? I argue that this is fundamentally linked to the disembedding of the carnivalesque as an integral dimension of social practice.

"It Kind of Lures You In": Transgression, Ecstatic Experience, and Subjectivity

> Well, Jerry Springer is the favorite of mine cause he's got—I don't know so much gossip and so much trash on his show. I guess [laughs] that's what I'm attracted to watch. I don't know why—like, you know, I even notice that people say, "Oh, I don't watch talk shows. It's a bunch of garbage." I was over at my sister's house the other week and *Jerry Springer* was on. And somebody was sleeping with someone else. And my sister was [laughs] looking at the TV. And she had her head turned for a while [laughs]! And she says she doesn't watch it. You know

that got her attention. So I think stuff like that gets people's attention to watch them. And then they keep you watching them whenever they get a chance. That type of thing. So it kind of lures you in. But it's all a bunch of trash [laughs]. (Jamie)

Like, you know, a lot of times people are on with these really screwed-up relationships and really bad family ties [said in a rhythmic cadence] and things like that. And it's sort of like—I really personally think that's probably a lot of their lure. (Susan)

I just leave whatever I need to do and just watch it. It's like, "Oh, a couple of minutes [laughs]." I end up staying for about two hours. (Claudia)

I used to love them so much. Like, I mean, you wouldn't understand how we couldn't wait to get home. We would be like, "Oh my God! We have five minutes.!" We'd . . . step on the gas. Run in the house. It was so gross. (Joanie)

I mean, to hear people talk about who they're sleeping with and what they're doing. Like, of course it's going to grab you. Because these people are talking about themselves. (Amanda)

While their specific language varies, the women who watch talk shows as entertainment share a sense of "attraction" to the shows, a sense of being *acted upon* or *pulled* to the shows in a way they cannot fully explain. "I couldn't not stay up," it "grabbed my attention," the shows "lure" and "fascinate" the women. This is the case even though the women actually always have control over their viewing. The women don't really *have* to watch; they can flip to another show or turn off the television altogether. Here, I more carefully consider the "luring" character of the attraction the women are attempting to describe but are unable to fully convey in words.

Up until this point, I have relied on a theoretical framework that emphasizes the role of language and the discursive in its social and historical aspects. But in trying to think through the "lure" of the talk shows, an analysis that foregrounds language is inadequate, since it is precisely the women's difficulty with finding words to explain their attraction that interests me the most. Attempting to understand experiences that language seems to elude requires additional conceptual tools.

In framing my explanation, I invoke Gordon's (1997) concept of *haunting* as a means to understand the lure as a "social symptom." I use the word "symptom" literally rather than metaphorically here. By approaching the lure as a social symptom, I am suggesting that it is a manifestation of a social phenomenon, observable in individuals through certain indicators. In this case, the symptoms I observed were as follows: the women's inability to find words to explain their attraction to the trash talk shows and the pleasure they experience in watching them (in contrast to their being quite articulate about shows they watched more seriously); their mood of giddiness as they spoke about watching the shows; and the laughter that interspersed their attempts at explanation. In diagnosing these symptoms, I engage eclectically with a range of concepts. I work with aspects of Lacan's psychoanalytic theory, which considers both how language "moves" us as well as experiences we have outside of language. I also draw on several less academic but nonetheless historically grounded concepts that deal with the varieties of ecstatic experience in the Christian, Buddhist, and Greek traditions.

The Lure as a "Haunting": The Inarticulate Experience

When asked what compelled them to watch the Springer show (and other shows generally categorized as "trash talk"), the women with whom I spoke frequently laughed and commented, "I don't know." Many also shared that they laughed a lot while watching the shows. As each woman attempted to pinpoint her attraction to the shows, the language she employs and the mood in which she spoke indicated an experience in which she felt "something" acting on her, which, while she was unable to explain it, produced an undeniable sense of pleasure. I suggest that this inexplicable attraction, this "inarticulate experience," can be explained by what Gordon refers to as a *haunting*.[14] Haunting, Gordon suggests,

> describes how that which appears to be not there is often a seething presence, acting on and often meddling with taken-for-granted realities, the ghost is just the sign, or the empirical evidence, if you like, that tells you a haunting is taking place. . . . The ghost or the apparition is one form by which something *lost, or barely visible*, or seemingly not there to our supposedly well-trained *eyes*, makes itself known or apparent to us, in its own way, of course. . . . Being haunted draws us affectively, sometimes against our will and always a bit magically into the structure of feeling of a reality we come to experience, not as cold knowledge, but as a transformative recognition. (Gordon 1997: 8)

This attraction toward the shows that the women experience as "luring," and "fascinating" them and "grabbing" their attention is an instance of their being "drawn affectively" toward something, sometimes apparently even against their own "better" judgment. The haunting is apparent through the moods in which the women speak about their attraction and the laughter, which intersperses that which they *can* articulate. Their symptoms of giddiness and their laughter constitute the "ghost" in this case. These are the indicators of something "barely visible," "not there to our supposedly well-trained eyes." They hint at the "structure of feeling," a distinctive sensibility into which the women are drawn.[15] There is an undeniable and distinct energy embodied in this experience, pointing to "the immense forces of 'atmosphere' concealed in everyday things" as mundane as trash talk (Benjamin, cited in Gordon 1997: 204).

Gordon frames haunting in a sociological sense, emphasizing that "haunting is a *shared* structure of feeling, a shared possession, a specific type of sociality" (Gordon 1997: 201). While experienced individually, the phenomenon is social. So, what is this "seething presence," the source of this "ghostly" laughter and giddiness? If the women who watch and derive pleasure from these shows are being "haunted," what, specifically, are they being haunted by? What distinctive sociality is trying to make itself known to the women? What *kind* of "ghost" is this?

Ecstatic Haunting

I suggest that what *pulls* the women I spoke with to watch trash talk shows is the carnivalesque quality at the heart of the shows. More specifically, what lures the women is what the carnivalesque itself embodies—this hyperexpressive, raucous, sexual, bodily, collective sociality "calls" them and grabs their attention. It is this distinctive sociality in which they find themselves involved and immersed in, after the fact.

Across the scholarship on this phenomenon, the carnivalesque is characterized by its violations of mainstream cultural conventions shaped by prevailing discourses of rationality, autonomy, and utility. In academic literature and in public commentary more generally, the carnivalesque is understood in binary opposition to the practices and sensibilities of civility. It points toward a sociality distinct from the routines of everyday life in contemporary Western society—the experience of collective and bodily exuberance and excess. I am proposing, however, that rather than ascribing to the carnivalesque a status of the devalued "other" of civility, it ought to be considered on its own positive terms. When considered this way, the core characteristics of the carnivalesque share much with the "ecstatic" experience.

The "ecstatic" experience is pointed to across a range of literatures: the various ecstatic religious experiences of the Judeo-Christian tradition, the "whirling dervishes" of Sufism, the possession by "loa" of Voodoo (Ventura 1985), Lacan's *jouissance* (Verhaeghe 1999), the Buddhist experience of egolessness (Chodron 1994, 2001), the Greek Dionysian (Johnson 1987), Bataille's "expenditure" (Bataille 1991, 1985), Durkheim's "collective effervescence" (Durkheim 1999), for example. These experiences vary in some important ways, but central to each is an experience of ego-death. In each of these experiences, one's identification as an autonomous, sovereign individual/subject gives way to another, more undifferentiated state. Contained individual energy is unbounded into a sense of merging with a greater, collective energetic state. This is, literally, an extraordinary state, one we do not generally access in the course of the routines of everyday life. While experienced by the individual, it is characterized by the individual's sense of connection to some larger entity or energy.

In their being "lured," the women's accounts indicate that they access a distinctly different energetic experience, something they don't "decide" to engage in per se, but rather something to which they find themselves "called."[16] This being "called" operates through a psychic process of *interpellation*, in which cultural artifacts (texts, images, rituals, etc.), by virtue of their imagery (actual or evoked) and sound, work *on* us to produce certain subjective experiences. Haunting can be understood as a process of "interpellation," a process in which cultural

artifacts (texts, images, etc.) "call" to us, engage us, and potentially move us such that we find ourselves involved in ways that exceed our rational understanding.

In the Face of the Haunting: Dealing with the Lure

While all the women I spoke with seem subject to the "lure" of
the shows, their reactions in the face of being lured vary. All ac-
knowledge the pleasure derived by watching the shows, but how
they articulate this pleasure and the mood in which they do so
show distinctive differences.

> Like, I think Jerry Springer is like the really, the really weird
> one. Like the really crazy one. Which is why, I guess, it's kind of
> fun to watch. But [laughs], you know, I'm in college, like I
> don't care. You know what I mean? Like, I just watch them for
> the fun of it really. She'll [Ricki Lake] intentionally, I think,
> put people on that'll just, like, she'll have a mistress or some-
> thing, and then like somebody's wife. You know, for the pur-
> pose really of, you know, having a fight and stuff like that. But,
> I don't know. I guess it's pretty twisted to watch them. But, I
> don't know. (Susan)

> I make jokes through the entire thing because I am a very sar-
> castic person. And I feel like I have to make fun of everyone on
> the show. I guess it's, like, after I go to my classes, like, and I'm
> kind of stressed. And I go to the library, and I get stressed. And
> I'll come home, and I'll just laugh at the TV for like an hour
> before I do my work. It kind of just relieves everything.
> (Karen)

> It's like the cases that they have are so far out there. They're so
> extreme that it's amusing to watch. . . . Like you feel bad some-

times that like these people are sitting there like going through this, like in front of other people. But it's—it's entertaining. (Colleen)

These women enjoy their practice of watching talk shows. The pleasure they derive is within a dynamic of attraction/ repulsion, in which they not only distance themselves from the shows, but also are disparaging of them. Theirs is a pleasure tinged with sadism and voyeurism, grounded in the "discriminating gaze" (Stallybrass and White 1986: 187) of the bourgeois social imaginary. I refer to their pleasure as *disparaging pleasure* in that the experience they describe seems to be one in which their pleasure is mediated by a negation that ranges from mild ridicule to contempt. In some cases, as with Susan, for example, the women are even self-critical of their own pleasure as well as of the show itself. Each woman assumes a superior status to those she encounters on the shows. If the shows embody a sociality that runs against the grain of that in which the women invest their identity (i.e., as rational, productive, sovereign subjects) and, moreover, evokes their pleasurable involvement with that sociality, it makes sense that these women *must* negate the shows and even their own pleasure. Who and what they encounter is constituted not just as different, but as embodying qualities that must be excluded as inappropriate, bizarre, and so on. Their disparagement allows them to return to the safety of the identity in which they invest themselves. What Bracher suggests in his discussion of jouissance is fitting, that "[t]he desire for this lost jouissance or being runs counter to conscious desire: here, 'what [the subject] desires presents itself to him as what he does not want'" (Bracher 1993: 43). In this case, while each of these women is pulled toward the sociality embodied in the shows and finds herself participating with it, *once she see this she is compelled to refuse it.* She cannot "want" it, given the kind of subject she is invested in being.

In contrast, Tina, Janice, and Claudia speak about the pleasure they derive in a distinctively different mood:

It's just stuff that, you know, I've seen. And I heard a lot of things in my life. And when something new, that I've never seen or heard, it just catches my attention.∫(Tina)

I think the topics are funny. . . . Like, what was the show she did that was funny? Oh—"I'm fifteen." Something like that. Something about, "I'm fifteen and why can't—why didn't you allow me to have sex in my house?" Did you see that part? No [laughs]? I thought that was a funny show. They were talking about younger kids talking to their mother about why, "Why don't you let me have sex in my house" [laughs]. I thought that was a funny topic. (Claudia)

They are fun type shows . . . I think it was one where they have the spikes. . . . Like the one guy who actually implanted spikes in the top of his head. Did you hear? That was a weird show— the earrings and the tongue—yeah. It was all about that kind of stuff. And that was, like, really "Wow!" It was crazy that night. It was really—he had a bunch of wild people on, you know. But it was fun. I liked it overall. I thought it was kind of a crazy show. Like I couldn't not stay up to watch it. (Janice)

These women speak about the pleasure they take in watching the shows with a sense of affinity, even affection. While they speak about the shows as "wild," "crazy," judging what they see as "strange" and different from themselves, their curiosity is less distanced and more participatory than that of the other women. In their narratives, they don't seem to assume a superior position. Even when they used some of the same descriptors as the other women, including, for example, "ridiculous" or "stupid," the mood in which they spoke was neither disparaging nor dismissive, but rather affectionate.[17] These women are not disparaging about the pleasure they encounter, nor are they self- critical about their enjoyment of the shows. What they watch is often constructed as "other," but not a *negated* other. Rather, they articulate a curiosity that is playful. While voyeuristic, it lacks the sadistic and moralistic tone of the women who assume a disparaging relation to the shows.

While clearly each of the women speaks from a materially situated social location (in terms of class, race, gender and age, for example), the kind of pleasure each articulates seems connected to her sense of herself as the subject, which, while mediated by her material circumstances (i.e., actual social location), is not determined by it. Rather, each woman's account of her pleasure involves how she locates herself as a subject within the dominant discourses of rationality and productivity and within a particular type of "life trajectory." The women who appear to locate themselves squarely within dominant cultural discourses as rational, productive subjects or who aspire to this position (Susan, Karen, Colleen, and Natasha) are attracted to the shows, but experience the pleasure that I characterize as "disparaging pleasure." It is not surprising that these women *must* negate the shows and even their own pleasure since the carnivalesque they encounter "denies with a laugh the ludicrous pose of autonomy adopted by the subject within the hierarchical arrangements of the symbolic" of rationality and productivity, what Stallybrass and White refer to as the "bourgeois subject" (Stallybrass and White 1986: 184). Who and what they encounter is encountered not just as different, but as embodying negative qualities that must be excluded as inappropriate, bizarre, and so on. It is notable that Susan, Karen, and Colleen are all white, middle-class college students. Natasha, who is black and grew up in the suburbs after her parents moved the family from the inner city, attended two years of college and planned to return after getting her beautician's license. She viewed her work in a salon as supplemental to her future career as a lawyer.

In contrast, the women who seem less fully invested in identifying themselves as productive, rational, and autonomous appear to allow themselves to experience a pleasure that I characterize as "affectionate pleasure." Tina's and Jamie's narratives, for example, show that they seem less hooked into these dominant discourses as the fundamental basis upon which they identify themselves as subjects.

Conclusion: Talk Shows and Cultural Sensibilities

Unpacking cultural common sense about "trash talk" presents an opportunity to understand the operation of cultural classificatory systems and their relation to subject formation. Most commentary or analysis of these shows is uncritically grounded in dominant discourses of rationality and productivity. These analyses are grounded in a morality founded in these dominant discourses and therefore (based in the logic of my analysis) negate the shows out of hand. (See, for example, Abt and Mustazza 1997.) Others (Shattuc 1997; E. Willis 1996; Carpignano et al. 1993) analyze these shows in the context of their embodying the possibility of a popular public discourse forum. While, like mine, several other analyses of talk shows, suggest that the shows embody representations of the carnivalesque (see Shattuc 1997; Masciarotte 1991), they do not engage the issue of how viewers encounter the shows in this way and the historical role of the carnivalesque as integrated into larger social practices. In this chapter, I have attempted to shift the terms of analysis. Situating these shows within a context of public discourse (with the standard being discourse among citizens about issues of common concern) focuses one's analysis of how the shows fulfill or violate the dominant standards for public discourse or open new possibilities for it. Here, I foreground these shows as embodying a different sensibility altogether. I am suggesting that the shows embody a carnivalesque sensibility, which operates as and is encountered by viewers as a powerful symbolic inversion, a function distinct from providing a public discourse forum. Analyzing the shows on these terms opens the possibility for analyzing the workings of culture, the workings of dominant historical discourses, and their relation to subject formation.

It is here that Gordon's notion of *haunting* as an analytic term becomes useful. I suggest that the shows these women watch as entertainment and from which they derive pleasure attract them through their evoking something that *haunts* us as a culture. What haunts us is a sociality missing in an integral way from our society.

The sociality of the carnivalesque, it's uselessness, excess, expenditure, even merging impulse and sensuality and, perhaps most importantly, its collectivity, are denied or devalued within the terms of dominant discourses. Discourses of purposefulness, economy, rationality, and productivity and their accompanying sensibility provide the terms through which we encounter the world and make sense of day-to-day life. The carnivalesque draws us in (the luring is accomplished) through a process of interpellation to a sociality we have lost, or at least devalued.

The varying ways the women find themselves experiencing the pleasure they derive in watching the shows reveals the ways in which they locate themselves as subjects within dominant cultural discourses and in their material circumstances. It reveals that how we locate ourselves as subjects matters with respect to the kind of pleasure we allow ourselves and, conversely, this pleasure can be unpacked in order to understand subject formation.

While I argue that these talk shows (like the Springer show) work to evoke the carnivalesque impulse that is generally denied us or devalued, I am not suggesting that this contemporary form operates as did, for example, fairs and carnivals in premodern, precapitalist western European societies at a time such rituals included the whole community. As a commodified form, produced, distributed, and controlled by highly rationalist organizations for the purpose of generating profits, these shows simulate the carnivalesque sensibility in a fragmented and displaced manner. The carnivalesque embodied in these shows is not a "break from production" (Pfohl 1992: 213). Rather, it is itself a product of production, whose intent it is to be productive (in terms of generating advertising revenue), thus making the aesthetic of uselessness useful.

My analysis raises the issue of the absence of collective spaces of the ecstatic in contemporary society, rituals that are integrated into the larger matrix of social practice. While talk shows and other forms of entertainment such as World Federation Wrestling powerfully simulate the carnivalesque, they are disembedded from the larger collective social practice in which the carnivalesque plays an integral role within the community. Moreover, given that these are commodified forms, they constitute yet another form of the prevailing social practice of consumerism.

Understanding talk shows as embodying the carnivalesque and recognizing the haunting they evoke opens the possibility for examining other forms that operate similarly to talk shows. For example, the raucous, bawdy, and often (materially and physically) destructive annual college student ritual of "Spring Break" can be understood this way. It provides a clear example of a "break" from productive activity and the intensely individualistic, ego-building endeavor of college. Again, however, as with talk shows, spring break is a highly commodified embodiment of this aesthetic, with travel agents and beer companies capitalizing on the compulsion students feel for this break from their "ordinary" day-to-day routines that carry at least the expectation of productivity. The contemporary "rave" can also be understood as a ritual that accesses this aesthetic. Interestingly, the drug "Ecstasy," a drug inducing a euphoric state in which ego boundaries are at least muted, is commonly used at such events. Rock concerts and the "be-ins" of the 1960s are also examples of the phenomenon. It is no mistake that these forms are dismissed by many as "decadent" and "excessive" in mainstream discourse, rather than as a signal of the foreclosed possibility of carnivalesque rituals as integral to the symbolic activity of contemporary society or as positive rituals allowing access to more collective ways of being.

Related to this, recent calls for "civility" (Putnam 1995; Sandel 1996) are, clearly, important (and needed) but neglect the yearning for this other symbolic dimension of society. This raises a question as to whether, given prevailing discourses within which subjectivity emerges, such rituals could be incorporated into the larger matrix of social practice without their being negated. I am not advocating public opportunities to "blow off steam" or individualized practices that are decidedly private. (Hence the concern when such practices spill over into the public domain.) Rather, I am advocating the recognition of the carnivalesque sensibility as a valid, positive sensibility, rather than simply as the "other" side of civility. The sensibility it embodies gives access to a particular dimension of being human for which people across history have yearned and which are accessed through a wide range of methods and rituals.

6. Utopian Hauntings?

Willis suggests that "mass culture is haunted by the desire for non-alienated social relations." She argues for a criticism and practice in which "[t]he goal is to recognize in all our commodified practices and situations the fragments and buried manifestations of utopian social relationships," emphasizing how this appears in the most routine activities of everyday life (S. Willis 1991: 34).

After listening to the women who participated in this study, I can conclude that Willis's instructions provide a useful orientation in trying to make sense of talk shows. What do we learn about how talk shows function in contemporary American society if we take Willis' instructions to heart?

I am careful to emphasize that, while I look for the "fragments and buried manifestations of utopian social relationships" that we may find in analyzing women's engagement with talk shows, I am not a champion of the talk show form. Also, that talk shows may provide or evoke certain experiences for the women who watch them does not alter the fact that this result is relatively incidental to television industry executives: their decisions about the programming lineup are driven chiefly by a show's profitability in terms of its advertising revenues. This figures as an important factor in my analysis.

If the women's experiences with talk shows are "haunted by a desire for non-alienated social relations" then it is because these relations are missing in their lives. But, as my analysis shows, different women engage with the shows differently. Some engage with certain shows as legitimate discourse and find them meaningful in this regard. On the other hand, there are certain shows that almost all the women watch for entertainment. How does this "yearning for utopian social relations" operate in each case?

Important to this argument, Willis asserts that we "recover use value in daily-life social practice" (S. Willis 1991: 13–14). Using the example of the popularity of historical theme parks, Willis suggests that, by virtue of the way these parks are set up, visitors are facilitated in imagining life in a culture where "use values more directly shaped lives and relationships than they do in late twentieth century capitalism" (S. Willis 1991: 13–14). What is key here is that in these theme parks, historic material culture is *enacted* rather than simply displayed. This type of enactment, Willis argues, is distinctive from museum display. Enactment *performs* "use-value" whereas museum display only *refers* to it and does not evoke the visitor's imagination in such an active manner. In a historic theme park, "the visitor is not only a spectator, but a participant in communication with the role-players and in the recreation of the world of the past" (S. Willis 1991: 15).

So, how do theme parks relate to my analysis of talk shows? The key to this connection is *performance* and what it evokes.

The Use of Talk

First, it is notable that those who dismiss talk shows out of hand often do so on the grounds that the shows are simply a "spectacle." In contrast, many of the women who watch more seriously describe a more active engagement with the shows.

These women commonly told me that they often interacted with the shows by speaking to guests or the host as if forgetting they could not actually hear them. While it would be easy to dismiss this occurrence by calling the women "cultural dupes" (Garfinkel 1984) or, in more straightforward language, "losers with nothing better to do," I challenge this facile assumption.

For these women, talk shows are not a display of issues and people (as they are for the women who dismiss the same shows as purely "entertainment" or trivial). Rather, in a dynamic such as the one Willis attributes to visitors to historic them parks, the women encounter the shows as *enacting* discourse about relevant issues by people with whom they identify. As evidence of this, many of the women indicate that the shows they watch make a positive difference in their everyday lives. These women become participants in the discourse of talk shows. Thus, for these women, the shows are useful: they provide a public discourse forum that is otherwise lacking in their lives. In Willis's terms, this relation to the shows is symptomatic of "the desire for unalienated social relations," in this case a desire to engage with others about issues of common concern.

Willis's argument draws on Marx's concept of use-value—that the utility of a thing (a commodity) makes it a "use-value": "Use-values become a reality only by use or consumption" (Marx 1978: 303). But rather than the use-value's inhering in material characteristics (as it does for commodities like corn, iron, or a car, for example), the use- value is derived from the meaning a show holds for a particular viewer.

This analysis may seem like an overly burdensome variation of the theoretical perspective that celebrates a "cultural economy" in which individuals appropriate commodity forms and produce alternative or even oppositional readings that may leave them *feeling* empowered but not necessarily any better off (Fiske 1987, 1989b). I emphasize that this is not the case. It is central to my analysis that many women engage the shows as a "use-value"; particular shows are useful to them as legitimate public discourse forums. I am interested in the questions and issues raised by this fact.

A key concern mentioned earlier is that talk shows exist by virtue of being a revenue-generating vehicle for television industry management. This means that as ratings drop and sponsors become less enthusiastic about advertising in a particular time slot, a show runs the risk of being canceled by station management. Whether or not "we" think a show has value as legitimate discourse, the show's existence as a forum for those who do find it valuable is tenuous and clearly out of their control.

What are the implications of these shows being a discourse forum for the women who watch them? I have two concerns here. First is the fact that the shows are not designed with the goal of providing a forum for public discourse. Rather, they are produced as "entertainment television." In the view of those who produce the shows, the fact that some viewers may find the shows meaningful, in a serious sense, is an unintended consequence. There is no obligation of television industry management to provide a meaningful forum for this market segment.

Related to this is the question: What other forums are available to these women in which they can engage with issues of common concern, in a manner that is comfortable for them. Most of the women who report engaging seriously with certain talk shows do not participate in other forums.[1]

The rich diversity of contemporary U.S. society and the reality of its stratified social arrangements generate a social structure in which certain groups have more power than others—as well as power *over* others. Multiple discourse forums for multiple publics would contribute to addressing a need for "open access, participatory parity and social equality" (Fraser 1994: 118). Multiple discourse forums that involve distinctive publics, some heterogeneous, some homogeneous, would enhance the possibility for individuals and collectivities to speak, be heard, and be taken seriously.

Socioeconomic as well as racial, ethnic, and gender stratification also makes the issue of whose conventions govern public discourse forums important. Mansbridge's observations of gender differences in the process of deliberation have applicability to broader dimensions of difference:

> Even the language people use as they reason together usually favors one way of seeing things and discourages others. Subordinate groups sometimes cannot find the right voice or words to express their thought, and when they do, they discover they are not heard. . . . [T]hey are silenced, encouraged to keep their wants inchoate, and heard to say "yes" when what they have said is "no." (Mansbridge 1990: 127)

Availability of and accessibility to more homogeneous public discourse forums may facilitate groups that have been historically marginalized from mainstream public discourse in articulating issues of common concern for them. Such a space can provide a group the chance to better develop its voice and thereby contribute to a more robust heterogeneous public discourse (Fraser 1994).

There is a potential role here for locally produced commercial and community access (cable) programming. Such programming would need to match the professional production values of syndicated talk shows, but would focus on issues identified by members of the community. These shows would be not be geared for mass broadcast, but for specific local publics or communities. Such a project could work to facilitate the emergence of "publics" in discourse on their own terms. There is evidence that this already takes place among immigrant groups and African American communities, for example.

Useless Being

The issue of how useful talk shows are or can be has been the basis for most of the debate about them. However, this fully overlooks another dimension important to analysis of the shows—that talk shows ought to be considered precisely for their "uselessness." This useless space of the carnivalesque can be understood affirmatively rather than pejoratively. Baudrillard, in his critique of Marx, explains why our society has such difficulty with the idea of an affirmative "useless" space:

> Everywhere man has learned to reflect on himself, to assume himself, to posit himself according to this scheme of production which is assigned to him as the ultimate dimension of meaning and value. . . . Here man is embarked on a continual deciphering of himself through his works, finalized by his shadow (his own end), reflected by this operational mirror, this sort of ideal of a productivist ego. (Baudrillard 1975: 19)

A discourse of productivity dominates contemporary society, wherein play (that which is "useless") not only constitutes a break from more serious work, but also functions as a recuperation *for* labor (Marcuse 1955; Baudrillard 1975). Play is promoted within appropriate limits and is individualized and placed squarely within the private sphere of family and friends. So, while celebration, excess, sensuality, sex, emotion, and expressivity are permissible and even promoted, these are generally lodged within the sphere of personal life, even when enacted collectively. Certain experiences that are collective and public (sports events and rock concerts, for example), do have a ritualistic quality and even a sense of community (in terms of community of interest). However, in these cases, access to the community depends on one's capacity, literally, to buy one's way into the community.

In addition, this orientation is grounded in a discourse that is generally not reflected upon, in which human beings are fundamentally and most importantly, *productive* beings. This discourse informs our common sense about people and becomes an explicit standard against which they are judged. In mainstream American discourse, "productivity" is regarded as a moral good as opposed to laziness, inaction, pleasure, and other activities considered nonproductive. This dichotomy is grounded in historically and culturally specific discourses.[2]

I do not argue with the importance, or even the necessity, of an ethic of productivity in society. However, positioning production as that which most fundamentally constitutes a human being is problematic. This ontological stance devalues that which is not regarded as useful. This is not to say that what is "not useful" or "useless" is always denigrated, it just does not hold the same status as that which is assessed as productive.[3] The talk shows that are the focus of this study, in particular those that the women I spoke with consistently watched as "entertainment," place in-your-face all those characteristics that are the antithesis of the productivist discourse. Critics object to and some viewers characterize these shows as "pointless" talk, excessive rather than efficient, unabashed rather than appropriate, wild rather than civil, full of yelling and screaming rather than economy of utterance in which the point is to get to the point. The emotional and moral force that critics voice can be understood as an indicator of the level of imagined threat this kind of display poses to the productivist identity.

These talk shows appeal to that which is excluded by production. They evoke a social space in which the constraints of the productivist discourse give way to robust, collective expression that includes the body and the sensual. The shows enact a thoroughly noninstrumental relationship among people. At its core, this experience is about being together beyond the restraints of our autonomous, ego-identified self. Even the confrontations that routinely occur on trash talk shows enact this relatedness at the level of the body.[4] The connection I refer to is not a cognitive "meeting of the minds," but rather a more immediate and sensual connection, an experience we crave but lack within the logistics, routines, and norms of everyday life, where we are focused on getting things done. This yearning is manifested in many ways, some more dramatic than others. Depending on our level of investment in a productivist ego ideal, we give ourselves permission to, and are more or less able to, tolerate this other experience of relatedness.

This raises a question similar to the one raised regarding spaces of public discourse. What spaces exist in our society for collectively accessing the type of sociality that underlies the carnivalesque, a space of connection beyond autonomous ego boundaries? Indeed, manifestations of the carnivalesque sometimes serve to inhibit accessing a connection. Think of World Federation Wrestling and college spring break, for example. In these cases, while the activities they involve embody the carnivalesque, the frenzy of these activities can actually inhibit human connection. Moreover, both are highly commodified experiences with the purpose of generating revenue for their producers. In the end, they are not really "useless."

The spaces closest to what I aim to describe are ironically those of religious practice. For example, worship practices in some black churches often embody a wildly energetic space of the celebration of faith. This is not an instrumental space. It is an expressive community space. In addition, this practice is integrated in a routine way into the lives of participants.

This is not a call to hedonism. Nor is it to idealize or romanticize the sociality embodied by the carnivalesque, which can be harmful in its recklessness. Rather, I point to the impulse underlying this sociality which, I have suggested in a desire for a space beyond ego, which, ironically, the ego resists and by which it is threatened. The impulse toward a relation beyond the productivist ego ideal manifests itself across history. Recognizing it as such, rather than getting caught in the dismissal, condemnation, or even celebration of its manifestations can alert us to a dimension of society and of being human that we undervalue and neglect to honor. Some critics point to talk shows as an example of what's wrong with society. Perhaps they are right, but not in the way they think. Perhaps, what's wrong is that we deny ourselves access to a sociality that is fundamental to our being human.

Appendix A

Methodology

Design of the Study:
Interviews and Photo-Ethnography

To study how viewers make sense of talk shows, I chose to conduct semistructured in-depth interviews with thirty women who watch these shows on a regular basis. I defined "watching talk shows on a regular basis" as watching talk shows at least twice a week. The talk shows the women watched included *Jerry Springer, Ricki Lake, Jenny Jones, Montel Williams, Maury Povich,* and *Sally Jessy Raphael. Oprah Winfrey* and *Rosie O'Donnell,* two popular shows categorized as talk shows, were not among those I considered, as these shows do not fall into the "trash" talk category in mainstream discourse, which was the criterion for this study. This definition arose from mainstream discourse, as indicated in newspaper articles and other commentary, including, for example, television and advertising industry journal articles or lists of "worst offenders" in the talk show genre.

Since I wanted to interview people who fit the shows' target demographics, I looked into sites where I would likely find women between eighteen and thirty-four years old, many of whom would likely be working class and lower income, with a significant proportion of women of color. I contacted most of the women through a local beauty school. At first I wanted to post a flyer, but the school's director suggested instead that I come in and speak directly with the students about my work, enlisting interviewees in person. The students had class in the early morning, but the bulk of their day was spent practicing hair- cutting and make-up application skills. The beauty school had three floors, and each floor had students at a different point in their eight-month program. On my first visit, I introduced myself to the instructor in charge and explained my project. She was quite receptive and suggested that I speak to the students as a group. She assembled the students, who, it turned out, included well over 50 percent women of color. I interviewed most of the women over lunch, which I bought for them. This worked well, since the instructors allowed the women to take more than their normal one-hour lunch break. I interviewed several of the women while they cut or set hair or applied makeup. Several of these women provided me with the names of other women (friends and relatives) who might agree to be interviewed. Most of these women were interviewed in their homes.

Most interviews lasted about one hour. At the end of each interview I explained to each woman that I was interested in finding out a bit more about her everyday life—her daily routines, things of importance to her, the people with whom she interacted, her family and friends—in order to better understand how watching talk shows fit into her life and how she made sense of them. To accomplish this, I asked each woman to take pictures that, in her view, would give me a sense of her everyday life. For the women who agreed to participate, I offered a twenty-four- exposure, single-use camera, which they would return to me to have the pictures developed. We would then meet again to discuss the pictures. I was not concerned with the quality of the photographs each woman took, but rather I wanted them to serve as an opening for further conversation about her everyday life, her routines and concerns. These vignettes would present a glimpse of the broader context within which each woman's practice of watching talk shows is situated, itself a mundane, generally daily routine. Note that I did not expect the women to provide a "realist" visual ethnography of their lives. Rather, I was interested in seeing how they chose to represent their lives both in terms of what they included and did not include in their pictures as well as how they talked about their lives.

I adopted this photo-ethnographic method from the work of Carolyn Wang (Wang and Burris 1994), who employed what she called a "photo-voice" method in her work with a rural development project in China, in which she focused on issues of women's health and well-being as they related to development. This was a participatory action research project in which each woman took photographs that represented key issues or concerns related to women's health and well-being. For example, one woman took a picture of a pond where her child had drowned, citing the need for children's supervision while mothers worked. The women's stories about their photos were written down and then served as the basis for articulating recommendations to their local officials. Clearly in this project, the women participating had a strong investment in the project's outcome. In my project, the women were only doing me a favor and were therefore less invested. As a result, some of the women never finished taking their pictures, and others took longer than I had anticipated, although when I called to check in, they did not seem to be offended. (I made it clear that they should not feel obliged to complete this part of the project, although most did.) Each woman who participated in the photo-ethnography project was given a set of the pictures she took.

Half of the women I interviewed agreed to participate in the photo-ethnography project, and most completed the task and met with me for a second interview session. Second interviews also lasted approximately one hour.

Interviews took place over a six-month period in the spring, summer, and fall of 1997. All interviews were tape-recorded and transcribed. The transcriptions were done in a way that preserved each woman's way of speaking, in terms of dialect, including structure (including repeated words, false starts, "hmm's," etc.). This approach was especially important since my analysis focused on how the women accounted for both their viewing practice and the talk shows themselves. While not generally making for a fluid "read," in my judgment "cleaning up" the women's responses would have been counterproductive, serving to move their way of speaking more closely toward idealized (middle- class, educated, bourgeois) models, thus undermining my analytic focus.

Appendix B

The Women Who Participated in the Study

Iris

Iris was an eighteen-year-old self-identified Hispanic young woman, who just graduated from high school and was the new single mother of a two-month-old baby boy. At the time of our interview she was on AFDC. She was enrolled in a junior college program for the fall semester and was planning to work part time while attending college. Her older sister, Claudia, introduced me to her.

Claudia

Claudia, the twenty-year-old sister of Iris, was a single high school graduate, enrolled in beauty school at the time of the interview. She also identified herself as having grown up "lower income." She had briefly attended three different colleges, and was not satisfied with her experience at any of them. She was artistic and shared some of her artwork and fashion designs with me. In addition, Claudia was interested in modeling. After completing the beauty school program, she planned to move to New York, where she felt she could better pursue modeling and her artistic and fashion design interests.

Joanie

Joanie, a thirty-year-old, single, working-class white woman was a high school graduate. Currently attending beauty school, she had been laid off from a supervisory job at a large local insurance company. Upon receiving her license, Joanie said she wanted eventually to open her own day spa.

Susan

A twenty-one-year-old white college student, Susan grew up middle class in upstate New York. She was a finance major. After graduation she planned to work for a few years, and then return to school for an MBA, envisioning a career as an accountant.

Jamie

Jamie was an eighteen-year-old, black, recent high school graduate. She attended a technical training school and was enrolled in a program to prepare her to work as a medical assistant. Jamie lived in a predominantly black inner-city Boston neighborhood, but had grown up mostly in Florida.

Karen

Karen was a nineteen-year-old white college student at a midsize suburban university. She had grown up middle class, close to Philadelphia. She attended schools that were fairly mixed in terms of income, race, and ethnicity.

Tina

Tina was an African American woman enrolled in an eight-month cosmetology program. She told me that she'd been "doing hair" for fifteen years and was finally getting her license. She had previously worked in an administrative job at a university. She was single and had a young daughter.

Tyra

Tyra was an eighteen-year-old black high school graduate. She identified herself as having grown up working class. She was enrolled in an eight-month program at the local beauty school working toward getting her cosmetology license.

Sonya

Sonya was a twenty-three-year-old black woman. She was a high school graduate, in a committed relationship, and had two children, ages eight months and eight years. She grew up lower middle class and was currently enrolled in an eight-month training program at a local cosmetology school, working toward her license.

Sarah

Sarah was a twenty-four-year-old white woman with a high school GED. She grew up in a family with fluctuating income. Sarah had a history of abusive relationships and saw her enrollment in cosmetology school as a way of moving her life forward.

Gina

Gina was a twenty-four-year-old biracial high school graduate. She reported being in a committed relationship and having a six-year-old son. She had been enrolled in medical assistant and accounting certificate training programs prior to beginning the eight-month cosmetology program in which she was enrolled at the time of the interview. She identified herself as having grown up working class.

Amanda

Amanda was a twenty-four-year-old white sophomore at a large urban university. She reported growing up upper middle class, had lived in several countries, which seemed to give her some perspective on American culture. While she participated in it, she was also critical of it. She shared that she had attended a private girl's boarding school. She was single, but dating.

Joy

Jill was a twenty-year-old white woman with a high school GED and reported growing up lower middle class. She was single and had recently left an abusive relationship. Her enrollment in the cosmetology program was her attempt at getting her life together.

Janice

Janice was a forty-three-year-old black woman. She had two children, ages 14 and 23. Over the course of my two interviews with her, she became engaged and was living with her fiancÈ and teenage daughter. Janice had attended two years of junior college, and had an Associate's degree. She had taken some other college-level courses, but not completed her Bachelor's. Janice said that she had grown up middle class. At the time of the interview she lived in a primarily black Boston neighborhood. She shared with me that she wanted to move to a neighborhood in which she felt safer. Janice had worked for a number of years at a clinic, moving from receptionist to doing some counseling. At the time of the first interview, she was enrolled in cosmetology school. She was then terminated for poor attendance due to health problems and, at the time of the second interview, was making plans for how to proceed with her career. She shared that she wanted to open a small salon in her home.

Carla

Carla was a twenty-five-year-old black woman, a recent college graduate majoring in sociology, originally from Bermuda. She was working as a security guard at the time of the interview but aspired to work in the field of law. Shortly after our interview, she got a position working in the district attorney's office. In the course of the interview, Carla also shared that she was lesbian.

Kirsten

Kirsten was a twenty-three-year-old white woman who grew up in Denmark. She was a high school graduate and had attended trade school for one year. At the time of the interview, she was completing an eight-month cosmetology program. Kirsten reported that she grew up middle class. She was married and had no children. Through the interview I learned that Kirsten was a born-again Christian.

Michelle

Michelle was a black nineteen-year-old college sophomore at a midsized suburban university. She grew up middle class in Boston. Until her last two years of high school, she attended school in Boston suburbs through a special program. She returned to Boston for her last two years of high school, sharing that she was tired of being one of only a few black students. Michelle planned to become a lawyer.

Natalie

Natalie was a twenty-year-old Puerto Rican woman. She was single and had a four-month-old baby. She graduated from high school and was enrolled in an eight-month cosmetology program at the time of the interview. She reported having grown up working class.

Olivia

Olivia was a twenty-one-year-old black high school graduate who lived in a predominantly black neighborhood in inner-city Boston. She shared that she had grown up "lower income," although she had spent the first six years of her life living with a white family in a more suburban, middle-class section of Boston. At the time of our first interview, Olivia was enrolled in an eight-month cosmetology program. At our second interview, Olivia shared that she had been "terminated" from the program for poor attendance and was working in an administrative job at a local hospital.

Natasha

Natasha was a twenty-year-old black woman. She had completed two years of college and at the time of the interview was enrolled in an eight-month cosmetology program. She shared that she had originally wanted to attend the program after high school, but on her parents' objections she enrolled in college instead. She planned to return to college to complete her degree. Natasha grew up middle class in a Boston suburb. She was living with her mother and her aunt in an inner-city neighborhood at the time of the interview.

Betty

Natasha introduced me to her aunt, Betty, a black woman in her fifties. Betty lived in a black Boston inner-city neighborhood, sharing an apartment with two of her sisters. She had worked in a production job for a large local manufacturer for many years, and as a seamstress; she had also worked as a foster parent. At the time of the interview, Betty was not working outside the home. While she had an adult daughter, she had recently adopted a three-year-old girl who had been in her foster care.

Dorothy

Dorothy was one of two women who responded to an ad I placed in a community newspaper soliciting interview subjects. She was a forty-seven-year-old white woman, divorced with no children. She shared that she grew up in an upper middle class family in Michigan and had been in Boston since 1968. She is a psychotherapist in private practice.

Sandi

Sandi was a young black woman in her mid-twenties. She was single and had two children. She attended a local state university and started attending cosmetology school during the summer months. She thought of getting her cosmetology license as a backup for her other career plan of becoming a lawyer.

Patti

Patti was an eighteen-year-old white high school graduate who had attended college for half of a semester. She grew up lower income in Boston. At the time of our interview, Patti was enrolled in an eight-month cosmetology program.

Chandra

Chandra was a twenty-four-year-old black woman. She had recently graduated from a local community college majoring in English. She was single and had one child. She shared that she had grown up poor. She had begun a cosmetology program after wanting to go into the field for a long time, but felt others wouldn't respect her wanting to "do hair," especially after having earned her Associate's degree. Chandra said that recently she had come to terms with the fact that this was the career she wanted for herself.

Irene

Irene was a thirty-five-year-old African American woman. She was married, although she and her husband were separated. She had three children, ages twelve, six, and two and a half. She was a high school graduate and grew up middle class. As a child she had moved a lot since her father was in the military. Irene shared that this experience exposed her to lots of different kinds of people in terms of nationality, race, and ethnicity.

Stella

Stella was a twenty-seven-year-old Hispanic woman. She was married and had a fifteen-month-old baby. She was a high school graduate and had emigrated to the U.S. from El Salvador. Her answers made it apparent that Stella was quite religious. At the time of the interview she was enrolled in an eight-month cosmetology program in Boston.

Sharon

Sharon was a white, working-class woman in her thirties. She was one of two women who responded to an ad I placed in a community newspaper soliciting interview subjects. Sharon grew up and currently lived in a working-class Boston suburb, working at a state administrative job in Boston.

Victoria

Victoria was a twenty-six-year-old black woman living in Boston, originally from Georgia. She was single and had a five-year-old daughter. She was a high school graduate and had done some training as a dental assistant and had also attended a program training her in business skills and carpentry. She had completed an eight-month cosmetology program, worked in a salon, and was now an instructor in the program.

Colleen

Colleen was an eighteen-year-old white college student who had just completed her freshman year at the time of the interview. Amanda referred her to me. Colleen was single. She had grown up middle class in suburban Boston.

NOTES

NOTES TO CHAPTER 1

1. Nielsen Media Research for February 1998 indicates, for example, that on average 4.26 million households were tuned to *Jenny Jones*, 7.33 million to *Jerry Springer*, 3.29 million to *Maury Povich*, 4.5 million to *Montel Williams*, 3.87 million to *Ricki Lake*, and 4.02 million to *Sally Jessy Raphael.*

2. Nielsen Media Research calculates their ratings based on a base of approximately 98.5 million "television households" in the United States. (A "television household" is a home in which there is at least one television.) A "rating" is "the estimated percentage of TV households viewing or listening to a specific program" (Dominick, Sherman, and Copeland 1996: 423). Illustrating the demographic spread of viewers, Neilsen Media Research data for February 1998 indicates that for *Jenny Jones*, 4.6 percent of all television households in the United States were tuned into her show, with 12.4 percent of all black television households; 4.5 percent of households with income of $30–39,999 were tuned in, and 2.8 percent of households with income of $75,000 or more; 2.5 percent of households with women 18–34 years old were tuned in, versus 2.4 percent of households with men of the same age. *Jerry Springer* shows a similar pattern: 7.5 percent of all U.S. television households, 19.9 percent of all black television households; 8.2 percent of households with an income of $30–39,999, 3.9 percent of households with income of $75,000 or more; 6.1 percent of households with women 18–34, 4.9 percent of households with men 18–34.

3. I found that as I spoke informally about these shows with people that I knew, their experience of the shows (if they had any direct experience at all) was also commonly a result of "flipping" through channels.

4. Later in this chapter I clarify how I use the word "public" in relation to other scholars' use of the term.

5. It is relevant to note here that since Masciarotte's 1991 article, Oprah Winfrey has taken a stand that her show will not engage in the sensational topics offered by the proliferation of talk shows since 1993 (following the debut of *Ricki Lake*). While her show continues to feature personal experience, the shows are oriented toward informing and teaching as well as interviewing celebrities. Many of the women I interviewed noted this change in her show. They indicated that as a result of it they no longer watched the show, considering it, for example, "boring," "not interesting," or that Winfrey had gotten "too high class."

6. All the women I interviewed told me they watched talk shows at least twice a week. For a full description of the sample of women I interviewed, see appendix B.

7. I explain the poststructuralist perspectives I incorporate later in this chapter.

8. Barrie Thorne (1993) provides numerous illustrations of the material effects of gendered discursive practices in *Gender Play: Girls and Boys in School*. For example, she shows that the consequences of a boy being called "sissy" were far greater than a girl being called a "tomboy." Madonna also makes this point explicit in her song "How It Feels." In the spoken introduction to her song, she says that it's okay for a girl to have short hair or dress like a boy, but a boy, while he might wonder what it's like to be a girl, finds the idea of being a girl degrading.

NOTES TO CHAPTER 2

1. The one exception is *The Sally Jessy Raphael Show*, which debuted in late 1983.

2. Rivera produced highly rated but critically disliked specials, including "Sons of Scarface: The New Mafia," "American Vice: The Doping of America," and "The Mystery of Al Capone's Vault"(Haithman 1987: 1).

3. All ratings cited are season-to-date averages, August 31–November 29, 1991, based on Nielsen Syndication Service (McClellan 1992: 24).

4. This characterization of the large number of new talk shows in the same style and aimed at the same 18–34 female market as *Ricki Lake* is made by Scott Carlin, Warner Bros. domestic TV executive vice president, cited in *Broadcasting and Cable* (McClellan 1995: 38).

5. The use of a discourse of "pollution" as a way of framing the situation regarding talk show content is more fully discussed both substantively and theoretically in chapter 5.

6. While TPP was not formed in response to Bennett's campaign against talk show content, the collaboration with Lear was the first series it attempted. (TPP had already worked on *The World Music Awards*.)

7. Moving the *Springer* show to an early fringe time period elicited some protest in the Detroit community. Protesters complained that moving the show to 4 P.M. would mean that it aired at precisely the time when unsupervised children would be mostly likely to watch it. The station refused to change the show's time slot (Trigoboff 1998: 11).

NOTES TO CHAPTER 3

1. Lodziak (1986) addresses the significance of individuals' routine of watching television in critiquing the "uses and gratifications" approach to audience research. Citing Sahin and Robinson, Lodziak (1986) notes that their

study indicates that "the gratifications viewers claim to derive from viewing are, by their own admission, of little importance. In other words it would seem that the reported satisfactions derived from television are trivial. . . . What uses and gratifications research fails to do is to address the question of the *significance of* the needs which are supposedly met through television viewing" (133). Based on my research, I argue that Lodziak's statement overgeneralizes the extent to which viewers find their practice of watching talk shows trivial. My findings indicate that the significance of watching television generally, and watching certain programs in particular, varies. I address this in my analysis later in this chapter.

2. Husserl and Merleau-Ponty both address consciousness as always being about something in their phenomenological philosophical works.

3. Talk shows as a genre lend themselves to this kind of segmented, repetitive viewing, given that their format is one of a series of discrete, bounded segments versus, for example, the open, ongoing, unending narrative of soap operas.

4. For example, a mood of sadness can be characterized as grounded in a sense of loss (of a valued person, object, or possibility), in which the loss will be irretrievable in the future; therefore, one's possibilities are reduced to some degree. A mood of resignation can be characterized as grounded in a sense that current circumstances that one finds problematic will continue unchanged in the future; therefore, one's possibilities for the future are imagined as constrained or frustrated. A mood of optimism can be characterized as grounded in a sense that one's possibilities for the future are imagined as open and likely to be beneficial to oneself. I take this understanding of mood, which draws on Heidegger, from Solomon (1983) and from my work with Fernando Flores. While both Solomon and Flores discuss this conceptualization as one that may not occur reflexively, they do not engage with the possibility that the assessments inherent in mood may occur in the psychic domain. While it is beyond the scope of this study to work through this argument, I suggest that mood may have much to do with psychic processes. In addition, both Solomon and Flores address the issue of mood at the level of the individual. I suggest that mood can also be understood as a social phenomenon, along the lines of Raymond Williams's notion of "structure of feeling."

5. It is important to note that not all interviews took place in the women's homes. Many were conducted during the lunch hour in the student lounge area at a local beauty school or in restaurants close by. However, of those whom I interviewed in the home, most did have the television on during the interview.

6. Even as I cite "psychological" factors potentially underlying Olivia's having "nothing to do," I am skeptical and cautious about conceptualizing even these apparently individual factors as too clearly distinguished from the social context in which they occur and through which I suggest they are constituted.

7. The issue of varying and distinctive pleasures is examined more fully in chapter 5. In that chapter, I distinguish "disparaging" pleasure from "affectionate" pleasure, each of which seems grounded in a different status relation between the viewers and the shows they watch. This analysis seems to explain how it is that while all the women seem to enjoy watching various talk shows, they assume differing relations to the show.

NOTES TO CHAPTER 4

1. Typically when I spoke with people in my everyday life about talk shows both prior to and during my research, their response was, "I can't believe that stuff is on TV!" (The exclamation here is meant to denote the emphatic quality of people's statements.)

2. I refer here to the usually pejorative use of the phrase "It's *just* semantics!" in which the use of particular vocabulary is trivialized as really not mattering *that* much.

3. There are many feminist scholars whose analysis makes explicit the gendered character of classifications of "public" and "private." See, for example, Landes (1995), Ryan (1992), and Fraser (1994).

4. This is illustrated, for example, in psychoanalytic theory, theories of moral development, and social theory. See Dorothy Smith's *Conceptual Practices of Power: A Feminist Sociology of Knowledge* (1990) as an analysis of the hegemony of classificatory systems grounded in the (white, European) male experience.

5. I refer to this analysis as "dated" because it is widely recognized (by the women I interviewed as well as by mainstream cultural commentators) that Oprah Winfrey has shifted the focus of her show. While she did formerly focus on narrative display, many of the women I interviewed now viewed her as moving in the direction *of Donahue.* Oprah is seen to want to "teach" or "make a point." More recently she has been attempting closure on issues, looking for solutions or resolutions.

6. This issue has been present in the news as of late, with the charges being made that guests on *The Jerry Springer Show* (at this point the most popular daytime television show, according to television industry ratings) are coached by producers to be outrageous and begin fights. Beyond the scope of this dissertation is the interesting issue that it was a show known as "tabloid" TV (*Extra!*) that broke the story in which they interviewed former *Springer* guests. Because his show's ratings surpassed those of *Oprah Winfrey* (who held the top-rated daytime slot for years), *Jerry Springer* has been featured in a piece on *Dateline* and was interviewed on *Larry King Live!* In both cases, he was confronted about charges of fraudulent guests and of the show's encouragement of guests fight-

ing. Springer also appeared on *The Tonight Show*, where he tried his hand at stand-up comedy.

7. For research on soap operas, see Modleski (1983) and Brown (1990b, 1994). For research on prime-time drama, see Ang (1992) and Liebes and Katz (1990). For television programming more generally, see Press (1991).

8. See, for example, Livingstone and Lunt (1994).

9. It is worth noting here that while Susan (as well as several other women I interviewed) regarded Oprah Winfrey and her show as the prototypical "good" talk show, several of the women I interviewed (in particular, black women), noting the change in Oprah's show, reacted to it very differently. These women charged Oprah with getting "too high class," being "boring," with "nothing going on," and not being concerned enough with inner- city blacks ("She doesn't come around this neighborhood anymore!").

10. Bennett, along with Sen. Joseph Lieberman (D- Connecticut), has spearheaded a campaign, organized through his conservative advocacy group Empower America, to ask advertisers to withdraw support from shows featuring "salacious" topics. Calling these talk shows "cultural rot," he charged that "every society has its red-light district," but that it must not be allowed to infiltrate "our main streets." He suggests that we clean out our "cultural air ducts." This campaign is discussed in chapters 2 and 5.

11. Fiske and others (many of them in communication studies, media studies, and sociology) draw on a key work by Hall (1981) entitled "Encoding/Decoding." In this article, Hall expands on models of communication that focus on the ideological coding of texts (in all forms, including print and visual media). He suggests that individuals may make dominant, oppositional, and negotiated "readings" of a text. That is to say, they may interpret a text according to the dominant meaning encoded in it by constructing a resistive interpretation that opposes the dominant meaning, or a negotiated reading that modifies but does not fully reject or oppose the dominant meaning. While an oppositional reading can often embody an explicit critique of the dominant meaning, a negotiated meaning generally does not.

12. See, for example, historians Joan Landes (1995), Mary Ryan (1992) and Geoff Eley (1994), and political theorists Nancy Fraser (1994) and Iris Marion Young (1990).

13. See Habermas (1991). This work has provoked a wide range of responses and critiques. Most scholars of political theory, and of democracy in particular, have been compelled to take Habermas's work into account whether or not they agree with his analysis.

14. In *The Semisovereign People: A Realist's View of Democracy in America*, Schattschneider (1975) discusses the important issue of who shapes the public agenda as central to understanding power in a society.

15. Shattuc (1997) attributes at least some degree of this change to the feminist movement of the 1960s and its promotion of "the personal is the political," which situates women's issues that were historically regarded as "personal" and "private" concerns as part of the larger cultural and social terrain.

16. I suggest that non-black Americans also access these discourses, but generally in a less connected, more commodified form. For example, it is not uncommon for white American young women to say, with clearly black inflection, "Don't go there!" or "You go, girl!" or for white suburban teenage boys to appropriate a walk clearly inflected with the black cultural style, practices usually accessed through the mass media. A classic example of the fragmented and commodified appropriation of African American cultural practice and style is in the Disney animated film, *Hercules*. The movie's opening shot focuses on a close-up of a Greek vase with a picture of Hercules painted on it, with a grouping of women above him. As the camera pulls in for a "tight" shot, the group of women becomes animated. These women are black, and, further, as they begin to talk among themselves introducing the film (operating as the chorus), they are clearly recognizable as African American in terms of what they say (e.g., "You go, girl!"), their speaking style, and their breaking into a gospel- style musical number.

17. When a show is encountered as entertainment, however, this is an entirely different case. (I discuss this in chapter 5.)

NOTES TO CHAPTER 5

1. Not only did *The Jerry Springer Show* surpass *The Oprah Winfrey Show* in the Nielsen ratings to become the most watched television talk show, but it held on to this position for over twenty weeks (K. Johnson 1998: 1). For example, for the week ending May 31, 1998, *The Jerry Springer Show* averaged a 7.2 rating (indicating 9.4 million viewers on average per show), to top *Oprah Winfrey's* rating of 6.0 (just over 7 million viewers).

2. In televised interviews, lectures, and a personal conversation, Springer distances himself from television industry management and its business-driven practices. Consistent with this, he sees the categorization of his show as a "talk show" as part of television industry practices. Springer consistently tends to position himself as naive, simply "doing a job" (for which he acknowledges he is being handsomely compensated), not caught up or involved in the business dimension of his show.

3. Most of this list is drawn from the transcript of a press conference with Malcolm Forbes, Jr., William Bennett, and Sen. Joseph Lieberman (October 26, 1995).

4. This line of thinking is developed further later in this chapter.

5. As cited in the previous chapter, Masciarotte's (1991) analysis of the "old" Oprah suggests that it was precisely this characteristic of teasing out the story, the display of narrative in all its permutations, that distinguished Oprah from Phil Donahue, whom Masciarotte analyzes as working toward closure and consensus. Masciarotte also positions Winfrey as an embodiment of the "Other," Stallybrass and White would surely identify her, with her fluctuating weight, as an embodiment of the grotesque body—curvaceous, round, and excessive. It is interesting to note that Winfrey's decision to move her program away from the sensations and more toward a Donahue-like format coincides with her losing weight, moving her body more toward the thin ideal of mainstream culture.

6. As with Greek plays and Shakespeare in the eighteenth and early nineteenth-century United States, the audience was familiar with the story unfolding on the stage.

7. This sense of being "compelled" to talk or being acted upon in some way will be discussed in the second part of the chapter, in which I focus my analysis on the operation of the "lure of the show."

8. Similarly, the name "Mardi Gras" means "Greasy Tuesday" and refers to feasting (on fatty meats) on the last Tuesday before to the Lenten fast/abstinence (Stallybrass and White 1986: 182). In New Orleans, where Mardi Gras is celebrated, this day is still referred to as "Fat Tuesday."

9. In voodoo practice, dance was associated with the *loa* (gods), each *loa* having its own dance, recognizable to participants by its distinctive rhythm and movement. Participants in voodoo ceremonies were recognized as being possessed by particular *loa* depending on the dance they performed (see Ventura 1985: 103–62).

10. This includes talk that appears to be "social" (or just for pleasure) rather than instrumental. For example, while "schmoozing" with colleagues or attending social events among professionals, one may be able to enter into "small talk." This socializing generally has the instrumental intent of establishing useful relationships (which may facilitate professional possibilities) for at least one of the participants. (This is not to diminish the fact that participants may also find small talk itself pleasurable.)

11. Looked at together, Allen (1991) and Levine (1988) show that critics of burlesque and popular theater shared a strikingly similar rhetoric.

12. Bennett, along with Sen. Joseph Lieberman, launched a campaign in 1995 aimed at getting talk shows to "tone down" their "salacious" content. Their strategy was vehemently not one that advocated government regulation, but rather focused on encouraging sponsors to withhold their advertising revenue from shows that continued to feature topics deemed unacceptable.

13. Relevant to this claim, in his lecture at Emerson College in November 1997, Springer reported that at that time his show was the number-one rated daytime television show in Amsterdam.

14. Gordon's (1997) notion of "haunting" draws on Freud's (1919) notion of the "uncanny," something she makes explicit in her own discussion.

15. "Structure of feeling" is a concept Gordon (and I) draw from Raymond Williams (1977). Citing Williams, Gordon explains that a structure of feeling "methodologically . . . is a cultural hypothesis, actually derived from attempts to understand . . . specific feelings, specific rhythms . . . and yet to find ways of recognizing their specific kinds of sociality, thus preventing that extraction from social experience which is conceivable only when social experience itself as been categorically (and at root historically) reduced" (Williams 1977, cited in Gordon 1997). Gordon goes on to suggest that "haunting is the most general instance of the clamoring return of the reduced to a delicate social experience struggling, even unaware, with its shadow but exigent presence" (Gordon 1997: 201).

16. In Althusser, Lacanian psychoanalytic theory, the work of cultural studies, and screen theory, the phenomenon of being "called" is discussed analytically as a process of "interpellation" (see Chapter 1, section on "Audience Reception").

17. For example, this reminds me of the term "gordita" or "gordito" in Spanish. The term, while technically meaning "little fat one," is generally used affectionately, as a term of endearment, not as an insult.

NOTES TO CHAPTER 6

1. I asked in my interviews about communities with whom they participate and places where they discuss issues.

2. This is evident, for example, in Weber's classic analysis of the "spirit of capitalism," which promoted increased productivity and accumulation of capital, which could be reinvested to make a business more productive.

3. As evidence for this, think of the disparaging mood in which a person often says to another, "That's not useful," or "That's useless," or, more pointedly, "You're not being useful," "Do something useful," or "You're useless!"

4. Along these lines, Bataille notes the closeness between violence and the ecstatic.

Bibliography

Abt, Vicki, and Leonard Mustazza. 1997. *Coming after Oprah: Cultural Fallout in the Age of the TV Talk Show*. Bowling Green, OH: Bowling Green State University Popular Press.

Abt, Vicki, and Mel Seesholtz. 1994. "The Shameless World of Phil, Sally and Oprah: Television Talk Shows and the Deconstructing of Society." *Journal of Popular Culture* 28 (Summer): 171–91.

Advertiser Syndicated Television Association. 1993. "Syndicated Talk Shows Advertising Revenue 1987–1993." *Broadcasting and Cable*, December 13, 80.

Allen, Robert C. 1991. *Horrible Prettiness: Burlesque and American Culture*. Chapel Hill: University of North Carolina Press.

———. 1992. "Introduction to the Second Edition: More Talk about TV." Pp. 1–30 in *Channels of Discourse, Reassembled: Television and Contemporary Criticism*, vol. 2, edited by Robert C. Allen. Chapel Hill: University of North Carolina Press.

Allinson, Ewan. 1988. "It's a Black Thing: Hearing How Whites Can't." *Cultural Studies* 2 (October): 438–56.

Ang, Ien. 1990. "Melodramatic Identifications: Television Fiction and Women's Fantasy." Pp. 75–88 in *Television and Women's Culture: The Politics of the Popular*, edited by Mary Ellen Brown. London: Sage.

———. 1992. *Watching Dallas: Soap Opera and the Melodramatic Imagination*. London: Routledge.

Barnouw, Erik. 1975. *Tube of Plenty: The Evolution of American Television*. New York: Oxford University Press.

Bataille, Georges. 1985. *Visions of Excess: Selected Writings, 1927–1939*, edited by Allan Stoekl. Minneapolis: University of Minnesota Press.

———. 1991. *The Accursed Share*, vol. 1, *Consumption*. Translated by Robert Hurley. New York: Zone Books.

Baudrillard, Jean. 1975. *The Mirror of Production*. St. Louis, MO: Telos Press.

———. 1988. *Jean Baudrillard: Selected Writings*, edited by Mark Poster. Stanford, CA: Stanford University Press.

———. 1993. *Symbolic Exchange and Death*. London: Sage.

Bennett, William. 1995. "Empower America Launches Campaign Against Daytime TV Talk Shows: Statement by William J. Bennett." *Empower America Highlights* 3 (2), Fall (www.townhall.com/empower/benno216.html)

———. 1996. "In Civilized Society, Shame Has Place." *Los Angeles Times*, January 26, B9.

Bobo, Jacqueline. 1995. *Black Women as Cultural Readers*. New York: Columbia University Press.

Bourdieu, Pierre. 1984. *Distinction: A Social Critique of the Judgment of Taste.* Translated by Richard Nice. Cambridge, MA: Harvard University Press.

Bracher, Mark. 1993. *Lacan, Discourse, and Social Change: A Psychoanalytic Cultural Criticism.* Ithaca, NY: Cornell University Press.

Broadcasting and Cable. 1994a. "NATPE Survey '94." *Broadcasting and Cable,* January 24, 66–67.

———. 1994b. "Star Talker: The Next Generation (Talk Shows '94)." *Broadcasting and Cable,* December 12, 56–57.

Brooke, Jill. 1998. "Can We Talk?" *Adweek* (Eastern Edition), February 23, 17–18.

Brown, Mary Ellen. 1990a. "Introduction: Feminist Cultural Television Criticism: Culture, Theory, and Practice." Pp. 11–22 in *Television and Women's Culture: The Politics of the Popular.* London: Sage.

———. 1990b. "Motley Moments: Soap Operas, Carnival, Gossip, and the Power of the Utterance." Pp. 183–98 in *Television and Women's Culture: The Politics of the Popular.* London: Sage.

———. 1994. *Soap Operas and Women's Talk: The Pleasure of Resistance.* Thousand Oaks: Sage.

Browne, Nick. 1984. "The Political Economy of the Television (Super) Text." *Quarterly Review of Film Studies* 9 (Summer): 174–82.

Brunsdon, Charlotte. 1989. "Text and Audience." Pp. 116–29 in *Remote Control: Television, Audiences, and Cultural Power,* edited by Ellen Seiter, Hans Borchers, Gabriele Kreutzner, and Eva-Maria Warth. London: Routledge.

Burris, Mary Ann, Xiang Yue Ping, and Caroline Wang. 1996. "Chinese Village Women as Anthropologists: A Participatory Approach to Reaching Policymakers." *Social Science and Medicine* 42 (10): 1391–4000.

Butler, Judith. 1993. *Bodies That Matter: On the Discursive Limits of "Sex."* New York: Routledge.

———. 1997. *The Psychic Life of Power: Theories in Subjection.* Stanford, CA: Stanford University Press.

Cable News Network. 1998. "Jerry Springer Answers His Critics," from *CNN Larry King Live!* May 8. Transcript 98050800V22.

Caputi, Mary. 1994. *Voluptuous Yearnings: A Feminist Theory of the Obscene.* Lanham, MD: Rowman and Littlefield.

Carbaugh, Donal. 1989. *Talking American: Cultural Discourses on Donahue.* Norwood, NJ: Ablex.

Carpignano, Paulo, Robin Andersen, Stanley Aronowitz, and William DiFazio. 1993. "Chatter in the Age of Electronic Reproduction: Talk Television and the "Public Mind." Pp. 93–120 in *The Phantom Sphere,* edited by Bruce Robbins. Minneapolis: University of Minnesota Press.

Chodron, Pema. 1994. *Start with Where You Are: A Guide to Compassionate Living*. Boston: Shambala Books.

———. 2001. *The Places That Scare You: A Guide to Fearlessness in Difficult Times*. Boston: Shambala Books.

Clegg, Stewart R. 1989. *Frameworks of Power*. London: Sage.

Collins, Jim. 1992. "Postmodernism and Television." Pp. 284–326 in *Channels of Discourse, Reassembled: Television and Contemporary Criticism*, 2d ed., edited by Robert C. Allen. Chapel Hill: University of North Carolina Press.

Collins, Patricia Hill. 1991. *Black Feminist Thought: Knowledge, Consciousness and the Politics of Empowerment*. New York: Routledge.

Conlin, Michelle. 1998. "Taming Jerry Springer." *Forbes*, May 18, 44.

Connor, Peter Tracey. 2000. *George Bataille and the Mysticism of Sin*. Baltimore: Johns Hopkins University Press.

Debord, Guy. 1983. *Society of the Spectacle*. Detroit: Black and Red.

De Certeau, Michel. 1988. *The Practice of Everyday Life*. Translated by Steven Rendall. Berkeley: University of California Press.

DeCoursey, Jennifer. 1995. "Advertisers Choosier in Talk Show Spending." *Electronic Media* (November 6): 79.

Dewey, John. 1991 [1927]. *The Public and Its Problems*. Athens, GA: Swallow Press.

Dominick, Joseph R., Barry L. Sherman, and Gary A. Copeland. 1996. *Broadcasting/Cable and Beyond*, 3d ed. New York: McGraw-Hill.

Donovan, Sharon. 1997a. "New Highs—And Lows—In Daytime." *Broadcasting and Cable*, December 15, 42–44.

———. 1997b. "Known Names Sought to Fill Host Chairs." *Broadcasting and Cable*, December 15, 45–54.

Douglas, Mary. 1995 [1966]. *Purity and Danger: An Analysis of the Concepts of Pollution and Taboo*. London: Routledge.

Dreyfus, Hubert L., and Paul Rabinow. 1983. *Michel Foucault: Beyond Structuralism and Hermeneutics*, 2d ed. With an Afterword by Michel Foucault. Chicago: University of Chicago Press.

Drotner, Kirsten. 1994. "Ethnographic Enigmas: 'The Everyday' in Recent Media Studies." *Cultural Studies* 8 (2): 341–57.

Dubois, W. E. B. 1989 [1903]. "*The Soul of Black Folks*. New York: Bantam.

Dubrow, Burt. 1992. "Burt Dubrow on the Two Faces of Talk." *Broadcasting and Cable*, December 14, 38.

Durkheim, Emile. 1999 [1912]. "The Cultural Logic of Collective Representations." Pp. 89–99 in *Social Theory: The Multicultural and Classic Readings*, edited by Charles Lemert. Boulder, CO: Westview Press.

Eley, Geoff. 1994. "Nations, Publics, and Political Cultures: Placing Habermas in the Nineteenth Century." Pp. 289–339 in *Habermas and the Public Sphere*, edited by Craig Calhoun. Cambridge, MA: MIT Press.

Ewick, Patricia, and Susan S. Silbey. 1995. "Subversive Stories and Hegemonic Tales: Toward a Sociology of Narrative." *Law and Society Review* 29 (2): 197–226.

Fick, Bob. 1998. "Idaho Legislator, Clinton Critic, Admits to an Affair." *Boston Globe*, September 11, A1, A21.

Fiske, John. 1987. *Television Culture*. London: Routledge.

———. 1989a. "Moments of Television: Neither the Text nor the Audience." Pp. 56–78 in *Remote Control: Television, Audiences, and Cultural Power*, edited by Ellen Seiter, Hans Brochers, Gabriele Kreutzner, and Eva-Maria Warth. London: Routledge.

———. 1989b. *Understanding Popular Culture*. London: Routledge.

Fiske, John, and John Hartley. 1978. *Reading Television*. London: Methuen.

Foucault, Michel. 1973a. *The Order of Things: An Archaeology of the Human Sciences*. New York: Vintage Books.

———. 1973b. *The Birth of the Clinic: An Archaeology of Medical Perception*. New York: Pantheon.

———. 1977. *Language, Counter-Memory, Practice: Selected Essays and Interviews*. Edited with an Introduction by Donald F. Bouchard. Translated by Donald F. Bouchard and Sherry Simon. Ithaca, NY: Cornell University Press.

———. 1980. *Power/Knowledge: Selected Interviews and Other Writings 1972–1977*. Edited by Colin Gordon. New York: Pantheon.

———. 1983. "Afterword: The Subject and Power." Pp. 208–26 in *Michel Foucault: Beyond Structuralism and Hermeneutics*. 2d edition. Chicago: University of Chicago Press.

———. 1984a. "Nietzsche, Genealogy, History." Pp. 76–100 in *The Foucault Reader*, edited by Paul Rabinow. New York: Pantheon.

———. 1984b. "Truth and Power." Pp. 51–75 in *The Foucault Reader*, edited by Paul Rabinow. New York: Pantheon.

Fraser, Nancy. 1994. "Rethinking the Public Sphere: A Contribution to the Critique of Actually Existing Democracy." Pp. 109–42 in *Habermas and the Public Sphere*, edited by Craig Calhoun. Cambridge, MA: MIT Press.

Free, Valerie. 1985. "The Elusive Female." *Marketing Communications* 10 (8): 33–59.

Freeman, Mike. 1992a. "Daytime: Lots of Talk, a Little Romance." *Broadcasting and Cable*, January 21, 35–36.

———. 1992b. "Can We Talk? New for 1993." *Broadcasting and Cable*, December 14, 26–30.

———. 1993a. "Talk of the Town: More Faces Crowd Mike in '92." *Broadcasting and Cable*, January 18, 36, 40.

———. 1993b. "Talk Trio Crowded Field." *Broadcasting and Cable*, January 25, 36, 46, 50.

———. 1995a. "Murder by Television? 'Jenny'-Related Shooting Has Raised Concern over Talk-Show Content." *Mediaweek*, March 20, 9.

———. 1995b. "Ax Looms over Talk Shows." *Mediaweek*, May 15, 14–16.

———. 1995c. "Putting Out the Trash." *Mediaweek*, November 6, 13–16.

———. 1996a. "Talk-Show Shakeout; More First-Year Television Series May Be Canceled." *Mediaweek*, January 1, 10.

———. 1996b. "Pondering Povich's Future." *Mediaweek*, July 1, 5–6.

———. 1997a. "The End of the World as We Know It; the Government and TV Viewers Have Forever Changed the Syndication Business." *Mediaweek*, January 6, 26–28.

———. 1997b. "Talk Shows' Blue Sweeps." *Mediaweek*, March 3, 12–14.

———. 1997c. "Talk Coup." *Mediaweek*, November 17, 9.

———. 1998a. "The Other Jerry." *Mediaweek*, January 19, 31–33.

———. 1998b. "Springer Shakes 'em Down." *Mediaweek*, February 2, 8–9.

Freeman, Mike, and Scotty Dupree. 1995. "Advertisers Dump 'Trash'; Broadcasters See Clients Fleeing from Controversial Talk Shows." *Mediaweek*, December 11, 5.

Friedman, Wayne. 1993. "Tight TV: Talk Shows." *Inside Media*, January 20, 1.

———. 1995. "Advertisers Developing Safe Talk Shows." *Inside Media*, December 13, 5.

Gamson, Joshua. 1998. *Freaks Talk Back: Tabloid Talk Shows and Sexual Nonconformity*. Chicago: University of Chicago Press.

Garfinkel, Harold. 1984 [1967]. *Studies in Ethnomethodology*. Cambridge, MA: Polity Press.

Gatens, Moira. 1996. *Imaginary Bodies: Ethics, Power and Corporeality*. London: Routledge.

Giddens, Anthony. 1986. *The Constitution of Society*. Berkeley: University of California Press.

Gilroy, Paul. 1993. *The Black Atlantic: Modernity and Double Consciousness*. Cambridge, MA: Harvard University Press.

Goodman, Fred. 1991. "Madonna and Oprah: The Companies They Keep." *Working Woman*, December, 52–55, 84.

Gordon, Avery F. 1997. *Ghostly Matters: Haunting and the Sociological Imagination*. Minneapolis: University of Minnesota Press.

Gray, Herman. 1995. *Watching Race: Television and the Struggle for "Blackness."* Minneapolis: University of Minnesota Press.

Grossberg, Lawrence. 1988. "Wandering Audiences, Nomadic Critics." *Cultural Studies* 2 (3): 377–91.

Habermas, Jürgen. 1991. *The Structural Transformation of the Public Sphere: An Inquiry into a Category of Bourgeois Society*. Cambridge, MA: MIT Press.

Haithman, Diane. 1987 "Rivera Vows Talk Show to Be Hot, Heavy." *Los Angeles Times*, September 4, 1.

Haley, Kathy. 1992a. "Still Talking After All These Years." Advertising Supplement: Donahue 25th Anniversary. *Broadcasting* 122 (45), November 2, S2.

———. 1992b. "From Dayton to the World: A History of the *Donahue Show*." Advertising Supplement: Donahue 25th Anniversary. *Broadcasting* 122 (45), November 2.

———. 1992c. "Talking with Phil." Advertising Supplement: Donahue 25th Anniversary. *Broadcasting* 122 (45), November 2.

———. 1992d. "Producing *Donahue*: The Three C's: Controversy, Continuity, Camaraderie." Advertising Supplement: Donahue 25th Anniversary. *Broadcasting* 122 (45), November 2, S22.

———. 1993. "Celebrating Sally." Sally Jessy Raphael Anniversary Supplement. *Broadcasting*, November 15, D1–16.

Hall, Stuart. 1981. "Encoding/Decoding in Television Discourse." In *Culture, Media, Language*, edited by Stuart Hall. London: Hutchinson.

———. 1996a. "Postmodernism and Articulation." Interview with Lawrence Grossberg. Pp. 131–50 in *Stuart Hall: Critical Dialogues in Cultural Studies*, edited by David Morley and Kuan-Hsing Chen. London: Routledge.

———. 1996b. "Cultural Studies: Theoretical Legacies." Pp. 262–75 in *Stuart Hall: Critical Dialogues in Cultural Studies*, edited by David Morley and Kuan-Hsing Chen. London: Routledge.

———. 1996c. "The Problem of Ideology: Marxism without Guarantees." Pp. 25–46 in *Stuart Hall: Critical Dialogues in Cultural Studies*, edited by David Morley and Kuan-Hsing Chen. London: Routledge.

Halonen, Doug. 1995. "D.C. Heavyweights Take on the Talk Shows." *Electronic Media*, October 30, 1.

Haraway, Donna. 1989. *Primate Visions: Gender, Race and Nature in the World of Modern Science*. New York: Routledge.

Hay, James, Lawrence Grossberg, and Ellen Wartella, eds. 1992. *The Audience and Its Landscape*. Oxford: Westview Press.

Heath, Rebecca Piirto. 1998. "Tuning into Talk." *American Demographics*, February, 48–53.

Heaton, Jeanne Albronda, and Nona Leigh Wilson. 1995. *Tuning in Trouble: Talk TV's Destructive Impact on Mental Health*. San Francisco: Jossey-Bass.

Hermes, Joke. 1993. "Media, Meaning and Everyday Life." *Cultural Studies* 7 (3): 493–506.

Hobson, Dorothy. 1982. *Crossroads: The Drama of Soap Operas*. London: Methuen.

———. 1990. "Women Audiences and the Workplace." Pp. 61–71 in *Television and Women's Culture*, edited by Mary Ellen Brown. London: Sage.

Horkheimer, Max, and Theodor Adorno. 1987. *The Dialectic of Enlightenment.* New York: Continuum.

Hyatt, Joshua. 1987. "The INC. 100 Portfolio." *Inc.,* May, 58–60.

Johnson, Kevin V. 1998. "Springer More, Wilder and Crazier This Fall!" *USA Today,* September (www.tvtalkshows.com/jerryspringer/ news/1998/wild).

Johnson, Robert A. 1987. *Ecstasy: Understanding the Psychology of Joy.* San Francisco: Harper and Row.

Jones, Alex. 1987. "Television: 'Geraldo' Gambles on Talk." *New York Times,* September 6, sec.2, 21.

Kellner, Douglas. 1995. *Media Culture: Cultural Studies, Identity and Politics between the Modern and the Postmodern.* London: Routledge.

Kelly, Frank. 1992. "Paramount's Frank Kelly: Anatomy of a Deal." *Broadcasting and Cable,* December 14, 34.

Kohler Riessman, Catherine. 1987. "When Gender Is Not Enough: Women Interviewing Women." *Gender and Society* 1 (June): 172–207.

Kristeva, Julia. 1982. *Powers of Horror: An Essay on Abjection.* New York: Columbia University Press.

Lake, Ricki. 1994. "Star Talker: The Next Generation." *Broadcasting and Cable,* December 12; 56–57.

Landes, Joan. 1995. "The Public and the Private Sphere: A Feminist Reconsideration." Pp. 91–116 in *Feminists Read Habermas: Gendering the Subject of Discourse,* edited by Johanna Meehan. New York: Routledge.

Lash, Scott, and John Urry. 1994. *Economies of Signs and Space.* London: Sage.

Lears, T. J. Jackson. 1983. "From Salvation to Self-Realization: Advertising and the Therapeutic Roots of the Consumer Culture, 1880–1930." Pp. 3–38 in *The Culture of Consumption,* edited by Richard Wightman Fox and T. J. Jackson Lears. New York: Pantheon Books.

Lefebvre, Henri. 1971. *Everyday Life in the Modern World.* New York: Harper and Row.

Levine, Lawrence W. 1988. *Highbrow/Lowbrow: The Emergence of Cultural Hierarchy in America.* Cambridge, MA: Harvard University Press.

Liebes, Tamar. 1992. "Notes on the Struggle to Define Involvement in Television Viewing." Pp. 177–86 in *The Audience and Its Landscape. Cultural Studies.* Edited by James Hay, Lawrence Grossberg, and Ellen Wartella. Boulder, CO: Westview Press.

Liebes, Tamar, and Elihu Katz. 1990. *The Export of Meaning: Cross-Cultural Readings of "Dallas."* New York: Oxford University Press.

Littleton, Cynthia. 1995a. "Stations Talk Back to Talk TV." *Broadcasting and Cable,* November 13, 12.

———. 1995b. "A Question of Content: Politicians Want Talk Shows to Change Their Ways." *Broadcasting and Cable,* December 11, 64.

————. 1995c. "Talk's Veterans Hang Tough." *Broadcasting and Cable,* December 11, 50–52.

————. 1995d. "Syndicators Keep on Talkin'." *Broadcasting and Cable,* December 11, 56, 58.

————. 1996a. "'Gabrielle,' 'Charles Perez' Talked Out." *Broadcasting and Cable,* January 8, 40–42.

————. 1996b. "Talk TV Toughs It Out." *Broadcasting and Cable,* January 15, 59, 66.

————. 1996c. "The Remaking of Talk." *Broadcasting and Cable,* January 22, 46–50.

————. 1996d. "Kids Shows Sell Despite Crunch." *Broadcasting and Cable,* February 5, 34–36.

————. 1996e. "Talk Is 'Scared Straight' for May Sweeps." *Broadcasting and Cable,* April 29, 26–27.

————. 1996f. "MCA Eyes Gannett's Multimedia." *Broadcasting and Cable,* October 7, 12.

————. 1996g. "The Many Faces of Talk TV." *Broadcasting and Cable,* December 2, 26–28.

————. 1996h. "New Talkers Look for Listeners." *Broadcasting and Cable,* December 2, 32–38.

————. 1997a. "Talk Show Turnaround." *Broadcasting and Cable,* January 6, 40, 44, 50.

————. 1997b. "Universal Adds Povich to Talk Arsenal." *Broadcasting and Cable,* June 9, 32.

Littleton, Cynthia, and Steve Coe. 1996. "Ad Dollars: Syndication's Not-So-Hidden Persuaders." *Broadcasting and Cable,* February 19, 21–24.

Livingstone, Sonia M. 1992. *Making Sense of Television: The Psychology of Audience Interpretation.* Oxford: Pergamon Press.

Livingstone, Sonia, and Peter Lunt. 1994. *Talk on Television: Audience Participation and Public Debate.* London: Routledge.

Lodziak, Conrad. 1986. *The Power of Television: A Critical Appraisal.* New York: St. Martin's Press.

Lull, James. 1990. *Inside Family Viewing: Ethnographic Research on Television's Audiences.* London: Routledge.

Mandese, Joe. 1995. "TV Talk Shows Send Chill through Advertisers." *Advertising Age,* March 20, 34.

Mansbridge, Jane. 1990. "Feminism and Democracy." *American Prospect* 1 (Spring): 24.

Marcuse, Herbert. 1955. *Eros and Civilization: A Philosophical Inquiry into Freud.* New York: Vintage Books.

————. 1969. *An Essay on Liberation.* Boston: Beacon Press.

Marx, Karl. 1978 [1867]. "Capital, Volume One." Pp. 294–438 in *The Marx-Engels Reader*, 2d Edition. Edited by Robert C. Tucker. New York: W. W. Norton.

Masciarotte, Gloria Jean. 1991. "C'mon Girl: Oprah Winfrey and the Discourse of Feminine Talk." *Genders* 11 (Fall): 81–110.

McClellan, Steve. 1992. "Look Who's Talking." *Broadcasting and Cable*, December 14, 22, 24.

———. 1993a. "Ricki Tops New Talkers." *Broadcasting and Cable*, November 22, 12.

———. 1993b. "Daytime Network Talk: 10 Years Too Late?" *Broadcasting and Cable*, December 13, 68.

———. 1994. "Young-targeted Talkers Take Off." *Broadcasting and Cable*, July 4, 18.

———. 1995. "1995 NATPE Survey." *Broadcasting and Cable*, January 16, 34, 38.

———. 1996a. "New Talk Sinks, Sitcoms Soar." *Broadcasting and Cable*, January 1, 22–28.

———. 1996b. "NATPE Survey '96." *Broadcasting and Cable*, January 15, 26, 34.

———. 1996c. "Tough May for Talkers." *Broadcasting and Cable*, June 24, 10.

———. 1996d. "MCA Buys Multimedia Shows." *Broadcasting and Cable*, December 2, 39–42.

———. 1997. "NATPE 1997." *Broadcasting and Cable*, January 6, 24–25.

———. 1998. "'Springer' Up in Flat May." *Broadcasting and Cable*, June 29, 62.

McClellan, Steve, and Mike Freeman. 1993. "Surviving the Shakeout in Daytime Talk." *Broadcasting and Cable*, December 13, 54–60.

McRobbie, Angela. 1978. *Jackie: An Ideology of Adolescent Femininity*. Birmingham, UK: Centre for Contemporary Cultural Studies, University of Birmingham.

Mifflin, Lawrie. 1995. "Talk-Show Critics Urge Boycott of Programs by Advertisers." *New York Times*, December 8, A22.

Modleski, Tania. 1983. "The Rhythms of Reception: Daytime Television and Women's Work." Pp. 67–75 in *Regarding Television*, American Film Institute Monograph Series, edited by Ann Kaplan. New York: University of America Publications.

Morley, David. 1981. "Texts, Readers and Subjects." Pp. 163–73 in *Culture, Media, Language*, edited by Stuart Hall et al. London: Hutchinson.

———. 1986. *Family Television: Cultural Power and Domestic Leisure*. London: Comedia.

———. 1989. "Changing Paradigms in Audience Studies." Pp. 16–43 in *Remote Control: Television, Audiences, and Cultural Power*, edited by Ellen Seiter, Hans Borchers, Gabriele Kreutzner, and Eva-Maria Warth. London: Routledge.

———. 1992a. "The Geography of Television: Ethnography, Communications, and Community." Pp. 327–42 in *The Audience and Its Landscape*, Cultural

Studies, edited by James Hay, Lawrence Grossberg, and Ellen Wartella. Boulder, CO: Westview Press.

———. 1992b. *Television, Audiences and Cultural Studies*. London: Routledge.

Mundy, Alicia. 1995. "Bill Bennett's Big Bet." *Mediaweek*, November 20, 20–21.

Munson, Wayne. 1993. *All Talk: The Talkshow in Media Culture*. Philadelphia: Temple University Press.

Nickles, Elizabeth. 1981. "The Newest Mass Market—Women Go- Getters." *Advertising Age*, November 9, 56.

Nielsen Media Research. 1996. *Nielsen Ratings Report*.

———. 1998. *Nielsen Ratings Report*.

Noglows, Paul. 1994. "Oprah: The Year of Living Dangerously." *Working Woman*, May: 52–55.

Parkin, Frank. 1971. *Class Inequality and Political Order*. London: Paladin.

Peck, Janice. 1995. "TV Talk Shows as Therapeutic Discourse: The Ideological Labor of the Televised Talking Cure." *Communication Theory* 5 (1): 58–81.

Peiss, Kathy. 1986. *Cheap Amusements: Working Women and Leisure in Turn-of-the-Century New York*. Philadelphia: Temple University Press.

Peterson, Eric E., and Kristin M. Langellier. 1997. "The Politics of Personal Narrative Methodology." *Text and Performance Quarterly* 17 (2): 135–52.

Pfohl, Stephen. 1992. *Death at the Parasite Café: Social Science (Fictions) and the Postmodern*. New York: St. Martin's Press.

Plume, Janet. 1997. "Network Talk Shows Remain Scarce." *Broadcasting and Cable*, December 15, 50–54.

Postman, Neil. 1985. *Amusing Ourselves to Death: Public Discourse in the Age of Show Business*. New York: Viking Penguin.

Press, Andrea L. 1991. *Women Watching Television: Gender, Class, and Generation in the American Television Experience*. Philadelphia: University of Pennsylvania Press.

———. 1992. "Toward a Qualitative Methodology of Audience Study: Using Ethnography to Study the Popular Culture Audience." Pp. 113–30 in *The Audience and Its Landscape*, edited by James Hay, Lawrence Grossberg, and Ellen Wartella. Boulder, CO: Westview Press.

Priest, Patricia Joyner. 1995. *Public Intimacies: Talk Show Participants and Tell-All TV*. Cresskill, NJ: Hampton Press.

Putnam, Robert D. 1995. "Bowling Alone: America's Declining Social Capital." *Journal of Democracy* 6, no. 1 (January): 65–78.

Rabinow, Paul. 1984. "Introduction." Pp. 3–29 in *The Foucault Reader*, edited by Paul Rabinow. New York: Pantheon.

Radway, Janice. 1988. "Reception Study: Ethnography and the Problems of Dispersed Audiences and Nomadic Subjects." *Cultural Studies* 2 (3): 359–75.

————. 1991. *Reading the Romance: Women, Patriarchy, and Popular Literature.* Chapel Hill: University of North Carolina Press.

Rattansi, Ali. 1995. "Just Framing: Ethnicities and Racisms in a 'Postmodern' Framework." Pp. 250–86 in *Social Postmodernism: Beyond Identity Politics,* edited by Linda Nicholson and Steven Seidman. Cambridge, UK: Cambridge University Press.

Reuters, Limited. 1995. "U.S. Campaign Launched against 'Trash' TV Shows." *Reuters North American Wire,* December 7. Available from Lexis-Nexis.

Richardson, Kay, and John Corner. 1986. "Reading Reception: Mediation and Transparency in Viewers' Reception of a TV Programme." *Media, Culture and Society* 8: 485–508.

Richman, Michele H. 1982. *Reading Georges Bataille: Beyond the Gift.* Baltimore: Johns Hopkins University Press.

Rosenzweig, Roy. 1983. *Eight Hours for What We Will: Workers and Leisure in an Industrial City, 1870–1920.* Cambridge, UK: Cambridge University Press.

Ryan, Mary P. 1992. *Women in Public: Between Banners and Ballots, 1825–1880.* Baltimore: Johns Hopkins University Press.

Sandel, Michael J. 1996. *Democracy's Discontent: America in Search of a Public Philosophy.* Cambridge, MA: Belknap Press of Harvard University Press.

Scannell, Paddy. 1996. *Radio, Television and Modern Life: A Phenomenological Approach.* Oxford: Blackwell.

Schattschneider, E. E. 1975. *The Semisovereign People: A Realist's View of Democracy in America.* Hinsdale, IL: Dryden Press.

Schleier, Curt. 1987. "TV Syndication: 'Donahue' Challenged by 'Oprah' Ratings Success." *Advertising Age,* January 19, S30.

Schlosser, Joe. 1997a. "Oprah Springs Eternal." *Broadcasting and Cable,* September 22, 23.

Schlosser, Joe. 1997b. "Jerry Springer: Punching the Envelope." *Broadcasting and Cable,* December 15, 32–33.

Schumuckler, Eric. 1995. "Daybreak for Syndication." *Mediaweek,* April 3, 5.

————. 1997. "Search for Tomorrow." *Working Woman* 22 (7) (July/August): 31–35.

Scott, Gini Graham. 1996. *Can We Talk? The Power and Influence of Talk Shows.* New York: Insight Books/Plenum Press.

Scott, Joan W. 1992. "Experience." Pp. 22–39 in *Feminists Theorize the Political,* edited by Judith Butler and Joan Scott. London: Routledge.

Seiter, Ellen, Hans Brochers, Gabriele Kreutzner, and Eva-Maria Warth. 1989."Don't Treat Us Like We're So Stupid and Naive: Toward an Ethnography of Soap Opera Viewers." Pp. 223–47 in *Remote Control: Television, Audiences, and Cultural Power,* edited by Ellen Seiter, Hans Borchers, Gabriele Kreutzner, and Eva-Maria Warth. London: Routledge.

Sennett, Richard. 1992 [1976]. *The Fall of Public Man.* New York: W. W. Norton.

Shah, Diane E., and Frank Maier. 1978. "Heeere's . . . Phil Donahue!" *Newsweek,* March 13, 85.

Shattuc, Jane M. 1997. *The Talking Cure: TV Talk Shows and Women.* London: Routledge.

Silverstone, Roger. 1994. *Television and Everyday Life.* London: Routledge.

Slack, Jennifer. 1996. "The Theory and Method of Articulation." Pp. 112–27 in *Stuart Hall: Critical Dialogues in Cultural Studies,* edited by David Morley and Kuan-Hsing Chen. London: Routledge.

Smith, Dorothy. 1990. *The Conceptual Practices of Power: A Feminist Sociology of Knowledge.* Boston: Northeastern University Press.

Solomon, Robert. 1983. *The Passions: The Myth and Nature of Human Emotion.* Notre Dame, IN: University of Notre Dame Press.

Spigel, Lynn. 1992. *Make Room for TV: Television and the Family Ideal in Postwar America.* Chicago: University of Chicago Press.

Stallybrass, Peter, and Allon White. 1986. *The Politics and Poetics of Transgression.* Ithaca, NY: Cornell University Press.

Stern, Christopher. 1993. "Cable Plugging into Talk Format." *Broadcasting and Cable,* December 13, 76–78.

Stewart, Kathleen. 1996. *A Space by the Side of the Road: Cultural Poetics in an "Other" America.* Princeton, NJ: Princeton University Press.

Thorne, Barrie. 1993. *Gender Play: Boys and Girls in School.* New Brunswick, NJ: Rutgers University Press.

Tobenkin, David. 1994. "Bumper Crop of Talk Shows Hopes to Tap 'Ricki's' Success." *Broadcasting and Cable,* December 12, 47–49.

———. 1995a. "Tough Talk and Times for Talk Shows." *Broadcasting and Cable,* January 16, 59–60.

———. 1995b. "1995 NATPE." *Broadcasting and Cable,* January 23, 48, 56.

———. 1995c. "Danny Bonaduce Is Latest to Join Ranks of Talk Shows." *Broadcasting and Cable,* January 30, 26.

———. 1995d. "Springer Buoyed by Remake." *Broadcasting and Cable,* February 27, 22–24.

———. 1995e. "Has Talk Gone Too Far?" *Broadcasting and Cable,* March 20, 22–23.

———. 1995f. "Springer Fever in February Sweeps." *Broadcasting and Cable,* April 17, 26.

Trigoboff, Dan. 1998. "Educators Don't Want to Keep 'Springer' after School." *Broadcasting and Cable,* March 30, 11.

Turner, Robert. 1993. "Multimedia's Turner: What Shakeout?" *Broadcasting and Cable,* December 13, 70–76.

Ventura, Michael. 1985. *Shadow Dancing in the U.S.A.* Los Angeles: Jeremy P. Tarcher.

Verhaeghe, Paul. 1999. *Love in a Time of Loneliness: Three Essays on Drive and Desire.* New York: Other Press.

———. 2001. *Beyond Gender: From Subject to Drive.* New York: Other Press.

Wang, Carolyn, and Mary Ann Burris. 1994. "Empowerment through Photo Novella: Portraits of Participation." *Health Education Quarterly* 21 (Summer): 171–86.

Warren Publishing, Inc. 1995. "'Trash TV' Attacked." *Television Digest,* December 11, 4.

Waters, Harry F., and Patricia King. 1984. "Chicago's Grand New Oprah." *Newsweek,* December 31, 51.

Weber, Max. 1958. *The Protestant Ethic and the Spirit of Capitalism.* New York: Scribner.

Weedon, Chris. 1997. *Feminist Practice and Poststructuralist Theory.* Oxford: Blackwell.

West, Cornel. 1988. *Prophetic Fragments.* Grand Rapids: William B. Eerdmans, and Trenton: Africa World Press, Inc.

———. 1999. "Subervise Joy and Revolutionary Patience in Black Christianity." Pp. 435–39 in *The Cornel West Reader.* New York: Basic Civitas Books.

White, Allon. 1989. "Hysteria and the End of Carnival: Festivity and Bourgeois Neurosis." Pp. 157–70 in *The Violence of Representation: Literature and the History of Violence,* edited by Nancy Armstrong and Leonard Tennenhause. London: Routledge.

White, Mimi. 1992. *Tele-Advising: Therapeutic Discourse in American Television.* Chapel Hill: University of North Carolina Press.

Williams, Monte. 1993. "Voices of 30–Plus Exclaim: 'Can We Talk?'" *Advertising Age,* March 8, S6.

Williams, Raymond. 1974. *Television: Technology and Cultural Form.* London: Fontana/Collins.

———. 1977. *Marxism and Literature.* Oxford: Oxford University Press.

Willis, Ellen. 1996. "Bring in the Noise." *The Nation* (April): 19, 22–23.

Willis, Susan. 1991. *A Primer for Daily Life.* New York: Routledge.

Wuthnow, Robert. 1987. *Meaning and Moral Order: Explorations in Cultural Analysis.* Berkeley: University of California Press.

Young, Iris Marion. 1990. *Justice and the Politics of Difference.* Princeton, NJ: Princeton University Press.

Index

ginalized discourses, 143, 149; on pleasure of watching talk shows, 190–91; on respectable behavior, 146; on talking with friends while watching, 169; on talk shows as repetitive, 174

Jenny Jones Show: audience participation increasing in, 39; audience size for, 219n. 1; as late-blooming, 35; as legitimate public discourse, 109, 113, 114, 116, 117–18, 122; and Lieberman-Bennett campaign, 44; NATPE survey of 1996 on, 48; premier of, 34; race, gender, and income and audience of, 219n. 2; ratings gains for, 36, 38, 52–53; *Regis and Kathie Lee* contrasted with, 44; as respectful of guests, 134; in second place in ratings in 1995, 47; secret-admirer shooting incident, 40–42; serious topics on, 103, 104; the show as getting out of hand, 129, 167–68; studio audience of, 133; time-period upgrades for, 47; trash talk on, 2; women 18–34 as core demographic of, 36

Jerry Springer Show, 54–56; advertising costs on, 56; audience participation increasing in, 39; audience size for, 5, 219n. 1; as carnivalesque, 161, 166–67, 172, 175; coaching of guests on, 222n. 6; containing and marginalizing, 180; dailyness of, 173; as displacement of carnivalesque, 172; as entertainment only, 99, 102, 115, 116, 117, 118, 131, 157, 167; as

fastest-growing talk show in history, 56; fighting on, 54, 56, 159, 222n. 6; as legitimate public discourse, 97–98, 121–31; license fees increasing, 55; as "low," 164; the lure of, 182–83; mainstream advertisers avoiding, 53; MCA buys distributor of, 51; NATPE survey of 1996 on, 48; as not a talk show, 159–61; and *Oprah Winfrey Show,* 54, 55, 56, 158, 224n. 1; as paradigm of outrageousness, sex, and fighting, 56; as performative, 161; as predictable, 173–74; race, gender, and income and audience of, 219n. 2; ratings down in 1995–96, 51; ratings gains for, 36, 39, 47, 52–53; reality of issues on, 123–24; serious topics on, 103, 104; sex as topic of, 160; Springer seen as good host, 129–30, 142; as symbolic inversion, 161–69; time-period upgrades for, 55, 220n. 7; as transgressing mainstream standards, 161; trash talk on, 2, 98, 122, 158; TV-M rating for episodes of, 52; videos of, 56

Joanie, 210; all-day television viewing as past practice for, 75, 77; discourse of productivity and television viewing by, 78, 92; life as in turmoil, 75–76; on the lure of talk shows, 183; negative reaction to talk shows, 76–77; on talking with friends while watching, 168–69; on talk shows as repetitive, 174; watching talk shows as central daily practice for, 65, 74–78

About the Author

Julie Engel Manga is a sociologist of culture, with a prior career as an organization development consultant. She has a keen interest in the intersections of cultural, social, political, and economic institutions and the everyday lives of individuals. She has a healthy disrespect for disciplinary boundaries, drawing on sociology, history, political economy, cultural studies, and philosophy in her analysis of contemporary society. She lives in Brookline, Massachusetts, with her husband and son.